YORKSHIRE TOUR

YORKSHIRE TOUR

Ella Pontefract & Marie Hartley

Smith
Settle

First published in 1939 by
J M Dent & Sons Ltd

This new edition published in 2003 by
Smith Settle Ltd
Ilkley Road
Otley LS21 3JP

ISBN 1 85825 182 6

Frontispiece: Ingleborough by Marie Hartley

Printed and bound by
SMITH SETTLE
Ilkley Road, Otley, West Yorkshire LS21 3JP

INTRODUCTION TO
THE 2003 EDITION

In 1938 Ella Pontefract and I had forged a partnership of author and artist, and had written and illustrated three books: *Swaledale*, *Wensleydale* and *Wharfedale*, published by J M Dent. At that time these were pioneer works, and has often been said they put the Dales on the map.

At the same time we had embarked on journalism by contributing for three and a half years an illustrated weekly on Yorkshire churches for the *Yorkshire Weekly Post* (now defunct). This had the important effect of introducing us to every region of the county, and the articles were published in book form — *The Charm of Yorkshire Churches*.

We then conceived the idea of compiling a book on the whole of Yorkshire, and in May 1938 we had a meeting in London with our publishers to ask if they would support us. They approved the project, but told us that such a book 'had to be a standard work on the county'. We returned home, and at once began planning an itinerary of intensive work. It lasted until we finished the book in June 1939, two months before the declaration of war, which had long threatened, on the 3rd September.

On re-reading *Yorkshire Tour*, two facts emerge. First, as the chapters unfold, there is a cohesion about the whole, and it becomes clear that this is an account of old Yorkshire with its three Ridings intact, written before the boundary changes brought about in 1974 by the Local Government Act of 1972. Encountering remarkably little opposition, edges of Yorkshire were nibbled away, and went to other counties. For instance Dentdale and Garsdale were swept into Cumbria, Saddleworth and Delph into Lancashire, and the Ridings disappeared until the East Riding was later restored. (Dissatisfaction still rumbles on.)

Secondly, in 1938 there might have been hints of decline, but the three historic industries — textiles, coal and steel — flourished in their separate districts. Now all has changed, and these industries have altered, diminished or gone. We drove on quiet roads. We saw smoke from mill chimneys and congested housing enveloping the textile towns, coal mines and colliery villages planted inrural countrysides, the smell of hot metal emanating from south Yorkshire, horses working in the fields, dialect spoken by the many, hard times remembered, churches, abbeys, castles and customs reminding us of times long past. The spirit of old Yorkshire is preserved in this book.

M H, 2003

Note to 1939 edition

Yorkshire is a large county, and no one volume could hold every aspect of it. We have been interested mainly in the social history from its faint beginnings to the fullness of the present time.

We owe a debt to the numerous authors who through the centuries have gathered together the lore of their own districts, but our gratitude goes particularly to the men and women who have given us pictures of the past from their own experiences or from reminiscences handed down to them from older generations. It would be impossible here to thank by name all who have helped in some way or other—those who showed us the intricacies of coal-mining; those who demonstrated to us the processes of the steel and woollen trades; those who introduced us to the smaller industries which are such an attractive feature of Yorkshire life; those who gave us some insight into country customs; those who supplied us with introductions or read part of the MS.—but we wish to express our appreciation of the kindness and welcome which have been extended to us from one end of the county to the other. Our journey has made us proud to be able to class ourselves along with those we met as Yorkshire people.

E. P.

June 1939.

M. H.

CONTENTS

ILLUSTRATIONS

DRAWINGS

PHOTOGRAPHS

MAPS

View from Sutton Bank

CHAPTER 1

YORKSHIRE

FOR most of us life lies in one or two small areas, and yet preoccupation with living or holidaying in these blinds us to their story. Few people go out of their way to see in their town a phase of life which does not ordinarily touch their own; or find time to climb from their country village to see the view from the highest hill. It is the distant and unfamiliar sights which send us on eager journeys, while we miss the drama at our more prosaic back-door.

A woman showing us over her house in one of the Bars in the walls of York lost some of her interest when she found that we lived only a few miles away. 'We get lots of American visitors,' she said. 'They know more than you do about the place. You see, they've read about it before they come.' Her 'you' was an impersonal one, but it was evident that her Yorkshire visitors had not expressed the same enthusiasm as those from longer distances.

But less obvious places have their separate stories, each forming a part of the whole. Because of the size and diversity of Yorkshire, they add up here to a rich and varied volume.

I

The scene must be peopled to be understood, for though the country has moulded the dwellers in it, they in their turn have made its history. Ancient camps on the hills, deserted roads, towns, and villages, ruined castles, abbeys, and cottages, unite to show how through farming and industry, progress and decline, man has written his story on the landscape; and his joys and sorrows, his hopes and disappointments can be read between its broad lines.

It was with some such glimmerings in our minds that we set out on our journey to discover the spirit of the Yorkshire to which we belong. The outline of the story we were to trace was already there; there were a few blurred pages in the regions we had passed through many times but never stayed in, or in the districts which we had visited with the limited tastes of childhood; and there were some well-filled pages representing places in which every house and turning, every lane and beck was familiar to one of us; but even they took on a fresh aspect as they fitted into the whole. The shape and contours of Yorkshire became a perpetual background into which, as our journey advanced, each particular district and each phase in the social life took its place.

That background grew increasingly necessary, for one day we would be on the slopes of Whernside, the next on the sandhills of Spurn, the next at a miners' meeting near Barnsley; or a day spent watching the Plough Stots at Goathland would be followed by a day on the Haworth moors.

We came to parts which were ugly and blackened, but much of our way lay amongst country which is singularly beautiful, a land of sheep-rearing fells and moors, of woods and waving cornfields, of meadows flowering beside rivers which see no land but Yorkshire on their courses, of rugged cliffs and low, wasting shores.

It is easiest to imagine the county as a whole under its early inhabitants, to think of the Bronze Age standing stones, the Devil's Arrows at Boroughbridge, and see the settlements round them at Aldborough and North Deighton; the Bronze

Age sites on the north - east moors where the surface is broken with burial howes; the highly developed cultures, some of the most important in England, on the Wolds; the Iron Age village sites with beehive dwellings under the scars of the Pennine Hills; the lake dwellings of Holderness and the Vale of Pickering. Many of our superstitions and customs originated with these people.

The Romans can also be imagined spread out in their camps, forts, and villas, wherever their roads went. It is not until the settlement of the Anglians and Norsemen that you begin to realize the separate districts. Many of the names which they gave to these divisions and to features of the landscape remain, our daily speech is based on their language, and we have inherited their legends.

From the stages during which the monks were developing the communities round the monasteries, and the village churches were being built, we come to that period when the county was settling itself after the upheavals of the Dissolution of the Monasteries and the Civil War. The seventeenth century does not seem very distant, because the field enclosures which the people made then are in use to-day, and houses and cottages which they built are still occupied. People had by that time adjusted themselves to their environment, and each district was forming its own social life.

The variety of Yorkshire scenery has divided it naturally into numbers of these small districts, each with its own customs and peculiarities. 'He comes out of yond country,' a man will say of another, as if he were a foreigner. In a distance of thirty miles you find a different scene, climate and farming system, and different looks and dialect in the people.

Thus it comes about that Yorkshiremen's visions of their county vary. To one man the mention of it brings a sight of the quiet country on the Plain of York where mellowed brick houses cluster up to churches with Norman doorways, trees overhang the lanes, and roads lead to where tall Georgian houses surround the squares of ancient market towns, and where across long distances there are sudden glimpses of the towers of York Minster.

To another it conveys a Pennine dale village circling a green where the houses, roofs, and walls are of grey stone quarried from the fells which enclose it, and a familiar scene is a shepherd starting out with his dog to round up the sheep. Another sees the heather- and bracken-covered moors of the Hambleton Hills bounding miniature valleys where corn-fields make a patchwork with the meadows, and a ruined abbey is sunk amongst trees.

To another Yorkshire is a colliery village where streets are lined with drab rows of houses, and the horizon is a jagged line of pit stocks, mine tippings, and railway trucks, which can nevertheless be lost in a sudden burst of fresh green country. Another's vision is of the West Riding woollen area where town runs into town, mill chimneys pierce the sky, and heavy traffic fills the roads, but whose hills and dales, once rural, have a mystical beauty at night when thousands of lights gleam in the valleys and mark the line of the roads.

One sees a village street leading past pebble-walled cottages and a fine church to where the low, lonely cliffs of Holderness are being worn away by the sea. Another, a band playing on the spa of a holiday resort while brown-sailed fishing trawlers come into the harbour under the shadow of the castle on the headland. A third, the red-tiled cottages of a fishing village rising one above another up a steep cliff from the sea. One man's country is the rolling cornland of the Wolds with roomy farmhouses sheltered by plantations of trees and looking over ploughed fields speckled with flinty chalk. Another's is where barges sail slowly down the canals of the flat land near Thorne.

Odd fleeting pictures which the seasons brought flash through our minds : the meadows and hedgerows under the Hambleton Hills, thick with flowers in the spring; the lime-stone country of Wharfedale and Littondale like an enormous rock garden; a jay chattering in a wood near Pickering; a woodpecker showing red and green on a hillside in Rosedale;

the brilliant colours of autumn in a gill in Wensleydale; the becks of Swaledale, dyed brown with peat after heavy rain, rushing down the fells; a heron, itself the colouring of the limestone rock, flying across Gordale Scar; men clearing out the bed of the river Cock, while a winter haze hangs over the frosty fields where the battle of Towton was fought.

Often such isolated incidents would transport us to other scenes. A kingfisher preening himself on the banks of the

Robin Hood's Bay

river Dee in Dentdale reminded us of the kingfisher seen occasionally by the edge of a mill dam near Leeds. Starlings coming down to their meeting-place in the marshy land near Spofforth, rising and falling like racing clouds, made us think of a little flock sweeping above the high fells of Teesdale in June. Plovers following the plough by the side of the Great North Road took us back to the moorland roads where these birds stand with their young ones on the grass verges.

The roads carrying the transport of the county echo its story. The Great North Road, along which the Roman legions came, is the spine, the way through, but the smaller roads tell the life of the varied districts which they serve.

Some of the drovers' tracks and the routes to markets and fairs are vanishing with the new transport and the dying of the smaller markets; the green tracks and paths which the lead miners used are sinking back into the moors; the paths of the alum workers run aimlessly now along the northern cliffs; and paved causeways along which fish and salt were carried from the coast are pavements to modern roads. On main routes or where industry still progresses many of the old tracks are widened highways, but stiles, turning from these, lead to trodden paths which the colliers take across the fields, or flights of stone steps end at paved 'ginnels' between walls, short cuts for the factory workers.

The roads are visible signs of the way in which industry originated in the rural districts. Winding over the fells from the villages of Hallamshire, they tell of the Sheffield cutlers working in the outlying villages before the slow movement to the towns began. Names of distant places on milestones in Craven, and the winding roads over the high hills round Halifax and Huddersfield, tell of an industry carried on for centuries in country villages where men were spinners and weavers as well as farmers.

It is from the grim towns in which the industries have become concentrated that the cutlery and cloth go out to far countries now. Perhaps under a heavy sky when the smoke hangs over them shutting out the sun it is difficult to connect them with romance, but by the skill and endurance of Yorkshiremen the enormous mills grew from cottages where cloth was woven on hand-looms, and the cutlery works from village forges. Step by step they advanced, son carrying on after father, until now they stand with a family tradition behind them, a tradition which was strong enough in master and men to last through the hard times, wrongs, and oppression which came with the quick development.

It was the Pennine Hills which enabled the woollen industry to be established in Yorkshire. The trade came from southern centres to a colder, harsher climate, for here, midway between

HESLEDEN BECK AND PENYGHENT, LITTONDALE

London and Edinburgh, we are definitely north. We realize the difference from the south in the variations in our own climate. Hedges are in full leaf round Selby when the first green buds break through on the northern plain. Lowland lambs are almost sheep when the mountain lambs first appear on the uplands. Snow-drifts block the Wold roads long after the villages round York have forgotten the snow. Life may be more of a struggle in this colder weather, but we like our bracing air, and after the month of June we feel stifled in the south.

The Pennines bound us formidably in a curve on the west, joining with the river Tees and the east coast to enclose the county, as in a smaller way our separate districts are enclosed. The hills have been one cause of the insularity which has been a characteristic of Yorkshire people, and which is only just breaking down to-day. They and the Cleveland moors give those vast open spaces where it is possible to stand and look for miles over unpeopled tracts. You can stretch your limbs and expand your soul on a Yorkshire moor. From the edges of these hills you get other kinds of extensive views, looking over the Vale of Pickering or across the wide acres of the Plain of York. These are expanses of hedged fields with villages and towns and church spires rising up from them. Let us stand on one of these points, and visualize the country to which we are going.

There are the ruined castles whose owners long ago helped to make England's history, and, generally within easy reach of them, abbeys which grew under their protection. The monks converted the 'waste' on which they were built into fine cultivated land, but it was the becks and rivers supplying water and drainage which made the great number of them possible here. They remind us of York Minster, and the full history of that second city in England. Amongst them are the houses of the yeomen who followed the monks, threading their way into every phase of life, owning lead and coal mines, selling wool, building up that stable English country life whose passing we mourn.

Perhaps because the peace of England is threatened to-day, we think a little of the sites of battles of long ago—Stamford Bridge, Towton, Marston Moor; and from them turn to the great aerodromes which are springing up with their surrounding villages on the flat central plain; and then remember how in the summer of 1938 the city of York thought it fitting to display on a carpet garden bed the motto: 'A city prepared. A city spared.'

More reassuring impressions crowd these out of mind. Blocks of new flats are housing people from the town slums. Pit baths enabling the colliers to return home clean are rising up near the pit-heads. Large schools with airy class-rooms are replacing inefficient ones. Youth Hostels by which walkers can see the beauty of their county inexpensively are being established in country places. Towns are holding festivals to encourage the interest in drama. Women's Institutes are bringing fresh interests into the lives of country people. New roads are being built.

And lastly there come quickly a few episodes which show the permanence of the life of the county and the stability of its people through change and progress: a man shaping knife-handles day in, day out, proud of his record of sixty-four years' work; a weaver week after week joining the thread in a shuttle; two men silently cutting peat on a northern fell; a farmer following the plough over a Wold field; children playing shuttlecock and battledore on the broad pavements of a new mining village; a group of haymakers working to race the weather under the shadow of Ingleborough. We shall find these among the rest as we pursue our journey.

Conisborough

CHAPTER 2

SOUTH YORKSHIRE

BAWTRY says 'Hail' and 'Farewell' to Yorkshire people, welcoming them home if they come north, and leading them to fresh sights and adventures if they go south. The little tongue of land on which it lies dips into Nottinghamshire, and makes a porch to the county to usher in the Great North Road. The atmosphere of travel and the life of the road yesterday and to-day are in its cobbled market-place. The tall brick ivy-covered houses, still reflecting the midlands, make it a half-way stage between them and the more sober north.

At Doncaster the midlands are left behind. You are really in Yorkshire now, though still a little conscious of the nearness of Lincolnshire on the east. Within the last twenty years Doncaster has changed from a country to an industrial town. Its fate was fixed when it became a railway centre, and the advance continued with the eastward spread of the coal mines, and the factories which have followed both these. In the name of progress many of its Georgian houses have been pulled down to make way for modern shops, and the ease of a country town has vanished. Bygone leisurely days flash back for a moment as you pass Parkinson's shop with its bow windows, and the sign over the door declaring their butter-scotch to be 'extensively patronized by the Nobility, Clergy, and Gentry'; but it is quickly lost again.

Doncaster is still an important market town drawing trade from a large and varied region. Farmers from quiet home-steads under the Lincolnshire Wolds bargain with Yorkshire farmers in the market-place, and jostle on the crowded pave-ments with railway workers, miners, factory hands, and their families. The rural and industrial elements are fighting for the mastery, and Race Week with its famous St Leger race proceeds as if no change had come. The fashionable crowd in the paddock, aeroplanes landing at the airport, the traffic of the Great North Road pressing through the town, white and gold ice-cream carts forming a fairy-tale guard round the market-place, are a few symbols of this strange mixture which is modern Doncaster.

The town is the centre of the newer part of the Yorkshire coal area, which stretches in a broad belt from the moorland country on the west to the flat land round Thorne on the east. It used to be thought that the coal seams stopped at the Don fault, but it is now known that these extend to the coast and under the sea.

The western area, of which Barnsley is the centre, was worked earliest because the coal was near the surface here. This is the district which first springs to mind when coal is mentioned. Its villages and towns present vistas of low rows of dreary brick or stone houses, many of them back to back and opening straight on to the street. Their soot-grimed walls are saved from absolute dinginess by the custom among miners' wives of scouring the steps and window-sills white or yellow. This decoration, which is varied to an astonishing extent, is always remarked upon by visitors from the south. Until recently Barnsley was merely a large edition of all this, but it has lately developed a civic pride and has a fine town hall and grammar school.

Pontefract and its neighbour, Castleford, are the centres for the middle district. This was developed sixty or seventy years ago, and from that time the third most picturesque town in Yorkshire quickly lost its character. Pontefract is still a more interesting place than Barnsley, but the ruined castle and Tudor hall seem to have taken the surrounding drabness into themselves.

> Castleford maids must needs be fair
> For they wash in Calder and rinse in Aire,

the old rhyme says of this town where the two rivers meet, but the result of such an act would be the opposite to-day. There is much the same type of building here as round Barnsley, and some of the villages are actually under the shadow of the pit hills turned out from the mines. The Doncaster development, which has come since the War, has favoured the garden city type of village, such as Woodlands, with trees and grassy spaces.

Once, on a road outside Doncaster, we met a man travelling with a roundabout on a cart drawn by a mule. He was collecting jam-jars and rags, and giving rides on the roundabout in exchange for them. He told us how he and his partner are the only men left in the trade, and how they are away for weeks at a time, travelling from place to place, and putting up at houses where they are known. He creates interest by giving free rides to children, or if trade is slack to a few large women whose shrieks are an effective advertisement.

'It's streets we want for our job,' the little man said. 'Streets is the only places which is any good. I've known mesen start first thing i' t'mornin' at one end, and it's been dinner-time by I've got to t'other. Aye, streets is the thing.'

His words seemed to echo in the air as he left, not knowing how perfectly he had described this stricken land. You see the names of the streets as you pass through the towns, Charlotte Street, Back Charlotte Street, Carlisle Street, Back Carlisle

Street—seldom roads; in Yorkshire you have gone up a stage in society if you move from a street to a road.

These are the congested, built-up districts which seem larger than they actually are because they join the woollen and steel areas on the north and south. Much of the surrounding country is still lovely with a luxuriant woodland beauty which made it a favourite residential part until the coal was exploited. The size of the churches, the richness of their architecture, their graceful spires and pinnacled towers, and the number of pretentious tombs show the wealth of this land in the periods in which they were built. They adorn the rural villages still, and are often the only significant features in places swamped by the mining growth.

A deep peacefulness prevails in many parts of this gracious country of South Yorkshire. You hear a ploughman whistling as he follows his pair of horses; watch a flock of rooks flying unconcernedly round a scarecrow in the newly sown soil; wave to a cartload of pea-pickers driving home from the fields. Down quiet roads there are mellowed farmhouses, and villages with ponds, and hollyhocks in cottage gardens. Birds are still country creatures where Campsall and Burghwallis are sunk among shady woods in the old forest of Barnsdale. The centuries roll back at Hooton Pagnell where the limestone ridge leaves a belt free from coal. Farmyards open on to the village streets at Badsworth and Darrington. At Ackworth you enter the gates of the Friends' School, and are taken back to the eighteenth century and the tradition and love of education which inspired an eminent Quaker to found a school here. Even at Conisborough where houses crowd the hillsides, the majesty of the site of the Norman castle with its great circular keep above the river is apparent.

The fact remains, however, that as the mines near a piece of country the heart goes out of the land. The advance of coal-mining is an insidious one, because so much of it is unseen. Levels are driven far underground without apparently disturbing the surface, but, quickly at the start, then slowly

SOUTH YORKSHIRE
COAL, STEEL,
AND MARSHLAND
Chapters 2, 3, 4.

but irresistibly, the development of that stretch of country begins. The opening of a new mine means work for many generations to come; thousands of men must be housed, new roads made, and all the facilities for a large community supplied. When that is finished, or long before, there will be another mine, another patch of development. Even now down many of the quiet roads you meet more colliers cycling or walking home from the pits than you do farm labourers. As you come over a rise from what seems the depth of the country, the un-lovely buildings and chimneys of a pit-head loom with a Heath Robinson effect on the horizon, and a red rash on the landscape marks a new village. Here and there an old village merges at one end into a mining one, and you know that presently the new will swamp the old, not only the buildings, but the people. A fresh community will arrive from Derbyshire, Durham, Wales, the Scottish Border, and overwhelm the farming community with its long tradition. The country, as country, is dying, for one of the essentials of farming is con-tinuity, a carrying on from father to son, from one family to another.

Another effect of tunnelling underground is subsidence of the land. Above old mines, where a certain amount of coal was left in for support, the ground has subsided unevenly. Cracks appear mysteriously in the earth, and in the walls of houses. We know a child who for weeks watched a crack widen in the wall between her bedroom and the next house, until she could see and speak to the people through it. It was some time before we realized that the many pinnacles and other church carvings which decorate the gardens of this district, were there because, through the undermining of foundations, they had become unsafe and had been replaced. Nowadays, when all the coal is taken out, a gradual subsidence of two-thirds of the height of the seam beneath, falling at the rate of two feet a year, can be definitely reckoned on. This is enough to cause ridges of hills to change their shape, ponds to disappear, and rivers to alter their courses, but it makes little difference to buildings. In a few years the ruins of Roche Abbey will be four feet lower than they are now, but it is not anticipated that the drop will cause any damage to them.

Coal was got in South Yorkshire in very early times, but it was not until the seventeenth century that it was worked to any great extent, and then chiefly because of the growing shortage of wood for charcoal. In 1714 Ralph Thoresby said that pits in the county were without number; and the coal was then being exported to other parts.

Early workers merely took coal where it outcropped on the surface. As this became exhausted, the seams were reached by what are known as 'day-holes,' that is levels dug straight or on a downward slope into the hillsides. A few day-holes are being worked to-day, but chiefly to get what was left by earlier miners. Short shafts followed these, and finally there came the deep shafts which are becoming increasingly necessary because of the dropping of the Barnsley seam as it runs east and south. It needs companies with large capital resources to work and equip these new mines.

In 1938 we attended a memorial service at Silkstone to twenty-six children between the ages of seven and fifteen, who had been drowned in a day-hole a hundred years ago. During a terrific storm floods rushed down the roadway, and the children were washed back as they struggled to reach the opening. After the service the Miners' Federation held a meeting in a large field outside the village, and a miner told how in his youth he had known an old woman who was one of the survivors from the Silkstone disaster. She had been saved by a man who had managed to climb on to a ledge at the side clutching at her hair as she floated past, and dragging her up. She always ended the story of her escape with the words, 'I were saved by the 'air o' me 'ead!'

He also told a tale of a woman named Nanty Paddle who slipped as she was climbing a ladder down one of the small shafts, and fell to the bottom. She was dazed but not hurt, and all she said when they carried her out was, 'I wouldn't 'ave cared a damn if I 'adn't splitten me clog soils.'

Those old days of hardship of which no Englishman is proud seemed to creep very near as we listened, sitting on forms in this open space with old and new mines on all sides. We were back in the times when children were 'hurriers,' dragging corves of coal to the surface, when men and women were working together half naked and up to their waists in water, when hours were long and wages poor, and yet the miners had to provide their own candles, keep their tools in repair, and pay the rents of their houses, which belonged to the owners. Attempts to enforce better conditions resulted in the men being turned out of their homes and the doors and windows being barricaded up.

Between ourselves and those oppressed days lie Shaftesbury's Act of 1842 and those which followed it, strikes and the growth of trade unions, and their amalgamation since the 1914–1918 War in the Miners' Federation. The good conditions of to-day, and the fact that the miners have a great deal of influence in the working of the pits, are due to the collaboration of owners and managers with the Miners' Federation.

A few months after this we went down the pit which was opened at Maltby in 1911. Frozen snow lay on the ground, and the grip of frost gave an air of unreality to the headstocks rising out of the quiet land at the edge of a wood. Conspicuous amid their stark outlines were the new buildings for the pit baths with their appropriate modern architecture.

Past the lamp-house, where men were recharging the electric lamps, now universally used, we came to the entrance. Here a fan, by creating a vacuum, draws the used air out of the pit up an enclosed shaft while fresh air continually rushes down an open one. The shaft at Maltby is half a mile deep, and the cage dropped in one minute. The wide, airy passage in which we landed might have been a subway anywhere, but for the slight feeling of suffocation which was probably due to the realization of how far away were the green earth and the sunshine. A hushed stillness gradually seemed to envelop us, a silence so deep that the footsteps and voices of the men, and later the clang of coal-tubs and the knocking of the picks, seemed to accentuate rather than pierce it.

Already there are twenty-seven miles of road in this pit, and it is seldom necessary to duck one's head on any of them. Of the three shifts, the night one is given over completely to making and repairing roadways, one of the most expensive and important parts of mine work. As the seams of coal are won, the levels to be utilized for carrying are made into roadways, and the rest filled in. The men are working continually against the natural inclination of the strata to close together again. One man explained it: 'You're always fighting against nature. You never get something for nothing in the universe.'

Older roadways are supported by pit-props in much the same way that the miners prop the levels as they advance into a seam. In the newer ones semicircular steel girders following the lie of the strata are used, so that pressure is lessened. We saw all types as we rode in the 'Paddy Mail,' the train of tubs run by compressed-air machines, which carries the miners to the various workings. As we reached the terminus we could see lights moving in the distance as in a scene on a darkened theatre stage. Here at the gleaming coal-face was a scene of activity after the empty roadway. The men, working in a line, wore nothing but shorts, for in spite of the good ventilation, it was hot. Persistently attacking the hard wall, advancing farther underground, the organized labour of these men can turn out from this one pit over a million tons of coal in a year.

The underground workers are paid by piece-work. A group will agree to take what is called a 'stall,' and if possible this is made a family concern. The drills are worked by compressed air, electricity being only used near the shaft bottom. There is still a considerable art in coal getting. A miner must have method in placing the pit props to bear the right amount of pressure, and now and again he can change on to night shifts and use his skill in road repairing.

The sky and trees and the tufts of grass showing through the snow seemed very desirable even on that dull winter's day as we emerged. On the surface again we watched the coal brought up the shaft, weighed and checked by two men, one appointed by the company and the other by the miners. and then washed and graded. Above us an overhead railway carried its loads of rubbish to the dirt heaps, fast growing into those pointed, artificial hills which surround pits.

From the pit-head the men go straight to the baths, leave their dirty clothes in one set of lockers, pass into the bath-rooms, and from there to where their clean clothes are in another set of lockers. The baths are provided by a government grant from mine royalties, but once they are built the owners keep them up, aided by a compulsory contribution of fivepence a week from each man. Their idea and accomplishment give one a pride in modern efficiency. The clean-looking zinc lockers, five thousand altogether, the enormous tiled bath-rooms filled with showers which the men regulate themselves, the canteen where milk is so much in demand that it seems to be ousting the miners' beer in popularity, are all that is needed and nothing more.

Within a fortnight of their opening, the majority of the men were using the baths, and appreciating being able to arrive home clean. The blacksmith, not being so grimed with coal-dust, was an exception. 'Well, I 'aven't used 'em yet,' he said, as he sharpened his tools. 'Once a week on a Saturday 's enough for me, I say.'

The shifts were changing as we came away, and processions of miners, many of them young boys learning their trade, passed us. In the yard a ballot was being taken to decide which of three weeks they would have for their first holiday with pay. There was a general air of goodwill between the men and the officials, as if they understood and respected each other, and we found the same cordial spirit in the homes.

The people were proud of their village, its church, grammar school, and Colliery Institute. This is a new village with good houses, and, surrounded as it is by open country, there does not seem to be the continual battle against soot and dirt which goes on in the older villages. Most of the women were baking, and a bowl of dough stood rising by the fire, or there came a smell of new bread as the oven door was opened. But even in the congested areas, miners' wives are notoriously house-proud, and their homes have more shining cleanliness and warm comfort than are found in many country cottages. One woman expressed their creed. 'It isn't the house that matters,' she said, 'it's what you make it.'

Modern improvements have lessened danger in the mines, but not wholly eliminated it, and there is still an element of risk about a miner's job. Inflammable gases are the chief cause of explosions, and it is compulsory for a certain proportion of oil lamps to be used in the pits because these show the presence of gas by the height of the blue halo above the yellow flame. Accidents are much less frequent under these precautions, but they are still recent enough in some pits for the tragedy of them to haunt the district.

Yet there are always more miners than there is work for. In the depression which has lately fallen on the industry men have waited years on the dole for the chance of another pit job. Once having been miners they do not wish to be anything else. The tradition has been passed down to them from father to son; it is only in recent years that there has been a tendency for miners and their wives to discourage their sons from going to the pit. The older men will talk eagerly about their work, of their first jobs as boys, of the proud moment when they were experienced enough to have boys in their charge, of locating the seams and knowing how far it is wise to go, of the fights for safer conditions.

Any one who has worked with him will tell you that the British miner is a fine type of workman, and a good companion. His work has made him nimble-minded, and this shows itself in his ready wit. There is a tale of a manager with a mop of ginger hair and a flowing ginger moustache, who was inspecting a roadway under repair. Water was dripping from the roof, and the men were continually asking for more corrugated iron sheets to protect them. At last the manager said: 'Nay, you don't want any more. Why, when I worked at the coal-face I used to get someone to throw a bucket of water over me.'

'Aye,' a miner retorted, 'but we don't want to go rusty.'

A miner who was a good workman but rather garrulous, coming up with a shift one day, remarked to the manager: 'By God, I 've lost some sweat this morning.' The manager said nothing, but picked up the telephone and asked for the under-manager.

'Oh, John,' he said, 'send two by-workmen down the road-way to find the sweat Tom Brown's lost this morning.' Every one on the pit-head heard, and it was many weeks before Tom was allowed to forget it.

As a workman the miner has a strong sense of responsibility towards his fellows, but that attitude does not as yet show itself greatly in his civic life, and his children are more than ordin-arily destructive. In one village we found scarcely any gates to the gardens, and were told that the boys had taken them all off and burnt them. The children go through the empty gateways and trample on the gardens, and they pull the copings off the walls and break the trees in the parks. Our roundabout man showed us where miners' children had broken the feet off his painted animals. To foster an early pride in the new garden villages seems one solution of the problem.

Standing in this mining community where men are gathered together by a common work in one corner of Yorkshire, you get flashes of what it stands for. Barges of coal glide down canals and rivers to the ports; long lines of trucks pass over railway viaducts; motor lorries and carts piled with coal wind along quiet roads; gas and electricity works rise on the land; a stoker mends his fire in a mill or a ship or a furnace; a night-

watchman bends over his glowing brazier; fires roar in the halls
of Yorkshire mansions, crackle in trim town houses, or blaze
in farmhouse kitchens. Far corners of England and beyond
rely for their warmth and comfort on this patch of Yorkshire.

The getting of coal may devastate the land, but always
somewhere gleams of country peep through, in the allotments
ringing the older villages, in the open commons, never far
away, where a miner can walk with his whippet. Once on
a quiet road with wide grass verges bordered by hedges, we
met an old woman gathering sticks for kindling, and piling
them into a shabby pram. A mile to the east, headstocks
and surface buildings towered into the sky, and smoke poured
from them. The woman came from the village beside them,
but she belonged in spirit to the fields and the quiet road.
She told us she often came there because it was so fresh.
She seemed as she worked in the evening light to express the
intermingling of town and country which is a characteristic
of South Yorkshire yet.

Lady Bridge, Sheffield

CHAPTER 3

HALLAMSHIRE

Sheffield made, both haft and blade,
London for your life, show me such a knife.

PRIDE in their work runs through the whole story of the
cutlers of Hallamshire, who early found themselves with no
serious rivals. The name Sheffield on cutlery came to be a
symbol of quality, and was jealously guarded by the smiths
themselves and by the Cutlers' Company, although it was only
in 1911 that a law was passed to protect it. Every child knows
that to be really worth having a penknife must be 'Sheffield
made,' and the giver of one without that mark suffers in his
estimation.

Yorkshiremen are proud of Sheffield's fame, but they only visit the city when necessary, for of all modern industries steel works blacken and devour their surroundings most. The district of Hallamshire, in which they are centred, is a vast area of towns and villages running into one another along the roads to Sheffield. The chimneys of its works and forges turn out an almost continuous stream of filthy smoke which spreads first into a thick cloud and then dissipates to fall gently to the ground in flakes of soot. The inky blackness coated on the walls gives an iron hardness to the buildings, as if they had been enamelled.

Standing on Lady Bridge near the centre of the city, you see the grimy buildings lining the river Don.

> The shelving slimy river Don,
> Each year a daughter or a son.

You try to imagine the scene before all this defaced it, when the hills rose unspoilt above the woods which overhung the river. For fourteen years Mary Queen of Scots, when she was imprisoned in Sheffield Castle in the custody of the Earl of Shrewsbury, looked out on a picture of loveliness here from the castle hill above the Don.

Reminders of this lost beauty remain in the country which runs in a bright green frill round the gloom of Hallamshire, and isolates this district which more than any other in Yorkshire seems to justify its division into a separate shire. On the north it is a belt of agricultural land dividing the steel from the coal areas, though at places along it the two overlap. To the east it is farming country where stackyards open from village streets, flowers bloom in cottage gardens, and here and there, as at Thorpe Salvin and Laughton-en-le-Morthen, there are graceful churches; a pleasant land, marred but slightly by the faint echoes of trade which reach it. The west is the bold moorland district above Bradfield and Bolsterstone with its memory of the potters and glass-makers. The building of reservoirs in the valleys here has taken some of the life out of the land, and has brought tragedy too, but it has also preserved it as open country. This merges into the Peak district and the Derbyshire dales, in which direction the residential part of Sheffield has grown, pushing farther into Derbyshire the people of a city which itself half belongs to that county in spirit and outlook and the dialect and names of its citizens.

The cutlery trade started in the wooded country of Hallamshire, chiefly in the valleys of the Rivelin, Porter, Don, and Little Don. It settled here because of the beds of iron ore, fire-clay, and ganister, gritstone for grinding, and limestone to act as a flux, and because of the streams to supply waterpower, and the great amount of timber to make charcoal for smelting.

Bloomeries on the hills tell of early mining for ironstone, and a smelt-house with a Norman doorway at Kimberworth of its working by the monks of Kirkstead Abbey. But the trade was really established, gradually but permanently, by the small cutlers, or knife-smiths as they were often called, working in the scattered villages, sometimes alone and sometimes employing one or two men. They had their own forges and wheels for grinding, and made the knives from beginning to end in their smithies. It was such a man who would make the knife for the miller of whom Chaucer says: 'A Sheffeld thwytel baar he in his hose.'

The work was then in the nature of a country craft, and the noise of the hammer on the anvil would sound pleasantly over the quiet land, but even in its simple early stages it had a devastating effect on the country. We read how the smoke from the forges used to curl up among the oak-trees of what was forest until as the industry increased the trees gradually vanished to supply charcoal for the smelt furnaces.

In the middle of the seventeenth century the famous oak-trees of Loxley Chase, which had supplied timber for the navy, were felled, and twenty years later the holly-trees, which had made a valuable winter feed for sheep, were sold to an ironmaster named Copley. The loss inspired the local rhyme:

> If Mr Copley had never been born,
> Or in his cradle had died,
> Loxley Chase had never been torn
> And many a brave wood beside.

In 1727 a man of eighty told how he remembered walking on Heigham Common, then quite bare, when there were so many large trees that the sun could scarcely shine on him. The charcoal was carried from the woods to the furnaces on horseback in baskets called 'banisters' which had loose bottoms and widened towards the top.

By the middle of the eighteenth century the country was so denuded of woodland that many of the great families left the district. Also about this time coal was first used extensively for smelting, and the great expansion which was finally to concentrate the industry round the town of Sheffield began.

The trade did not develop haphazardly. It was controlled at first by a court acting for the Earl of Shrewsbury, who also, by settling Huguenot refugees in the district, helped to establish the various branches of the industry, sickles, scythes, scissors, flatbacks, in particular villages. In 1624 the Cutlers' Company of Hallamshire, formed by an Act of Parliament, took the place of this court, and acted as a kind of trade guild with a master and various officers. Any man over twenty-one who had served his compulsory apprenticeship of seven years was admitted to the freedom of the company, and allowed to strike his own mark on his work.

The company, aided by Sir John Reresby of Thrybergh, fought against the hearth tax and other grievances, worked for a Bill to make the Don navigable, and distributed charities, but its chief work was always the granting of marks. It retained the control of these until 1888 when the Hallamshire Registry was appointed a branch of the National Registry in London. The first mark was issued in 1564 to Robert Boure. The rapid increase in number after the Cutlers' Company

was formed shows the advance of the industry. Cutlery
firms to-day have a great number of marks at home and
abroad, and pay large sums annually for these, but they are
proud of, and retain, the early marks of the cutlers who
established them.

Cutlery work differed from coal mining in that it was carried
on above ground in workshops where the doors could stand
open, but principally in that, whereas the opening of a new
coal mine meant the sudden settlement of a population from
another part, here the growth was in the same place, passing
from one generation to another, and expanding naturally in
its own tradition. The cutlers were known as 'Little Masters,'
expressed in the speech of the district as 'Little Mesters.'
They worked themselves, and employed a varying number
of apprentices.

The apprentices were an important part of the system.
They were bound for seven years, at the end of which they
were at liberty to start for themselves, ten pounds being a
sufficient amount to set a man up as a Little Master. The
popularity of a master depended a great deal on his wife, or
dame, as she was called, and the kind of food she provided.
Before the water was contaminated salmon were very plentiful
in the river Don, and some indentures stipulated that the
apprentices were not to have salmon more than twice a week.
The manual work was hard, and many boys developed knock-
knees through standing for long periods in awkward positions.
'As badly treated as any prentice lad,' became a saying in
Hallamshire. Apprentices who took a day off to go to Doncaster races were often so afraid when the time came to
return that they enlisted instead.

In medieval days Rotherham was much the largest town in
the district, chiefly because a good pack-horse road from it
to Doncaster enabled its manufactures to be shipped from
there by river to the port of Hull. Old books and documents
show it as a merry town with a weekly market and a great
annual fair attended by jugglers and minstrels chanting tales

THE PADDY MAIL [PAGE 17]

SHEFFIELD CUTLERS

of Robin Hood. Travellers entering the town stopped for a while at the chapel on the bridge to give thanks for a safe journey. Gradually the great families of the district acquired winter houses in the town which grew round the handsome church and fifteenth - century grammar school. With the founding of the Cutlers' Company much of its trade went to Sheffield, and though it is now a large industrial centre with that depressing mixture of steel and coal, it has never recovered its first place.

So it was to Sheffield that the Little Masters eventually brought their goods to sell, carrying them wrapped in straw and sacking on their backs. They were bought by chapmen, who took them away on strings of pack-horses. The chapmen had their particular hotels, and as they arrived the ostlers would go round and warn the cutlers. As they grew richer and the roads improved, some of the cutlers rode to London themselves to try to get better prices for their goods. They moved about that city, considerably awed, but keeping their Yorkshire spirit and bluntness, speaking a dialect that was like a foreign language to the south, and being very indignant when they were asked to give discount.

For a period after the aristocratic families left Hallamshire, the population was almost all busy with one work, and of one class—the 'apron men,' as they were called. In every village the noise of hammering sounded in the forges; the smoke rose from smithy chimneys; and the masters' grinding wheels lined the river banks. With the change to coal furnaces some masters began to build larger workshops and smithies and to employ more men. For a time they lived in their former simple style, then a few more ambitious ones built houses in the country round. Some built them too large and ruined themselves, but the wiser ones settled down to a comfortable social life, their wives and families going to York for the season.

The expansion of the trade which had brought this about brought also a growing working class which began to specialize in the various processes. There were grinders who because of the grit were subject to asthma, and had also to endure the danger of bursting grindstones; braziers who were paid large wages because they were scarce; and platers who were chiefly travelling tinkers who had settled here. These specialists were skilled at their jobs, but, perhaps because their work was hard and monotonous, they were on the whole a wild lot of men, given to drinking and occasional orgies, and easily stirred to rioting.

Animosity against the first Methodists was as great here as anywhere in England. Knives and other implements were flung irresponsibly from the gallery and pit of the theatre at performers of whom the audience did not approve. The lawlessness showed itself in the nature of the risings which accompanied the forming of trade unions. A group of men, chiefly grinders, led by William Broadhead, an innkeeper who had himself been a grinder, used rattening, blew up workshops and wheels, and even murdered men who refused to join the societies.

The modern end of the story is one of the gradual drift of the industry from the country districts to the towns. It came with the use of steam power which made becks no longer necessary, and was hastened by the making of canals, the improvement of the river Don for transport, and the building of better roads to the towns. One by one the outlying firms moved down to erect their factories by the river Don in Sheffield. The scope of the work was tremendously increased when about 1750 Thomas Bolsover invented the process of silver plating, and Benjamin Huntsman the making of cast steels. By the middle of the eighteenth century, travellers were talking of 'old smoky Sheffield,' and in 1760 Horace Walpole described it as 'one of the foulest towns in England, in the most charming situation.'

The Cutlers' Company to-day is shorn of much authority, but it still registers trade marks, and controls the charities with which it continues to be endowed. The first company

met in a tavern, but a hall was built in 1638, another replaced
it in 1725, and the present hall, where the annual Cutlers'
Feast is held, was built in 1832.

The feast is probably a continuation of a venison feast
originated by the Earl of Shrewsbury. As time went on it
became more elaborate, and the present feast, in which
many smaller ones are included, is given by the Master Cutler.
The principal guest is generally a man in a high position in
the Government. Ladies are only admitted as spectators to
the gallery, and this custom seems a reflection of the city
itself, which is essentially a man's place.

The present Cutlers' Feast represents an enormous industry,
making anything from tiny files, knives, and scissors to modern
armaments. Great forges prepare the raw material for many
firms, but the mammoth concerns take every process themselves, relying now chiefly on mass production. The show-
rooms displaying the decorative side of their output are like
enormous jewellers' shops. The firm of Rodgers have a
special show-piece known as the 'Year Knife,' a penknife
with as many blades as years A.D., all folding into one handle;
another knife, worth a thousand pounds, has views engraved
on its silver blades. These are all on a grand scale, but there
is some feeling of the old cutlers with their pride in their
skill behind them—the Little Masters.

The Little Master is not quite dead to-day, even if he is
dying. There is still a small place for him amid changing
modern conditions, although he no longer has his own mark.
He does not now take apprentices, but an older man often has
sons whom he has trained working with him. We found a
number of them congregated in an old factory which supplied
them with power, each renting a room or part of one which
he called a side. Climbing the worn steps, we came first to
where a Little Master and his three sons were assembling
penknives, boring holes in the parts and fastening them
together with steel wire. 'Our job's just makkin' holes and
fillin' 'em up again,' the Little Master said. He showed us

farmers' knives destined for Australia and Canada, and knives for the Royal Air Force. He had strange names for them: Banjos, Shove-'em-offs, Ranjapoos, but every one in the trade knows what these mean.

Next we found an old man and his son pinning (fixing) hafts (handles) on to butchers' and palette knives. They were journeymen or sidesmen, receiving the material for their work from the firm which orders it, whereas the Little Master buys his own material and sells his goods himself. The old man had worked at this for sixty-four years, and was content, though as a boy he had run away to be a sailor, and had been fetched back by his father who apprenticed him to himself to bind him.

In a smaller room, a man was forging blades, hammering them into shape purely by eye, and using his skill in tempering the steel to give it strength. Large firms used to employ between thirty and forty hand-forgers, but there are not more than this number now in the whole of Sheffield, although there is no blade to equal a hand-forged one. The smith forged a blade for us as we watched, and we took it down to another room where five or six men were grinding and polishing with stone, leather, and cloth polishers, smoothing the rough steel to a glimmering surface in a few minutes.

High up a narrow flight of stairs we came upon the buffers. These are women whose job of buffing is to polish the spoons and forks turned out in the mass-production factories. The business is conducted like that of a Little Master; one woman gets the orders and employs five or six under her. They stand at benches along the sides of the room, and with their blackened faces and aprons, and their hair tied back in red cloth, have an air of wild recklessness. They work at great speed, but on a Monday, which they call Saint Monday, they will as likely as not refuse to stay after the inns open at half-past eleven.

Time will eventually remove these strange communities, gathered together under one roof, keeping their independence, but as yet they are useful to the larger firms to execute small orders and do work which is not mass production. They are a strange survival amongst the mammoth factories.

We leave Sheffield for the country where the old cutlers began, and that beyond it, a district where ancient houses and buildings occur with a frequency not found in any other part of Yorkshire. A few stand in what are now built-up towns, but the majority are in quiet valleys and on the hillsides of the moorland districts.

When the making of reservoirs in the valleys necessitated the pulling down of some of these old houses it was found that many of them were built on cruck[1] frameworks. The oaks for the beams came from the forests which were later cut down for smelting. We saw a barn in Bolsterstone with the original beams, and a door in one corner which had led to what had been a dwelling-house next to the cow shippon. The thatched roofs of these barns and houses have been replaced by stone, and there are new doors and more windows, but otherwise the old buildings stand as they did, their workmanship so good that it has not been necessary to replace them, and they are still in daily use.

It was early summer when we saw the great half-timbered barn at Gunthwaite, near Penistone. The year's hay was nearly used, so that the sun streaming through the open door cast the pattern of the tie-beams and joists of the roof on the stone floor. The barn standing behind a cobbled courtyard is a long churchlike building with six large doors opening into it, and eleven bays in the interior. Godfrey Bosville, who lived at Gunthwaite Hall in the sixteenth century, is supposed to have built it. The hall was pulled down in the nineteenth century, but the barn stands as a memorial to it and the hearty life which went with its decline.

We walked down a stone causeway across the fields from the barn into the woods to find the sulphur well whose fame once made Gunthwaite into a spa. Two cyclists showed us

[1] Curved roof beams built up from the ground level.

where it stood deserted under a tree. In its heyday the spa attracted crowds from long distances, and its opening day in May was made a gala. Quiet, peaceful country lingers here just beyond the sounds of industry, and farmhouses rest in green fields among patches of woodland.

The three industries of steel, coal, and wool which envelop this land are reflected in the town of Penistone in its midst. The memory of the old pot-houses also lives here, it keeps its importance as a market-town serving the congested areas which surround it, and it is able to support a large agricultural show; but this complexity tears the place to pieces and robs it of much of its character.

South and west of Penistone, vast open moors stretch to the county border, making an outlet and breathing space for the people of the towns who flock to them at holiday times— you can tell the quality of their Yorkshire ham by the number of cars outside the inns. But these are real moors which roll back into lonely ferocity when the crowds go. They are part of the great western boundary of the Yorkshire Pennines. Wagoners coming over the Hazlehead Moors here from Yorkshire, Derbyshire, and Cheshire used to meet at the Millers' Arms at Saltersbrook where they were served with a special dish of Yorkshire ham and Cheshire cheese, cooked together in great brown jars, before they took their separate ways over the moorland tracks.

Selby Toll-bridge

CHAPTER 4

MARSHLAND

It used to be impossible to see anything of the port of Goole from Thorne Moor, but during recent years the land has shrunk with draining, and now from certain places there is a distinct view of the chimneys and roofs of that town. To a dweller in hill country this seems contradictory, but in flat country the horizon is very near, and only some form rising above it prolongs it.

The district round Hatfield and Thorne is like a slice out of Holland, with that excessive flatness which appears artificial. In some parts sunk ditches divide the large fields, and narrow bridges over canals and the sails of barges moving slowly along the water are the only features besides a few scattered trees in the level land. In the villages the mellowed brick of the houses makes faded frames for the old stone churches. Here and there towards the north a church is repaired with brick, proclaiming the lack of wealth to transport stone down the rivers any longer.

This is the marshland of Yorkshire. Names such as Fish-lake, Sykehouse, Reedness, Ousefleet, tell of watery sites. Its story is one of water, of attempts to drain it, and risings of the people against those attempts, of fights against flooding rivers, of the transport of men and materials along water-ways. Hatfield Chase is good agricultural land now, but the eerie stillness which broods over marshes has never really left it. You can imagine it still a watery waste, a hunting forest with red deer on the drier land, but its chief game wild fowl — geese, ducks, buzzards, kites, eagles, curlews—and now and again an osprey or a ruff and reeve. This was a royal chase, and the king also kept a protected swannery here with a 'meres man' to look after the birds.

There were other boats besides those of the hunters, for there were few roads, and water was the chief means of trans-port. Wedding and funeral parties rowed over it on the way to the parish church at Hatfield; one funeral party was so drunk that the boat was tipped over, and all of them were drowned. In winter the inhabitants were often marooned in the few villages because the ice was too thick for a boat to cut through, and too thin to skate on. Beggars and wild characters haunted the district, where there was always food to poach, and where they could hide successfully if necessary; and a hermit dwelt peaceably amongst them in a little hut.

In medieval days Gilfred de Gaddesley, a monk from Selby, worked for twenty-one years at draining a portion of Hatfield Chase owned by the monastery. His attempts angered the people, who imagined that the draining would deprive them of their free fish and fowl, and they appealed to Parliament against him. After his death 'certayn unknown persons' destroyed his work. No further important attempt was made until 1626 when the Dutchman, Cornelius Vermuyden, made a contract with Charles I to drain the Chase.

Vermuyden also met with opposition in the three years during which the work lasted. The people turned against him because his one serious mistake of altering the course of the river Don to drain into the Aire instead of the Ouse caused the land round Fishlake to become flooded. In order to remedy this he had to make a new river bed from Snaith to Goole, and the cut, which is always called the Dutch river, cost him twenty thousand pounds.

Vermuyden settled with his Dutch colony near Sandtoft, just over the Lincolnshire border, and built a chapel there, and a large house, 'Crow Trees,' which is now pulled down. When his work was finished he bought the manor at Hatfield from the king, but he soon lost interest in it, and moved to another part of the country, selling his estate among a number of Dutchmen. In 1686 the people of the Isle of Axholme in Lincolnshire burnt down the Sandtoft chapel, and the colony from Holland moved from there to settle round Thorne in Yorkshire, where they were joined by Huguenots and other refugees. They built many of the present houses in Thorne and Hatfield, and roofed them with red Dutch tiles. Dutch family names are still common, and Vermuyden's name is perpetuated on inns and streets. But the foreigners' greatest memorials are the corn-growing fields of this corner of Yorkshire, more than they themselves ever knew, for the draining continued.

The drained land was still liable to heavy floods. One of the worst of these was in 1687 when the farmers had to carry their cattle in boats to the higher ground, and besides the trouble of moving had to bear the expense of keeping them there for two or three months. Abraham de la Pryme tells in his diary of the Level banks bursting with a noise which could be heard miles away, and the water making such a large hole that the banks had to be remade in a wide curve round it. Another diarist, James Fretwell, records how in

1740 the floods froze, and 'the ice and snow was drove in heaps upon the Marsh, and froze together, so that they appeared like so many mountains. . . . For some days, when the water began to fall, the ice kept cracking day and night, like unto guns discharged at a distance.'

The waterways still attracted great quantities of game—in 1692 thirty-two pair of duck and teal were killed at one shot. De la Pryme tells of catching delicate fish in the river Went, amongst them 'such vast knots of eels, almost as bigg as a horse, that they break all their netts in pieces.' Ten years earlier he had found in the river Don at Fishlake, 'sea dogs, a hee and a shee, and a purpose, the last of which I saw.'

East of Hatfield and Thorne great tracks of peat moorland, covered with heather, mosses and low birch-trees, give some idea of the old wastes, though even these are now drained to a great extent. On a mild, sunny day in November we walked over Hatfield Moor, stepping straight on to it from the cultivated land. Bracken lay in golden patches on the darkening heather, though blackberries still hung thickly on the bushes by the roadside. The season for birds was almost over, but we saw a flock of rooks mobbing a marsh harrier, one or two of which birds usually visit the moor at this time of the year. Wild geese fly over in winter on their way to the corn stubble at the edge, and if overtaken by sudden fog alight and spend the night here. Grass-snakes about three feet long and venomous adders live on the moor. An old man named Henry Warburton used to collect adders in a stocking, spread them on the flagstones in Thorne churchyard to revive, and use them for medicine. In summer midges and flies can be unbearable. But these are all natural occupants of a moor; the great dread to-day is of fire, which in most cases is caused by careless visitors; in 1937 it broke out on seven successive Sundays. Once the fire gets a hold on the peat it will last for weeks, spreading quickly and taking everything before it, so that only blackened stumps remain to tell of what were fir- and birch-trees. The gamekeeper has known his cottage to be completely surrounded by flames, so that the noise and heat were terrifying.

In the midst of Hatfield Chase, just beyond the gamekeeper's cottage, a circle of grassland, about an acre in extent, rises suddenly out of the marsh. In the centre of this stands a substantial house with tall oak-trees beside it and a well-filled stackyard. It has a peculiar phantom effect, rising out of the boggy waste with no arable land in sight, and it is not surprising that legends and stories have grown up round Lindholme Hall.

The first inhabitant of this island on the moor was a hermit named William of Lindholme, who had a cell here in which he was eventually buried. Being something of a giant, he has taken the place of mythical figures in accounting for phenomena of the district. It was 'Billy Lindum,' as he is called locally, who threw the large stone a mile from his house to a cottage down the road. It is said that the devil, meeting him one night, offered to make a road over the moor if he did not look back. After a mile curiosity overcame the hermit, and turning round he had the wonderful sight of hundreds of devils, dressed in red, hard at work, before they disappeared for ever, leaving the road half finished—even to-day it is rougher beyond that point.

Billy is made a child to account for the white sparrows in the district. The tale goes that one day his parents left him to scare the sparrows from the corn while they went to Wroot Feast, but as soon as they had gone he shut the sparrows in a barn and went off to the feast himself. Next morning the birds which had not died had turned white, and ever since then there have been white sparrows at Lindholme.

The hall was built as a shooting-lodge near the remains of the cell, and is now a farmhouse. The farm land a little distance away was made about fifty years ago by dry warping from the bed of the old river Don. Men can remember standing inside the warping pit when it was thirty feet deep. It is now filled with water, and is known as Lindholme Lake.

The warp was spread six inches thick over the peat and the land grows good corn and potatoes.

On Thorne Moors, further north, peat was cut and dried for fuel until about a hundred years ago. Forty families worked at it, and the dry peat was carried in boats to Thorne, where it was shipped to York and Hull. The boats, called keels, were pointed at both ends because it was impossible to turn them round in the narrow drains.

Peat is still cut extensively on the Hatfield and Thorne moors, but little is sold for fuel now. It is made into peat-moss litter, packing, and patent manures, and a certain amount is sold wet for medicinal baths. This industry, too, is connected with Holland, from whom England formerly bought all her peat moss. At first Dutchmen were imported for the summer 'graving' (cutting) season, but now local men are employed to 'grave' all the year through.

The graving seemed hard work, but two old men whom we watched had been on these moors respectively forty-four and fifty years. They worked as partners, one graving and one carrying the blocks to dry. The graver wore sandals, made with wooden soles and leather toe-caps and heels, over his boots, so as not to kick up the soft peat. They showed us the roots, called 'rag,' inside the peat, and told how a man they knew had once had some of these spun and woven and made into a suit.

The blocks of peat are spread in various processes to dry, and are finally built into long stacks like enormous potato pies. These are carted as required to mills which surround the moor, and here they are ground, graded, and packed into bales. The whole industry with the elaborate draining, the good roads made as each new stretch is started, and the curious little mills, is strangely un-English still.

In the early days of the industry as the peat was taken the land was warped by means of drains and sluices from the tidal river Ouse, until it was covered with a sufficient depth of mud. This soil, which is practically without stones, makes some of the finest potato-growing land in the country. The sluices still open to the river, but no warping is done to-day, because it would cost as much as the land is worth.

South and west of Thorne Moor canals run through placid, contented country. Barges coming silently down them are often the only movement on the land, and their brown sails bring warmth to the scene in winter and colour in summer. So vividly does the water mirror them, that the reflection is as distinct as the reality.

If a keen wind blows they move briskly down the canal, but as it drops towards evening, they come so slowly on the last few miles to Thorne, that they scarcely seem to move. On such occasions there is time for conversation as they glide through the road gates.

'How's yon lad of yourn gettin' on?' asks the keeper of the gate.

'Oh, not so bad. He's up at Middlesbrough now.'

'Where's Harry? He's not been down lately?'

'On t' dole, I think.'

Then the gate closes, the barge with its load of wheat or cement glides away on its journey to Doncaster or Sheffield, to return another day carrying coal to Hull, and the keeper goes back into his cottage facing the canal.

The bargee, calling to us on the tow-path, told us that every year there were fewer sailing-boats, and soon there would be none left. 'You see,' he said, 'petrol's dearer, but it's sure.'

North of Thorne lies a forgotten corner which lost much of its life when the river Don was turned away from it. At Eastoft the old river bed runs as a dry ditch through the middle of the village with roads which are unnecessary now on either side of it. Beyond it the villages lie by the bank of the river Ouse in straggling lines of faded brick cottages sandwiched between white - washed ones. These seem in bright sunlight to be cut out of cardboard, but when the sinking sun casts its glow over them, they are like old prints. They are silent places whose lower windows face the floodbank which shuts off the river Ouse, but whose upper windows look over it to where the water rushes swiftly to become the Humber.   The road winds through them—Ousefleet, Whitgift, Swinefleet—to the growing port of Goole.

Great liners cannot reach Goole, but it is an important port for Scandinavian, Dutch, and German boats.   There was a German boat in, flying the Nazi flag, when we were there.

Whitgift on the Ouse

'That's t' Nazis,' an old sailor informed us.   'Aye, that's 'Itler, that is.'

The bulk of the coal which comes down the canals and rivers is shipped at Goole.   A form of water traffic used nowhere else in the world runs from here by river and canal through Ferrybridge, to Leeds.   It is a line of any number up to twenty barges, each carrying from forty to fifty tons of coal, joined by chains, and pulled by one tug.   The local name for it is 'Tom Puddings,' and it moves down the river like a snake.   As the whole contrivance takes only four men to run it, it seems strange that it is not more generally used.

Until 1650, Goole was merely a tiny hamlet in the parish of Snaith. Since then it has gradually drawn to itself the trade of smaller ports, such as Thorne and Selby higher up the river.

> Selby was a seaport town,
> When Goole was but a marsh,
> Now Goole it is a seaport town
> And Selby fares the worse.

Snaith is a striking example of the way in which the centre of a district can shift with changing conditions. Its large and very beautiful church, which belonged to Selby Abbey, tells of its past importance, when its parish stretched twenty miles from Adlingfleet on the east to Whitley Bridge on the west. Its enormous Methodist chapel was built for a large population only a century ago. Now it is a sleepy country town, scarcely more than a village, with a general air of sadness and decay about it; and only the annual calling of the Court of Piepowder tells of its fair and market when cattle filled its streets.

In the midst of its decline Snaith retains a vital local industry in the making of clog soles. Though mill-girls no longer wear clogs, and gum-boots have taken their place for many jobs on the farm, there is still a demand for a certain number, and when many firms have fallen out, the few that remain get the trade. Nothing keeps the wet out and the feet warm so well as clogs.

Machinery has replaced hand labour to cut and shape the soles, but the workshop has the attraction of any factory dealing with timber, the smell of newly sawn wood, heaps of sawdust on the floor, and piles of soles waiting their destination and completion. The soles are sent all over England, Scotland, and Ireland, and each district has its own preference as regards shape. Yorkshire demands a rounded toe, Lancashire a rather narrow, square one, and London a wide, square one. These go by the names of 'common,' 'square,' and 'London.' The wood is chiefly beech, alder, and sycamore, but Scotland prefers silver birch.

* c

There begins here a succession of magnificent churches whose Norman architecture is obviously influenced by that of the abbey church at Selby: Birkin with its Norman apse and carvings, the chancel arch and doorway at Brayton, the doorways at Riccall and Stillingfleet. The boldness of their conception is surprising in this land over which the memory of the marsh still hangs.

The abbey church which was their inspiration is the one monastic church in Yorkshire where worship has continued without any break since it was built. It began when Hugh Baldricson, sheriff of Yorkshire, noticed a cross on a wooden building as he was sailing down the river, and landed to find a monk who had come to settle here because of a vision. He brought him to the notice of William the Conqueror, who in 1069 founded here the first monastery in the north of England after the Conquest. Amongst its many beauties, the different types of Norman work, such as the north doorway and the arches and carved piers of the nave, are most memorable at Selby. In our own time the two west towers have been raised according to the first plan of the monks.

The church looks out on the life of the town, whose people have a strong affection for it and often turn into it from the street for a few minutes of its rest and peace. We heard a woman call out to a girl from some cottages near: 'I tell you what, Mary, you 'll have to get done early on Thursday, there 's four big weddings at the abbey.' The weekly market is held under the shadow of it. Selby is a favourite market, and though the stall-owners complain that it is dear, they continue to come on a Monday, erecting their stalls down the middle of the square, and crying their wares. Across the road the farmers' wives stand at the edge of the pavement with baskets of eggs, butter, and chickens to sell, and, according to the season, flowers, gooseberries, apples, and plums from their orchards. Many of them still spit for luck on the 'handsel,' the first money they receive.

New industries mingle with the old here, the flour mills

with their tall silos, the oil and cake mills landing their romantic cargoes from the river, the yards where fishing trawlers are made, the sugar beet factory organizing its autumn campaign.

All around is fertile agricultural land with fields of potatoes, peas, celery, and here and there a yellow square of mustard. Each crop brings its own activity and its group of outside workers. Such notices in shop windows as: 'Pea Pickers wanted for Mr Marshall, Wistow Lordship, for Monday. Bring own baskets,' tells that the pea-picking season has arrived. For a few weeks the pickers, stripping the plants and carrying their sackfuls to be weighed, bring colour and movement to the scene. Then they are gone, and as the potato-pickers take their place, long potato pies rise in the fields. Months later, when groups of men and women are sorting round the pies, you know that winter is over, as the life of the land follows the seasons.

North of Selby the story is still of water, of Tostig and Harold disembarking at Riccall to march to victory and defeat; the ironwork on Stillingfleet church doorway in the shape of a Viking ship commemorates this. Past Skipwith Common, where black-headed gulls nest, and Howden, with its lovely church, half in ruin, half in use, we are back at the Ouse again. A great iron bridge crosses the river at Boothferry now, saving the long journey round by Selby, and heavy traffic from Hull to the west booms over it. We lean over the bridge, looking across to where the Aire joins the Ouse, and remember not many years ago being rowed across the river in a ferry-boat. It was almost as quiet then as it must have been in 1600 when there was only a ferryman's cottage at the little place called Booth.

Hull

CHAPTER 5

HULL AND HOLDERNESS

A series of small wooded dales open out from the southern slopes of the Yorkshire Wolds to the flat land by the river Humber. From the high road which gathers each of them up you see the river, a broad silver band between the green fields of Yorkshire, and the mistier green of Lincolnshire beyond. It has grown far beyond the stage at which from a distance its course is marked merely by the trees which border it, and large boats move along it on their way to and from Goole.

The Humber is a tidal river with the smell of the sea over it, but, watching it here where it has gathered to itself most of the Yorkshire rivers, it is not of the sea to which it is going that you think, but of the country from which it has come. The tang of peat and heather, the green of mossy rocks, the scent of meadow flowers, the shade of thorn-trees, willows, and alders, the refuse of mills and factories are in the rushing stream. It bears the echo of the songs of curlews and peewits,

44

the whirr of snipe, the hum of swallows' wings, the bleating of lambs, the call of the shepherd to his dog, the sound of reaping, the voices of haymakers and harvesters, the splash of an angler landing fish, the shouts of mill-girls as they stream from the mills, the tramp of miners and cutlers on their way to work, the traffic of Yorkshire over hundreds of bridges. The waters of the Humber have drained a county.

Old prints show the countryside along the Humber bank dotted with windmills, but only one of the few which survive is working. This stands on a hill at Skidby, near Cottingham, its domed tower showing for miles round, a lonely remnant of a picturesque past. The manager, who has been at the mill most of his working life, led us up the first flight of worn stairs and out on to the low gallery where the sails, thirty-six feet long, swept past us. Inside again their long arms made flickering shadows across the windows, and their whirr was the only sound not muffled by the covering of white dust which lay thick on everything as we mounted to where the enormous grindstones were working at the top. The windmill is the first of a significant series, for the firm which works it also runs a water-mill at Welton and a steam mill at Hull.

It is to Hull, the third port in England, that the river and the roads are going. Its magnet quality is noticeable in the surrounding villages, which are fast becoming its suburbs. Hull differs from the towns of the industrial areas in being isolated. Its roads drift to the country instead of into another town. It rises from a sleeping land, a land many of whose industries and trades it has confiscated.

Modern Hull is a clean town with imposing official buildings, domed roofs, large department stores, and a flourishing repertory theatre. The main entries are broad streets with avenues of trees, and these are rapidly being flung further into the country to be as quickly surrounded by housing estates. In the city the streets are lordly in plan, taking in many cases the name of the man whose idea or gift they were. One of the newest is built over the Queen's Dock, where boats used to move in a romantic fashion through the centre of the city. Prince's Dock is the only one left with a nodding acquaintance with the town, so that what constitutes the real life of Hull is now on an edge of it.

The old town lies east of the newer development, and here down narrow alleys and in out-of-the-way corners there are relics of it, odd pages in the city's stirring story. This began when Edward I exchanged land in Wawne with the monks of Meaux Abbey for the two hamlets of Myton and Wike on the west bank of the river Hull, where its entrance into the Humber formed a natural harbour. He called his new town Kingston-upon-Hull, and merchants eagerly flocked to it because of the charter for markets and an annual fair and other privileges which he granted. William de la Pole was the first to come from the still flourishing port of Ravenser on Spurn Head, and other merchants followed him as the sea gradually inundated that port. The de la Poles rose in importance with the town, becoming bankers wealthy enough to lend money to Edward III for his French and Scottish wars, and in the third generation Michael de la Pole, as Earl of Suffolk, was the first English merchant to be made a peer.

Henry VIII widened the fortifications of the walled town to take in the village of Drypool across the river Hull. Charles I was lavishly entertained here in 1638, but only three years later he knocked in vain for entrance at the Beverley Gate, and the refusal of the Parliamentarians to admit him started the Civil War in England. That was Hull's last personal connection with the kings of England. To-day, though its royal name is used officially, it is always spoken of, and ordnance maps mark it, as plain Hull. It keeps its royal memories by naming its docks and many of its streets after kings and queens.

The stir and thrill of the early days when the port was growing and making history, when dignity was being added to the status of a merchant, is strong yet in this old part. It was from the beginning a brick town—the art of brick-making was revived here in the fourteenth century to build it; but the streets were paved with stone brought from Holland as ships' ballast. There is nothing left of the houses which the de la Poles and their fellow merchants built, but the memory of their gardens remains in the names of the streets made over them. The Land of Green Ginger tells of the potherbs grown there, and Bowlalley Lane runs where they played bowls. And there are still the churches whose walls echoed to their footsteps: St Mary's in Lowgate, where an archway supporting the tower now spans the pavement, and the beautiful church of Holy Trinity in Highgate, with its mixture of fourteenth-century brick and stonework, and where there are tombs and arms of the de la Poles. Some of the old spirit seems to return on market days when stalls are ranged under the walls of Holy Trinity church.

There are relics of the Elizabethan town in the Manor House, now the White Harte Inn, and the Merchant Adventurers' Hall where the grammar school was also held, but most of these earlier houses were rebuilt or restored out of recognition in the eighteenth and early nineteenth centuries. By this time large numbers of merchants had become wealthy, and had money to spare in ornamenting the new homes which they built with counting-houses on the ground floor in or round the High Street. Some of them also had mansions in the surrounding country, and kept their dignified Georgian town houses for the winter. One of the finest of these was the home of William Wilberforce, the slave emancipator, and is now a museum named after him. This is a land of offices and warehouses to-day, but it remained a residential quarter until well into the nineteenth century. In Victorian times there was a strawberry garden at Drypool where people from the town used to meet to gossip and eat strawberries.

The later nineteenth-century builders of the new town planned on a large scale, but even they would have been amazed at the Hull of to-day. The docks, the cause of it, stretch behind it for miles, extending almost to the old port of Hedon, whose trade long ago came to Hull. This is a

world in itself, an impassioned world where distance is eliminated and variety and strangeness have become commonplace.
Here is a mirror of Yorkshire industry: long lines of coal-
trucks with familiar names on them—Hickleton, Denaby,
Airedale—waiting on the sidings; steel goods from Sheffield
and Rotherham; woollen goods and machinery from the West
Riding. This utilitarian merchandise mingles with cargoes
from other lands, changing with the seasons. Bags of rice
powder and linseed from Rangoon are packed into barges for
the starch and seed-crushing works; cranes dangle bales of
Australian wool for the West Riding; bags of sprouts, onions,
and potatoes have come from Holland, boxes of eggs from
Denmark, timber from Norway, butter from New Zealand,
fruit from Canada; and barley, wheat, and maize from the
Dominions pour down the chutes on their way to the silos.

The fish dock, where during the last few years more fish
has been landed than at any other port in the world, seems a
forest of masts. It is very English here; local sailors man
the trawlers and the buyers and sellers are English.

At this older end of the docks you find the dingy streets
which made the nineteenth-century visitors shudder, but will
soon be things of the past. They are ripe for pulling down,
but something irreplaceable will go with them, the fantastic
and fascinating quality of a district which is cosmopolitan and
poor. Here are marine stores with long ships' masts reared
above the doors to proclaim them, and windows a mixture of
anything from oranges to sailors' socks. You wonder to what
country that blue sailor's jacket hanging on a bit of string will
travel, what sailor's child will buy those bright red sweets.
Those unkempt women coming out of the stores or gossiping
at their doorways have connections all over the world.

These people mix with the rural visitors and the town residents at Hull Fair in October. The mayor opens the fair,
and the charter granted in 1299 is read, but there is nothing
here in common with the old cattle and sheep fair. It is the
largest amusement fair in the north of England with all the

blatancy and tawdriness of a great modern feast, a blaze of light and a clang of noise with megaphones screeching against each other to tell of dwarfs and coloured boxers and serpent trainers, anything so long as it is sensational. Parents of families enjoy it most, because they loved Hull Fair when it was one of the few treats of the year—Hull Fer they call it in the East Riding. You wonder if the toffee apples and coco-nuts bring back childish experiences, and if they have any

Beverley

feeling that the joyous excitement which they remember has been replaced by the tired, strained air of a modern feast.

Where Hull is the commercial gateway to Holderness, the inland town of Beverley is an ecclesiastical one. It seems to connect with the magnificent Holderness churches, which are now so often too large for their needs. The town takes a little of its spirit from this flat land, a little from the rolling country of the Wolds, but most from its position round its two churches.

The white stone of the minster and the church of St Mary stands out in relief against the warm brick houses, and their buildings seem to draw into harmony those which came after them, the fifteenth-century gateway of Monk Bar, the market cross with its friendly turret, the dignified Georgian houses which are a delight in the main street. Modern buildings have not up to the present destroyed the uniformity, and the churches set their seal of dignity upon it whether you wander in their naves and aisles or see their white towers rising above the town as you approach over the grassy common of Westwood.

Beverley sank to great poverty when it lost its woollen trade in the sixteenth century, and vaulted cellars which had fallen in gaped in the streets. Much later Hull took its trade as a port, but it survives to-day as a busy market town.

The road slips unobtrusively out of it into the flat, sleepy land of Holderness. This is a remote, detached country, seeming always aware that the sea broke against cliffs between Hull and Bridlington and rolled into a bay at Driffield before there was anything of it at all. The peninsula is glacial moraine, formed during the Ice Age, and its first inhabitants were the Neolithic people who lived in lake dwellings on the series of lakes dotted with islands into which the country settled. Traces of these have been found at Ulrome and Skipsea along with a harpoon and other implements. They were probably reached by the kind of floating road which Holderness farmers still make over marshy pieces of land by binding birch twigs or bundles of grass into faggots, laying them across the marsh, and covering them with gravel.

Hornsea Mere, the largest lake in Yorkshire, is the only one of the glacial lakes which remains. It runs down from marshy, reedy land to the fringe of the old town. Rare birds haunt its shores, and at one end there is a heronry. In winter when the water freezes over, and the birds stand motionless on the ice, the mere gives some feeling of the scene which the water-logged land must have presented in winter. Even after centuries of draining, Holderness was for long a damp place, and its people were afflicted with ague, for which the local name was 'the shakking.'

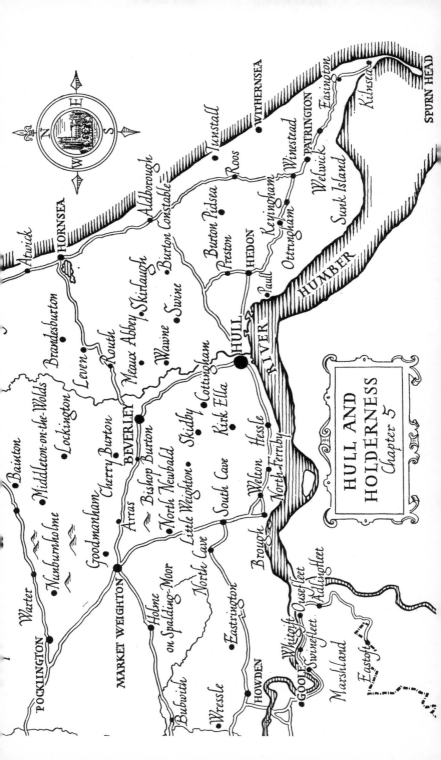

HULL AND
HOLDERNESS
Chapter 5

This flat country has not the Dutchlike quality which we saw round Hatfield, for low hillocks and clumps of trees break it in places. The villages are on the whole characterless, and roads open into them and pass them as if they had never been. But here and there a more striking one stands out, such as Patrington with its wide main street and beautiful church, or Easington whose houses and walls are built of large pebbles, and where there is a thatched tithe barn. Almost all of them are lifted from monotony by their lovely and varied churches.

At intervals large dikes for draining cut the country. Insistent draining, started first by the Knights of Holderness, resulted in the 'Rich Holderness—excelling for her grain,' of which Drayton makes the East Riding boast. Cobbett was amazed with the fertility of the land, which he says was the envy of agriculturalists, and grew such corn that merchants came long distances to buy it. It is now divided into large fields by hedges known as 'brushings,' after the old temporary hedges. Shire horses, for which the district used to be famous, are coming into demand again, and twelve or fifteen can be seen grazing with sheep and cattle in a single field.

The farmhouses seem to melt into the land, and their outbuildings and well-filled yards after harvest tell of rich acres. The stacks themselves are shapeless, and very few are thatched. They are merely protected by a layer of straw kept in place by a weighted net, a method which is effective, but seems to show a lack of pride in the work.

A kind of lethargy hangs over the whole promontory. It is as if the quietness and apathy which you might expect in country cut off except on one side by water were accentuated by the melancholy of land which the sea is wearing away. Seen from the shore, there is a look of hopelessness about the low, jagged cliffs of the wasting coast. The red, clayey land is bringing about its own destruction, for it is underground drainage which causes the ground to crack and fall; the sea merely carries away what would otherwise form a lower layer of land.

Open sea now rolls across what was once miles of green country with villages on the coast. Old maps mark their sites far out to sea—a tragic line, Hartburn, Cleton, Hornsea Burton, Old Aldborough, Old Kilnsea, and many more. They belong to a ghostly but not very distant past, for the sea is washing away the coast at the rate of seven feet a year— fifteen near Kilnsea. It has taken three and a half miles since the Roman occupation of Britain. 'Buried in the sea,' is the end of many Holderness stories.

Roads which once led to these villages now end abruptly at the empty shore and their signposts have merely the names of sands on them, or the simple words, 'To the Seaside.' Here and there along them you find an old house or inn whose doom is already sealed; an inn at Ulrome fell into the sea in 1938.

There used to be a peculiar haunting attraction about this coast with its low cliffs and little sandy bays in which you could be alone by the sea. Now, wherever a road leads out to the shore a summer camp, a conglomeration of huts and caravans, has been planted along it without place or order, and one sus-pects with the cliff as the only drain. They make one regret that campers of to-day are forsaking tents, which are attractive in themselves, and depart with the occupants.

The present villages lie a mile inland. The only places now actually on the coast are the two resorts of Hornsea and Withernsea, which are large enough to have been able to build promenades and breakwaters to keep back the sea. At Hornsea it is vital to keep it from the mere, which would flood the surrounding land.

Villages and buildings have also vanished along the Humber shore—the Early English door in Easington church was brought from Burstall Priory before it was buried—but here the tide has given as well as taken away. The district of Sunk Island was formed by mud washed from the seashore up the estuary. It appeared as an island in the middle of the seventeenth century: in 1767 it was a mile and a half from the coast, in 1771 little more than a mile, and by 1827 the channel between was no wider than a drain. Having risen from the sea, it was claimed by the Crown, which still owns it. Its rich warp land is divided into large farms, but has that detached air of all Holderness, intensified a hundredfold.

The silting up brought ruin to many small ports on the estuary. The streams, here called havens, and the drains running into the Humber formed natural harbours for the villages a little way inland, and as these filled up only small boats could reach them. Hedon shows its past importance in its beautiful church, but its harbour is now a grass field with an avenue of trees down the centre.

Sea and estuary shores draw together at Kilnsea, the gateway to Spurn Head. Here on one hand is the sea with its stretch of sand when the tide goes out, and on the other the river with its edge of sandy beach merging at low tide on to banks of mud. The land between consists of sandbanks covered with coarse grass and strange fleshy sea plants—sea holly with its silvery-grey leaves and blue flowers, sweet-smelling southernwood, clumps of sea purslane.

Old Kilnsea is in the sea, and for many years at certain low tides the ruins of its church could be seen. But Kilnsea seems secure compared with the narrow isthmus which runs out to the sea as Spurn Head. It shows plainly from here, a curving strip of land stretching for four miles, and widening out into a spoon shape at the end where, looking stronger than what it stands on, is the famous lighthouse of Spurn. It differs from schoolday imaginings and from the rocky headland which early writers who had never visited it describe.

There is no road beyond Kilnsea. You must walk over the soft, sinking sand to it or get a permit to travel in the army trolley. We rode out with the postman and a party of girl guides from Hull, who munched sweets and sang a lively song with a refrain beginning:

> For we 're all down in t' cellar 'oile,
> Where t' mud slarts on t' winders.

They seemed as unmoved by this strange scene as they would have been by a Hull street.

We passed men unloading blocks of chalk from a boat to strengthen the banks at the narrowest parts, and finally the sandy waste broadened and we stepped out between the lighthouse and a few scattered houses. There are no roads or attempt at lay-out, nothing but the deep, dry sand. Women and children came up from the cottages for their milk and parcels, and several dogs barked at us—there are eighteen familes in Spurn and sixteen dogs.

Three separate communities inhabit the headland: the War Department, grim but necessary, on the low, vulnerable shore; the lifeboat crew, the only permanent one in England, occupying with their families a row of houses which are lashed by the sea during winter storms; and the lighthouse keepers, living in cottages built snugly inside the circular foundations of an earlier lighthouse.

Water is pumped to the houses from a fresh-water spring discovered in the river bed when a fort was built there during the 1914–1918 War. Ballast collectors, until they were sent away, made a larger population at Spurn, and a cottage by the Humber was an inn which did a good trade with them and passing ships.

There is little to occupy the people except their work. The coxswain of the lifeboat has a garden, and squares are railed off for keeping hens or growing a few potatoes. It seems amazing that anything so earthy as a potato can mature in this sand, but at one time most of the people grew their own, manuring them with mud and seaweed from the shore. Formerly the lifeboat crew filled in time by fishing for crabs which they took across the Humber to Grimsby to sell, but this no longer pays them.

The first lighthouse on Spurn was erected by a hermit named Reedbarrow in 1428. In 1772 Smeaton built two towers, one for the river and one for the coast, and their several successors have stood on different sites owing to the shifting sand. Two keepers look after the present 519,000-candle-power light, whose chief use is to guide ships going north away from the Humber mouth. Red and white lights on lower levels guide the ships up the estuary.

The population is a moving one, and the children who meet in the little school are a cosmopolitan group. Of the nine whom we saw, two had lived in London, one in India, one in Egypt, and two in Mauritius. Yorkshire voices were least prominent amongst them. The children brought out their collections of flowers and butterflies and told us about the birds. Spurn may not have the normal excitements of modern life to offer, but for a child or an adult interested in nature study it is a paradise. There were rare butterflies in these cases, and specimens of peculiar sea plants of the kind any one living far inland seldom sees growing.

The whole of Spurn is a bird sanctuary. Terns, oyster catchers, and ringed plovers nest here; golden-crested wrens and woodcocks fly over; siskins feed on the mud shores in autumn until bad weather drives them further south or inland; skeins of pink-footed geese pass over to spend their nights on the sandbanks of the Humber and their days in the fields of Holderness and the Wolds. The promontory lies on the track of migrating birds, and hundreds used to beat themselves to death by flying against the glass of the lighthouse lamp. Now every spring and autumn perches are put out round the gallery for them to rest on, and there are few casualties except in foggy weather, when plovers and starlings are the most frequent victims.

Every year more sand and mud are silting up against the farthest point of the headland, the tip of the spoon. A military tower, now quite a way inland, was built over a dump on the high-water line during the War. On the new beach where a border of drift and seaweed showed the last tide line, we thought of vanished Ravenser, whose site, once on the Humber, is off the coast now, for the shape of Spurn has altered since its time. It began as an island thrown up by the sea and joined to the

SPURN HEAD

mainland by a rocky road. A man named Peter made a house on it in the wreck of a ship and sold provisions to passing ships until merchants were attracted to it and it became a prosperous port holding fairs and markets; and then the sea claimed it, and in the fifteenth century it was wiped out.

We imagined Henry, Duke of Lancaster, landing secretly on this silent shore some years after Ravenser was abandoned on his way to usurp the throne of Richard II, and finding a hermit named Matthew Danthorpe, the predecessor of Reed-barrow, building a chapel; and Edward IV landing here on his return from Holland, and spending the night in a poor cottage in Kilnsea.

But the ghosts of these visitors to Spurn are not here, where they merely landed on the way to other places, and as we turned from our dreamings of the past and looked along the narrow ridge we too felt glad to belong to the mainland beyond it.

A Wold Road near Sledmere

CHAPTER 6

THE WOLDS

EVERY year on the third Thursday in March the oldest horse race in England is run at Kiplingcotes on the Yorkshire Wolds. March is not always kind here, and the event is often held in a blizzard, or the course has first to be cleared of snow-drifts. In 1938, however, the sun was shining, and it was a mild spring day when the six riders and the few spectators, press photographers, and reporters gathered at the winning post.

The first prize is the interest on £360 given by fifty gentlemen in 1618 on condition that the race is always run. To comply with this, the entries have occasionally been cart-horses or horses drawing wagons. The second prize is the entrance fees, and, as these have been raised during the last few years, it exceeds the first in value—in 1938 it was three times as much.

The rules were read by a member of a family who have done it for generations, and the competitors set out for the starting-point, four miles away. The affair is no Derby or Ascot.

58

The route begins on the old race-course, now merely a rough track over fields, and ends on the grass verge of a modern tarred road. We watched the riders arrive along it one by one, looking hotter and more dishevelled than when they started out, then the money was paid, and every one went home.

We turned to a typical Wold scene. A capacious farmhouse, sheltered on the windward side by a dark clump of trees, stood on the hill slope below the road. In a field beyond it sea-gulls followed a labourer with a plough. Spirals of smoke rose from rubbish fires, and the scent of burning wood and grass wafted over to us. In the distance, across rolling fields bounded by hedges, were the red roofs of a village.

The Yorkshire Wolds are the northern equivalent of the South Downs. Like them they are a great escarpment of chalk hills ending in the white cliffs of the sea, but whereas the downs are chiefly grassland, the greater part of the Wolds is now corn-growing country, showing on its surface the changing colours of the harvest. Such districts are usually flat, but here you can stand on a rise and look over miles of billowing hills all brought into cultivation.

Two distinct types of villages rise from the rolling land. The lowland ones, built chiefly of dark stone, lie like Thixendale at the foot of treeless valleys, or like Bishop Wilton and Kirby Grindalythe in wooded hollows along one of the few streams. The upland ones, such as Fridaythorpe or Wetwang, straggle along open roads, and their white chalk cottages are mirrored in village ponds.

Between these are the sleepy market-towns of Pocklington and Market Weighton and the busier town of Driffield, the capital of the Wolds and the focus for its life. Almost every village and town are enriched by an ancient church. Pre-Conquest towers at Wharram-le-Street and Weaverthorpe show early occupation; the south doorway and font at Kirkburn, the west doorway and gargoyles at Garton-on-the-Wolds, and the lavish carving at North Newbald are fine Norman work; and the Decorated church at Bainton lifts the village out of the ordinary.

The good preservation of many of these churches is due to the zeal of the second Sir Tatton Sykes, a member of the noted Sledmere family. He spent a million and a half pounds on restoring and, where necessary, rebuilding the Wold churches, keeping as far as possible to the original structures and periods. and employing Italian artists for wall paintings and mosaics.

Few of the grassy valleys have water flowing down them. The large village ponds and the many dewponds scattered over the hills are signs of the shortage of streams and rivers. In times of drought some farms are over four miles from a water supply and have to fetch water that distance in tanks; and the nearest village pond is the only supply for cattle. These conditions are gradually being improved under a scheme by which water pumped to a reservoir from underground springs is to be laid to the farms and villages.

Here and there in wet seasons streams called Old Gypsey or Gypsey Race rise intermittently on the hillsides from subterranean reservoirs. The name gypsey appears to come from the Old Norse *geispa* to yawn, and well describes these currents, which work on the system of a siphon; race comes from Old Norse *ras*, a rush of water. The largest of these streams runs from Wharram-le-Street to Bridlington, and is more permanent than the rest, for at one time it supplied power for twenty-six mills. There was a superstition in the neighbourhood that the sudden rising of the Gypsey Race was a sign of some disaster.

The Wold hills are not high enough for their names to have more than a local familiarity—the highest is only eight hundred and eight feet. Roads and old drovers' tracks which are still used for driving cattle go over them. They give rolling vistas of farmland, but it is from the edges of the plateau that you get the extensive views towards the plain, the river Humber, and the sea.

Early people found these dry hills desirable for habitation

and one race after another stayed for a few hundred years, and were then driven further north by a more advanced one. Neolithic races were followed by Bronze Age people who built the huge monolith at Rudston and made a track over the Wolds as part of a route from Ireland to Europe, and they by the Parisii of the Iron Age with their higher culture. Ploughing has taken away the obvious traces of their occupation, but it and organized excavation have discovered arrowheads, spears, axes, swords, and chariot burials of all these people, as they have revealed the presence of Roman villas.

The church at Wharram Percy, with its blocked aisles and only a few humps to show where the village stood, is a relic of the Black Death. The rot which came to agriculture with this visitation sent much of the land back to waste, and until the enclosures the summits of the hills were given over to sheep walks and rabbit warrens. Apart from the turf walls topped with furze which surrounded these there were no hedges or ditches; it was one vast field with stones here and there to mark the boundaries.

The change came when, between 1771 and 1801, Sir Christopher Sykes of Sledmere enclosed his Wold estates and other owners followed his example. This enabled a good deal more land to be brought into cultivation, and trees were planted round the farmhouses and plantations made. The wide grass verges which edge most of the Wold roads were left so that the cottagers, deprived of their common land, could graze their cattle on them.

Sir Christopher enlarged the house which his father, Sir Richard Sykes, the first baronet, had built at Sledmere, and of which he was very proud, not being able to endure to hear of strangers visiting Castle Howard and not calling to see Sledmere also. The house was burnt down in 1911 and has since been rebuilt.

Sir Tatton, the son of Sir Christopher, was perhaps the most famous member of this progressive family. He introduced bone meal as a manure and further improved the land by draining, so that in some places it rose to eight times its former value. Sir Tatton was very proud of his Leicester sheep, and of his famous bloodstock stables, which are still kept up at Sledmere, the stock being sold chiefly as yearlings at the Doncaster horse sales in September. He was happiest tramping about his estates in an old coat, and would often take a turn at road mending or hoeing turnips. He loved the Wolds, and was not content to be away from them for many days. To him the Wold song, *The Statty Fair*, a ballad of the fair held at Driffield Hirings, was the best of all music.

Sir Tatton's elder son restored the churches; his younger son, Sir Christopher, was known as 'The Gulls' Friend,' because he introduced the bill for the preservation of sea birds into Parliament, thus stopping the wholesale shooting of gulls by visitors at Filey, Bempton, Flamborough, and Bridlington.

The Wold farms brought into being by the draining were imposing ones, and until the War were run on a lavish scale. The substantial farmhouses are more often away from the village than in it, standing with one or two cottages behind their shelter of trees. The workers included a foreman, wagoner, third and fourth lads, a wag, that is, a lad to help with the horses and ploughs, and a stable lad or, as he was locally called, 'Tommy Owt,' because he must be able to turn his hand to anything. A very large farm employed more men, but all relied a great deal on outside labour for haymaking and harvest. Irishmen are hired for this to-day, but in the days of hand-loom weaving, men came from the West Riding, and whether they were numerous or not depended on the state of the woollen trade.

However lonely the farm, there were enough people living actually in the house to give it a vigorous life of its own. On Sunday afternoons the lads from two or three farms would meet in turns in the stables of one of them. Another addition to the life of the farm were the shepherds or small farmers' sons, who brought flocks of sheep from Craven and the Pennine dales to winter on the Wolds. They arrived in October, having travelled by road with as many as a thousand ewes collected from several farms, and stayed until March, cutting turnips for the sheep, and looking after them.

At one side of the yard of a Wold farm is a long row of brick sheds to hold the wagons which are among the most important implements on the farm. The Wold wagon, which is peculiar to the district, is influenced by Flemish and German design, and has a distinctive craftsmanship and architectural beauty. It is a shallow wagon with wide overhanging sides to hold the corn, and instead of shafts has a single pole in the centre. The two horses are yoked on either side of this, and the driver rides on the near wheel horse. At one time four horses were used, and earlier still four oxen. Until the War a wagon and two horses were worth £140, and large farms would have ten. A wagoner's was, and is still, one of the most responsible jobs on a farm. He has the control of the farm hands when the foreman, or hind, as he is often called, is not there.

The War killed many customs connected with the harvest, but at Driffield a bell is still rung during the harvest month every morning and evening at seven o'clock except on Sundays. When work started earlier the morning bell was rung at five o'clock. It was a custom on the Mell Supper day to strew a layer of corn in the bottom of the last wagon, in which the children rode home singing:

> 'Here we are as nice as nip,
> We never fell over but once in a grip,
> The grip was wide, the horse couldn't stride,
> So hip, hip, hooray!'

The custom of tying the last few standing stalks into a little sheaf and burning it in the field has gone. This was known as 'Bonnin' awd witch,' and, like the making of the Mell Doll, which signified that the last sheaf of corn was sacred, had a pagan origin.

In some respects the harvest festivals of the churches have taken the place of the harvest customs, but these have not the

A WOLD POND AT FRIDAYTHORPE

same robustness. The old customs had their bad side, but they were an expression of pride and interest in the harvest, those qualities which made each man build his stack as a thing of beauty. Men's hearts were in the land then. A Wold farmer, after listening to a clergyman telling of his visit to Palestine, asked: 'And is there any good mangel-wurzels in that country?'

The story of Wold farming to-day is often one of depression, of farms going derelict or being worked by the owners for lack of tenants, of good land let for half a crown an acre, of men holding grimly on to farms which their forbears have worked for generations. Houses which were homes of prosperous farmers are now occupied by hinds and the long rows of wagon sheds are almost empty—though the use of tractors has had something to do with this. The granaries above them have stored little corn during recent years, and there have been few stacks in the yards. The farmer to-day wants ready money so badly that he threshes as soon as possible after harvest and does not trouble to thatch. In the once tidy yards and in the fields the straw is left scattered about for weeks after threshing for want of labour to clear it. Only on a few farms such as the Sledmere home farm are there thatched stacks now, and here they are still finished off with the ends curving into a fine point and a wooden ornament. In times of depression the Wold farmers feel the disadvantage of their height and the shallowness of the soil. They have to contend with a fairly late harvest. In the wet autumn of 1938 stooks of corn stood in the fields in November, each with a green cap, where the ears were shooting. Sugar beet, to which so many farmers have turned, does well in places, but the roots are small because of the shallow soil.

The tale of woe is worse in some parts than others. Apart from differences in soil, Wold farms vary according to whether or not they face south. There are still many which flourish without too rigid economy. Some of the finest of these are round Sledmere, the show farms of the estate. Here the

D

hedges are trimmed as if a gardener had cut them, and the well-tilled fields have scarcely a weed in them. 'Look at it,' a local man said. 'Look at it; just like a garden, isn't it?'

Good or bad as farming may be, the Wolds still present a scene of activity when the corn harvest begins. Standing at one point you see examples of every stage in process. On all sides the corn is falling to the reapers, and men are gathering it into stooks. In some fields it stands drying, in others it is being piled into Wold wagons, which will presently sway along the narrow roads to where the stacks are being built beside the houses. A few fields are still ripening in the sun, and here and there a tractor is already at work ploughing the gathered fields ready for the next harvest.

Sheep graze with their lambs in the pastures in spring and summer, and are folded in the turnip fields in winter. Here, besides fertilizing the land, they trample down the shallow soil and keep it firm, so that, apart from their own value, they give as much as they take out of it.

And there is life yet in the Martinmas Hirings at Driffield. We were told before we went that there would be little to see, but we found the streets crowded with men and boys and there was a general air of holiday, though the farms now have to compete for labour with the new aerodrome at Driffield. The chief hirings are on the Thursday after Martinmas. The farm hands leave their places the Saturday before this, those who are staying on starting their week or fortnight's holiday then, and those who are changing going home for a few days before getting hired. The men no longer wear slouch hats, corduroy coats, and bell-bottomed trousers, nor does the wagoner carry a whip with as many brass rings as he can afford on it, but many of them can still be picked out by the feathers in their hats. It must have been a farmer with ideas of his own whom we heard remarking: 'I allus pick a lad wi' a cap. He 'll be a better worker, will a lad wi' a cap.'

The boys stand in groups outside the butchers' shops whose windows are piled with hot pies; buy ties, scarves, and pipes at Woolworths; or examine the mackintoshes, breeches, and corduroy trousers hanging outside the shop windows, and the tin trunks underneath them.

Lads and men are now chiefly paid by the week instead of annually as the old custom was, and a boy will expect more than the five pounds he would have got for his first year fifty years ago, but they still buy most of their clothes at Martinmas. Mothers meet their sons in to see that they get new clothes before they spend the money on anything else. Nowadays the lads' washing is seldom done in the farmhouses, and women who do it for a shilling a week, drawing the money once a year, are generally early in Driffield too, to make sure of getting paid.

A farmer will pick a boy out of a group, sometimes because he likes the look of him, but more often because he knows something about him. If he engages him he pays him a 'fest,' that is a 'fast-penny,' which is anything from five shillings to a pound, to bind the bargain. If the lad changes his mind he must refund the fest.

The talk is chiefly of the hiring, and stray sentences sound above the rest: 'Arta stoppin' ?' 'Es tha gettin' 'od ?' 'Wheea 's ta gaein' ?' 'Es tha getten thi fest ?'

'Wheea 's George gaein' ?' asks a woman.

'He isn't gaein' annywheear yet. He 's got seven pun' ten left,' comes the reply.'

There are cheap-jacks on the look-out for guileless country boys, and there is still a mild fair to which the Corrigan family, who come from Driffield, bring some roundabouts and vans; but the Martinmas Hirings to-day are chiefly a meeting-place for families and friends who only see each other at this time of the year. Geniality seems to instil warmth into the cold air, for this holiday takes the place of the Christmas one for many of the farm workers. There will be parties and big meals and perhaps one or two toffee suppers where toffee is made round the fire and rolled and eaten while it is still warm.

An orderly crowd attends the Hirings to-day, but at one time there were wild scenes in Driffield streets on that night.   For a long period the whole standard of life on the Wolds was low. Many of the houses were squalid, there was much ill-feeling among the people, and the Church with many of its vicars and rectors living away had little influence.   It was the Primitive Methodist revival about 1760 which turned the fervour of riots and street scenes into better channels.   (It touched the same spirit of sacrifice which showed itself in the seventeenth century when the vicar and the whole village of Rowley sailed to Massachusetts and founded a new Rowley there because of their puritan belief.)

The early Methodist meetings were often held in small cottages, many of them with only one room in which the man and his wife and children would afterwards sleep.   The converts did much extempore praying and falling to the ground in religious zeal, but they showed a practical side by walking long distances to conduct services, often arriving wet through, and they cheerfully endured bad treatment.   These first local preachers were shoemakers and farm workers whose homely speech suited the simple congregations.

'Wakken 'em up, Lord, wakken 'em up!' a ruddy-faced labourer prayed.   'Big words are varry good, but big deeds are better.   Wakken 'em up, Lord, wakken 'em up!'

There is a tale of a young woman who at the time of the revival went into a Bridlington shop to buy ribbon for her summer bonnet.

'I 've got convarted,' she said, 'and I want a modest colour to correspond like.'

'Well,' said the shopkeeper, 'which shall it be, white, yellow, or lilac?   Make thee choice, lass.'

'Nay, ah think a bit bleead reead is as modest as owt going,' she answered, and went away with her conscience and her love of colour satisfied.

The restless element in the people found a different outlet in the Wold Rangers, the last of whom died only a few years ago.   They were a group of about fifty people who forsook a settled life and lived as gipsies, travelling about the Wolds selling articles which they made themselves. Many were skilled craftsmen, and apple scoops which they made by narrowing and hollowing the knuckle-bone of a sheep at one end are treasured in houses in the district.

The memory of these people still hovers over the Wold villages, but one wonders for how long it will do so, for the chalk cottages which are an essential part of them are fast being condemned and pulled down.

'Aye,' said an old man on the village seat at Wetwang, 'they've come round condemnin' 'em, and they're gaein' to rive 'em all up. Yer see, ther's neea drainage.'

No doubt the time has come for them to go, but their replacement by new houses built in squares beyond the villages will rob these communities of their air of clustering together for companionship, and many families will miss the pieces of land which belonged to the old cottages, and gave cobblers, tailors, and all the inhabitants a share in the farming life.

But change comes slowly in the country, and any journey across the Wolds still gives those pictures which have been a part of them for generations: Wold wagons rumbling along the roads with their golden harvest; a farm lad filling a tank in the village pond with the water up to his horse's knees; ducks and geese swimming in another pond or basking on the grass verges; a woman in a bright apron throwing corn to a flock of hens; potter women hawking in the villages while the men lounge with their dogs round their camp on one of the green roads called drives; sheep munching turnips in a field, their heavy earthy fleeces the colour of the soil; a newly ploughed field sprinkled with white flinty chalk; an open road over windswept pastures and corn-fields. 'It's nice an' 'ealthy like 'ere,' the old man told us, 'there's neea reeak fra t' fonnaces.'

Bridlington Harbour

CHAPTER 7

THE MIDDLE COAST

YORKSHIRE'S long coastline provides the county's playground. The majority of its people and many from other counties spend their annual holidays somewhere on the coast between the Humber and the Tees. This middle section of it, which rises from the wasting coast of Holderness through the chalk headland of Flamborough to the brown cliffs of Scarborough and beyond it, is an unbroken pleasure ground.

The three large resorts which have grown to serve the holiday-makers have developed in different ways, partly because of their sites and partly from the demand of the visitors who favoured them. Bridlington with its simple approach to the shore, its golden sands and large, safe bay, and its free and easy ways contrasts with Filey in its smaller bay, endeavouring against modern conditions to keep itself select; and both of them pale beside the size and magnificence of Scarborough, divided into two places by the castle headland, offering its spa and swimming pools and its ability to provide for all tastes.

The beautiful little bays in between these places—Primrose, Cayton, Cornelian—were until a few years ago lonely stretches of shore with paths winding up the cliffs to small villages. Their visitors came by the day from the larger places, but now holiday camps, caravans, and ribbon building have appeared on the cliff tops, and the occupants of these fill the beaches.

Flamborough's white headland has suffered the same fate in parts, but thanks to the efforts of Bridlington an enormous building scheme to occupy the space by the lighthouse has been stopped, and the cliffs which the fishermen were wise enough to leave open, building their village a mile inland, are to be left little spoilt.

We are apt to claim our favourite holiday resorts, to allow them no life of their own in our thoughts, so that it is well to realize the life on this piece of coast before seaside holidays were thought of, when the villages and towns only differed from the inland ones in their occupations.

Bridlington or Burlington, as it was called, had its monastery which owned great tracts of the surrounding country and land as far away as the Pennine dales; and pilgrims came to visit the shrine of St John, entering by the Bayle Gate, under which so many visitors pass to-day. The old town grew round the dissolved monastery, built largely with its stones, and the Bayle Gate became a prison. At Bridlington Quay on the coast a mile away, there were a few fishermen's cottages, and the only visitors were country people coming into the market from the surrounding villages. Those clean-looking villages which have the breezy atmosphere of the Wolds and the listening air of villages by the sea are little changed, and their upland spirit mingles with the spirit of the flat land of Holderness in Bridlington itself.

Bronze Age people built the great dyke at Flamborough as a defence across the headland, and later men, knowing nothing of these early inhabitants, named it Danes Dyke, after more recent Scandinavian conquerors. Up to the time of Henry VIII it was a custom for the head of the Constable family to shoot an arrow with a coin fixed in it into the sea once a year as a due for a grant of land from the Danes. Much later the rangers of Speeton would search the beach for wreckage; and on the cliffs above egg gatherers collected sea-gulls' eggs to sell to the sugar factory in Hull.

Filey was a fishing village clustered round the Early English church which looks from its raised site to where the rocky platform of Filey Brigg runs out into the sea.

The Norseman, Thorgils Skarthi, founded Scarborough about 967, and the little fishing village saw the Norman castle built, sheltered under its shadow for over five hundred years, and then saw it besieged and destroyed and the tower of the parish church ruined in the siege. Still it prospered as a fishing village with a growing harbour.

> The fishermen brave more money have
> Than any merchants two or three;
> Therefore I will to Scarborough go,
> That I a fisherman brave may be,

says an old rhyme. For a time ships were built here, but this industry declined because the harbour, with no river estuary opening into it, could not hold large ships.

The first move towards change in the life of the coast came with the discovery of medicinal wells. These were found at Hornsea, Bridlington, Filey, Scarborough, and Saltburn. A Mrs Farrow discovered a magnesia well under the south cliff at Scarborough as early as 1626, but for a long time it was only used locally, as were other spa wells scattered about the country.

It must have been some realization of the beauty of the coast and its suitability for holidays, as well as a growing desire among people for a change of scene, which started the custom of a man transporting himself and his whole household to the coast in order to take similar waters to those which he could have obtained quite near his home. The growth of the habit is shown in the development of Scarborough. The *Universal Spectator* reported of its 'Spaw Season' in 1732 that 'The Place abounds with all handsome Accommodations; the Conversation is elegant and polite; and a bright Constellation of Luminaries never fail to adorn the Hemisphere.' At first it was always written as Spaw, but the 'w' was omitted in the first minute book of 1826.

The novelty of the scene and the high, towering cliffs impressed the early visitors. In 1733 a Mr Edmund Withers came for a holiday and wrote to his brother, a clergyman, telling him how he had spent his time. He found the 'Place and Company' exceedingly diverting. They drank the waters between seven and ten o'clock, and then amused themselves on the sands, where, he says, 'High and Low equally privileged, pass and repass, mix and separate, as if it were in the Elisian fields.' He describes how to walk 'betwixt the impending Ruines of a prodigious precipice (for such the shore is all along for many miles) threatening to overwhelm, on one hand, and the rage of an impetuous and angry Sea, on the other, awakens a good deal of Horror in the apprehension,' but the sight of the harbour and ships with a view of the town, church, and castle behind, afforded him a 'Prospect too Romantic to be described.' Eleven years before this, by an agreement between John Bland and the corporation, the good carriage road known as Bland's Cliff had been made down to the beach. In 1739 the corporation erected a building over the well, and a Long Room for dancing was built where the Royal Hotel now stands. Many of the early patrons were titled people. Mr Withers mentions dukes, earls, and a marquess among the visitors, and 'Crowds of Scotch Gentry.' All through its holiday history, Scarborough seems to have had a large proportion of Scots visitors.

The wells provided employment for many people who had suffered some misfortune or accident on the sea. The water was served by widows; the first governor was a

*D

deformed man named Richard Dickinson, who was always known as Dicky; and the governor at the beginning of the nineteenth century was a Mr Pearson, who, while a sailor, had lost the use of his hands and feet by frost-bite. Before the cliff bridge was built in 1826, a blind man named Billy Donkin used to keep a plank across the stream for visitors to cross from the town to the spa.

The popularity of the other spas grew along with Scarborough, and Bridlington had a 'Spaing Season.' There was a certain amount of rivalry between them. Doctors wrote pamphlets on the merits of the various springs, and the names of the diseases which they were claimed to cure were as frightening as are the more subtle descriptions of modern advertisements.

By the end of the eighteenth century sea-bathing was added to the attractions, and the number of bathing-machines increased yearly. Again pamphlets were issued telling how to use this new pastime for the good of one's health, but the bathing marked the first turn of the places into holiday rather than health resorts. There were guides to help the ladies in the water. It was all very gay and not too strenuous, and there seems to have been that bustling importance which is a good ingredient for a successful holiday.

The spa season gradually gave way to the phase of the Victorian family holiday, but though the towns grew because of this the nucleus of the old spa was there, influencing the plan; in Scarborough the elegant Regency architecture persisted to a late period.

Purely Victorian building never seems so bad in seaside places as it does inland, perhaps because the high bay-windowed houses are associated in the mind with the joys of childhood holidays. They were ugly but suitable for their purpose; they held with ease the large families for which they were built, and their many stories give numbers of sea views to the visitors of to-day.

It was the Victorians who started the Cricket Festival at Scarborough in 1871, at a time when public schoolboys were being taught that to play cricket well was a badge of an educated Englishman. Cricket week at Scarborough in September, watching the season's Yorkshire eleven play its final match or a match against the Australians or South Africans, is still the holiday of the year for many men. We met a man in Pickering who has only missed one festival, and that because he was getting married. White figures against the green; strains of music floating across and then silence except for the click of the ball on the bat; the card-seller's voice, now near, now distant: 'All the score up to luncheon time, and the order of going in'; the applause as a ball hits the roof of the pavilion; these are not only moments to enjoy in the present, but reminders of earlier years. Each will bring its own reminiscences over the hotel fire that night, and will be a memory for another festival.

Little else is left so unchanged from those more spacious days. Bridlington has developed its south side and built what it calls a Spa to take the glory from its parade. Scarborough has connected the north and south by the cliff road of the marine drive, which was opened in 1908, having taken ten years, ten months, and ten days to complete. Again and again during this time months of work was washed down by winter storms, and heavy seas can still drive people off the road.

As in the spa days, there is a tendency yet for a district to keep to a particular place for its holidays. Before the railways came, holiday-makers chose the resort which was easiest to reach, and a special liking for that place seems innate in their descendants. South Yorkshire and the coal district choose Bridlington while Leeds gravitates to Scarborough.

Only two or three landaus standing to be hired on the foreshore remain of the long lines which waited to take people to Hackness, Forge Valley, Silpho Moor, and Hayburn Wyke, which were once day's outings. The landaus followed the jockey carts, low, light carriages whose drivers, in white breeches and jockeys' caps, rode postilion on the ponies.

You can capture some of the spirit of the times when these were familiar sights in the few weeks before the season starts, when there is an air of leisure and calm and the visitors are of the type which takes its holidays with pomp and dignity. An elderly lady told us how excited she was as a young girl to be taken for a holiday to Scarborough, and to have her first grown-up frock bought at Marshall's.

For a great part of the season the coast to-day means crowds of people and streams of cars, rising to a climax at holidays and week-ends. Between York and Malton a great new road, the first long stretch of dual and cycle tracks in Yorkshire, has been made to carry the traffic. Look for a moment at those places which we saw before the days of holidays. At Bridlington just before Whitsuntide the cobles and rowing-boats which have been used for getting crabs and lobsters during the winter are brought in and painted for the season, when their owners can make more money in hiring them out to visitors than in fishing. Catering for summer visitors, not fishing, is the real industry here now, and the quays have become largely parading piers or landing places for the yachts which crowd the harbour. Bridlington's visitors always seem to be on the move, rowing in hundreds of little boats about the bay, bobbing up and down in the sea, pacing the promenades. It is known familiarly as Brid, being one of the few places whose names are shortened.

In Filey also, men who have fished all winter make a living from visitors in the summer. This has become a favourite place for families with young children and nurses. Holiday-makers wear the latest beach clothes, and paradoxically congratulate themselves on not having to 'dress up,' as they would have in Scarborough. Filey prides itself on its smallness, but already there are plans for big developments on the cliffs.

Scarborough is a huge conglomeration of busy streets and shops, great hotels, and long promenades spreading out like an enormous wheel from the ancient centre of the harbour. The nineteenth-century houses make a dark ring between the red-tiled roofs of the old houses under the castle, and the outer rim of the modern development which is chiefly residential.

At the south side gay flower-beds decorate the promenade, shady gardens appear in hollows of the cliff, and a band plays to strolling crowds on the spa. The spa is mostly for amusement now, but at a modest little kiosk you may drink the iron

The Spa, Scarborough

or magnesia waters in orange-juice instead of the wine with which the early drinkers disguised the taste.

On fine nights the orchestra plays outside, people dressed to be seen wander up and down amid vivid lights and animated chatter, couples pass in and out of the dance-room, and the floodlit castle, the red-roofed houses, and the waiting boats in the harbour make a backcloth to the holiday scene.

Beyond the spa is the foreshore, the popular part, with a pleasure fair, knick-knack shops, shops selling rock and sugar pebbles, and amusement halls for the day tripper. Blackboards outside the huge restaurants announce the time of arrival of excursions varying from church choirs to workpeople from a laundry. Across the road stout fisherwives preside over stalls filled with crabs, lobsters, and plates of shelled cockles and winkles. Donkeys thread a patient way between the crowds on the beach, and a man with a Punch and Judy show searches for empty spaces.

The life of the harbour still goes on in this middle portion. During August and September the Dutch herring-boats put in at the week-ends for provisions, and Dutch sailors, parading the quay in their blue blouses and wooden sabots, bring the interest of the unusual. Cargo boats unload timber from Norway, and as evening comes the brown-sailed fishing-trawlers set out to sea.

Now and again a few people step out from the pacing holiday crowd to watch the life of the harbour. A man and his wife look down on a boat where a fisherman is mending lobster-pots. They are fascinated and a little bewildered by the sight, their urban minds unable to visualize all that it implies. The man tries to convey something of his feeling to his two children, but the older boy has turned to look at the wreck of a warship brought into the harbour for repair, and he says: 'It's got a propeller, Dad, a great long one,' and the younger boy interrupts with: 'Oo, look, Dad, speed-boat's goin' out.' The parents make no answer and continue to gaze at the man mending lobster-pots.

Only a few yards away, twopence will admit you into a shed to see a tunny fish. About 1930 it was discovered that tunny could be reached easily from here, and the only Tunny Club in England is now established in one of Scarborough's oldest houses, where you can see the tackle, learn the weights, and hear stories of this big-game-hunting of the sea.

Then round the marine drive with its border of waiting cars and buses you are at the North, where a frenzied life has overtaken the placid family scene of a generation ago. The stateliness of the south is thrown to the winds here, and the new swimming pool stands beside the roadside for passers-by to see. Beach bungalows line the promenade almost to Scalby Mills, which made a morning's walk or a long donkey-

SCARBOROUGH HARBOUR

ride in a calmer age. A first impression of the North on a summer's day now is a beach filled with camp chairs and hundreds of people lounging and sun-bathing aimlessly about it. Seeing them you realize that one great attraction of the sea to the town dweller is that he can be unashamedly lazy by it.

A modern development of which Scarborough is justifiably proud is the Open Air Theatre. There is something exciting and foreign in sitting in that vast auditorium with the dark, cool night round you, listening to opera performed on a stage which is an island on a lake.

In all these places something of the old peeps out among the new. More than any of them Flamborough retains the atmosphere of the past, in spite of the caravans, huts, and wooden shops which a more discerning generation will sweep from the cliffs. It is a large brick village with wide open streets, and though it is a mile inland there is a tang of the sea everywhere. The knowledge of the danger of the rocky coast is in the very air. It has come through centuries of women who have waited through storms for their men returning home in fishing cobles or watched them start out in the lifeboat to a ship in distress. Monuments in the street record disasters and rescues at sea. At the Head the lighthouse flashes its warning light, and a little way from it the old 'towre' remains from the days when a coal fire was lit as a beacon. John Matson built the present lighthouse in 1806 without the aid of outside scaffolding.

Herrings and other fish are displayed with the fruit and vegetables at the harvest festival at the chapel in Flamborough, and are appropriate offerings for a place which still gets much of its living by fishing. There are animated scenes at the North Landing when the boats come in. As each one arrives, the catch is tipped out on the sands and immediately sold by auction, and the boat is hauled by an engine to its mooring on the cliff-side. The buyers clean the fish on the sands and pile them and the wriggling crabs and lobsters into panniers which are strapped on to the backs of donkeys to be carried up the cliff to waiting lorries. There is something medieval about the simple scene, carried on as it must have been for centuries, isolated in the narrow bay shut in between cliffs.

The men working in groups do not wear gold ear-rings as the Flamborough fishermen used to do, but they still call each other by nicknames. The donkeys munch hay as they wait under the rocks for their turn to clamber to the shouts of their masters up the steep, winding path, and now and again they bray to each other across the beach. Then suddenly the shore is deserted, the men make for the village, and the donkeys are led to their night's grazing in fields or on the roadsides.

That moving inland as night comes on is fitting on this bleak headland. As the visitors depart, the cliffs should be left to regain their austerity amid natural sounds, the call of gulls returning to their nesting-places on the high cliffs at Bempton, and the lapping of the waves on the smooth chalk pavements of the bays.

Micklegate Bar, York

CHAPTER 8

YORK

WHEN a Yorkshireman or any one familiar with Yorkshire arrives at the top of a hill with a view he looks for York Minster. From the Wold hills, from the rises on the Plain of York, from the Pennine fells, his accustomed eye can pick it out on a clear day, a small white speck in a haze of blue distance. He uses it as a guide for other landmarks, a symbolical gesture towards a building whose city in olden times was the focus for the life of the north.

Standing at the junction of the three Ridings, York, as capital of the county, belongs to all of them, yet is actually in none. The city is complete in itself, enclosed by its modern development as surely as it was by the medieval walls. You enter it with the expectancy with which you would go to meet a famous person. Here are all the sights you have read about or seen in pictures, in their setting, not as separate, unrelated pieces.

To-day cyclists crowd the streets, more to the square yard than in any other town in England; cars pass through on their way to the coast, blocking the narrow roads; there are railway engine works, a sugar beet factory, huge cocoa and chocolate works with swimming baths, canteens, and welfare sections; but these modern characteristics fit happily into the whole, making an attractive pattern. They are part of the medley of York as are the residential houses in quiet corners only a few yards from the main shopping streets.

The city takes its tone from the seasons and the weather. Pale autumn sunshine lighting its walls and leafless trees blends the new and old together. Pace slows down in the languid drowsy days of summer when in the hazy enervating air it seems to slip back into the past. On bright winter days the buildings stand out sharp and clear as the sun illumines forgotten corners, fresh energy comes to it, people move briskly along the streets, and it seems a modern city.

There is a great charm in letting York discover itself, in walking its streets and coming across its relics, most of them still playing their part in the life of the city. You reach the centre of the town through one or other of the bars in the walls. Micklegate and Monk Bars are the most imposing, but Walmgate Bar retains its barbican. Traffic to and from Hull roars through it, and the top serves as a kind of roof garden for the cottage in the bar. In Elizabethan days this cottage was prolonged by a wood and plaster wall, and, perched in its ancient site, it still makes a cosy little home. Near Bootham Bar a piece of the wall which surrounded the Roman city of Eboracum can be seen.

The Multangular Tower stands as a glorious relic of the Roman era close to the ruins of St Mary's Abbey, but neither of these are cut off from the modern life, for the public library backs on to the grounds of the abbey.

YORK FROM THE CITY WALLS

The river Ouse, threading a way through the city, adds to the scene breadth and space in contrast with the narrowness of the streets. Views from its bridges where tall warehouses rise abruptly from the water have the tranquillity of a picture by Canaletto. On the south where it joins the river Foss the Ouse did away with the necessity for walls. It carried stone for the building of the abbeys and castles, wool and other produce of the market was shipped down it, and it supplied the water for the city. In severe winters it was used for weeks at a time as a roadway down which people skated into the town.

You pass from the riverside to narrow streets many of whose names have the Danish suffix 'gate,' meaning street. Skeldergate comes from the Old Scandinavian and means 'the shield-makers' street,' Pavement means 'a paved way,' as does Stonegate, 'the stone-paved street,' built over the Roman road; the old coffee-houses were chiefly in this street. Whip Ma Whop Ma Gate is called either from the local custom of whipping dogs here on St Luke's Day, or because it had the whipping post and pillory. The Shambles, 'the flesh benches,' where the upper stories of the wood and plaster houses overhang, is mentioned in Domesday Book. Coney Street, 'the king's street,' is still narrow though it is the principal shopping street; the old coaching house here, the Black Swan, now closed, has memories of famous visitors, Sir Tatton Sykes coming from Sledmere for York races, and travellers from the seventeenth to the nineteenth century using it as a stage on their journey to the coast. Petergate is the street near St Peter's, which is the minster.

Down High Petergate those curious fancy shops which are a feature of York come one after another with their jumble of ornaments, toys, and confectionery. Toys of a generation ago can be bought here, and the window of one is filled at Christmas time with old-fashioned Christmas cards in boxes, stiff gelatine cards with pleated ribbon edges and hearts and loving rhymes on them. You go into a little sitting-room at the back to choose them from an old woman who has sold them there for over thirty years.

In a few minutes you are round the corner at shops which cater for tourists and visitors, the sudden kind of change which parts of London give. The contrast brings a cosmopolitan atmosphere, and forms one of the links in the chain which makes York not merely a Yorkshire but a British city, a part of the Empire. Has any city except London been so much photographed? These newer shops exude photographs of the minster and the city in postcards, pictures, snapshots, and books; decorated ornaments and boxes fill the windows; and gifts with views of York go from them to all corners of the world.

Ancient relics are down these streets, wedged between shops and houses which themselves are old. There are the fourteenth-century Merchant Adventurers' Hall with its beautiful roof, telling of the old trades, the red brick hall of the Merchant Taylors, and the Guildhall, now the chief hall of the city. The roof of this is supported by wooden pillars, each made from a single oak tree cut from the Forest of Galtres. We saw it during repairs, and could only peep through the scaffolding at one or two of the beautiful bosses. We watched a young man bevelling the capital of a new oak pier; another pier had had a piece spliced on to it. The Mansion House just behind is still used by the Lord Mayor and Sheriff. The first Lady Mayoresses of York kept their titles all their lives whilst their husbands only retained theirs during their term of office. The custom accounts for so many names of apparently titled ladies on old gravestones.

> The Mayor is a lord for a year and a day
> But his wife is a 'Lady' for ever and aye.

The Blind School, once the residence of the Abbot of St Mary's Abbey, the Treasurer's House, the half-timbered building of St William's College, old inns such as the Black Swan in Peaseholme Green, the Blue-coat School, and many more you find as you travel York streets.

Amongst these and newer buildings, some wedged in so as to be hardly noticeable, the York churches rear their towers and spires to the sky—All Hallows' with its octagonal tower; All Saints' in Pavement with its lantern tower: St Cuthbert's where a recluse lived in the churchyard in the fourteenth century; St Dennis's in Walmgate, said to have been once a Jewish synagogue; the Decorated church of St Helen in Stonegate, the survivor of three churches in York dedicated to that saint; Holy Trinity, Micklegate, which once belonged to a priory of alien Benedictines; St John the Evangelist's in Ouse Bridge whose chancel has been encroached upon by the street; the old tower of St Lawrence; St Mary's, Bishophill Junior, with Roman stones in its tower, and probably standing on the site of the first Christian church in York, earlier than the first minster; St Mary's, Castlegate, where a Roman pavement lies under the foundation of the west wall. These seem to our changing age far more than the 'small ashes of antiquity' which early eighteenth-century writers described as all that was left of the city.

The churches radiate round the minster, reflecting its glory, and resting placidly under its protection. Its white walls rise from the midst of them in sudden exquisite beauty, and they and the houses and buildings connected with it make an oasis of space and quiet in the surrounding bustle.

We make no attempt to describe York Minster—that has been done often before. Each person takes away his own impression; for ourselves we never lose the wonder of the majestic conception of this cathedral church. Separate features are absorbing in their turn, the beautiful east and west fronts, the lofty arches, the intricate carving, the medieval glass which makes the finest collection in England; but it is the beauty of the whole which stays in the memory. We have inherited something so precious here that generation after generation has not grudged the enormous sums of money which have been necessary to keep it in repair. Men are employed continually in the workshop nearby, and thousands of pounds have been spent on the glass alone.

Just before Christmas a tableau of the scene in the inn at Bethlehem is set up with a lighted Christmas tree beside it in one of the aisles. We remember how two elderly ladies stood for a long time discussing whether they should put something in the collecting box for the particular charity it was helping, and then passed on without doing so. Another memory is of hearing the *Messiah* sung in the minster on the Sunday before Christmas. But it is good to sit quietly here in an afternoon and feel its life as a church round you. Clerks and priests move about the aisles. One steps up to the reading desk to open the Bible for evensong, another comes to see if it is correctly opened, and presently a third. They give a human feeling to the vast interior, a sense of the intimate worship for which the stones were raised.

The halls with their memory of the guilds regulating trade and dispensing charity also keep alive the tradition of the woollen trade which was started in York by William and Haukinus of Brabant under the protection of Edward III. Wool and cloth were taken down the passage under the Guildhall and shipped from its landing stage on the Ouse. The York merchant adventurers were the pioneers of commerce as we know it, and they conducted a large trade. A sixteenth-century song gives some idea of the importance of the city under their sway:

> Yorke, Yorke, for my monie,
> Of all the citties that ever I see,
> For merry pastime and companie,
> Except the cittie of London.

But woollen mills have never lined the Ouse or Foss, and the stringency of the guild laws was one of the reasons why the trade went westward. There is a saying that Leeds, Bradford, and Sheffield grew while York slept. When Defoe visited it he found no particular industry. Instead the city developed as a residential place. Families with country estates and mansions had town houses here; the Scropes of Masham had one in Coney Street; the Thompson family, a member of whom married General Wolfe, came from Long Marston for the winter months. Visitors also came in from all parts of the county for the social season when there were balls and brilliant gatherings at the Assembly Rooms. Defoe says of them: '. . . a man converses here with all the world as effectually as at London.'

It is sentences such as these which rouse waves of regret that York with its tradition of learning going back to the days of the scholar Alcuin has not become a university city. But it takes only a little time here to realize that the reason for this and its industrial limitations lies in those many churches and in the minster at their heart. It is the tale of all cathedral cities, as if the monks were guarding their memory from other influences and encroachment. In medieval times there were twenty-seven more churches than there are to-day, as well as several small monasteries, friaries, and hospitals.

York, as might be expected, is still ecclesiastical at heart. Its inhabitants, whatever their religion, are influenced by the nearness of the dean and chapter. You can pick a group of York people out of a crowd at a conference. They bring an air of importance with them, a curious blend of country, cathedral town, and long tradition, and this is displayed even in the clothes they wear. Its people are citizens, not merely occupants of a city. They have roots in it—they belong.

The town has inherited something from the old days of the assemblies. These gatherings reached their height during the Assizes and Race Weeks, and something of their spirit returns on race days to-day when traffic roars through the streets, crowds everywhere wend their way towards the Knavesmire, and the frocks of the women in the paddock are described in the newspapers.

For a long period the Knavesmire was undrained common land on which the freemen had the right to graze horses and cattle except on race days. Joshua Hedley, a Quaker, visiting his brother in York, says in his diary of 25th June 1815: 'Walked out in the evening with Hartas and little James to

Knavesmire, carrying the mare a feed of corn, crossed over from thence to Hob Moor. The Knavesmire Stock were to be removed to Hob Moor in a little time, as it had been clear of stock since May Day, so would be a bit of fresh meat for them.'

Gipsies used to camp along the sides of the road on Hob Moor, and people were afraid of travelling that way at night. Criminals were hanged and their bodies left in chains here. These were accustomed sights to York people, for executions and hangings were numerous outside the prison which is part of the old castle. The prison has now become a museum for household objects, but a menacing atmosphere, a mingling of old massacres and executions, imprisonments for belief, and election scenes, hangs over the space between it and Clifford's Tower opposite.

You can retrace the story of York looking down on to its outer and inner circles from the city walls. A gap between Layerthorpe Bridge and Red Tower shows where an impenetrable marsh made walls unnecessary. These fringes of it were strategic sites which were continually being attacked.

From one part you see beyond a daffodil-covered bank the great modern railway station and junction. George Hudson, the railway magnate, had been a York draper, and it is told that when he was asked about certain projected lines he said: 'Mak all t' railways cum ti York,' this being convenient for his home at Londesborough.

From another part there is a sight of the market where sheep and cattle waiting their turn in the auction mart across the street are folded in pens close under the wall. Black Irish cattle form the main part of the stock, and the high-pitched voices of their drovers mingle strangely with the deeper Yorkshire voices. Thousands of sheep and cattle change hands in a week here. The climax comes with the Christmas Fat Stock Show when stock is shown one day and sold the next. In the weeks before Christmas many a butcher in neighbouring villages and small towns displays in his shop window a carcass with a colourful rosette on it and a notice that it is a prize winner at the York Fat Stock Show.

Some of the stock has come to its destiny here along the winding country roads which surround York. This is sunken, quiet land, out of the beaten track, with hedges bordering green fields, trees overhanging winding roads, and here and there a circle of willows round a still green pond. Some of the most perfect churches in England are to be found in the villages which sleep in its gracious arms — Wighill and Healaugh with their magnificent Norman doorways and arches; the exquisite little Early English church at Nun Monkton, part of a priory of nuns; Kirk Hammerton, whose south aisle is a Saxon church.

Bishopthorpe, which has been the Archbishop of York's palace since the thirteenth century, lies to the south of this country, northwards was the Forest of Galtres, and to the west lay Knaresborough Forest through part of which the men of Acomb used to guide pedlars. The old wapentake of the Ainsty on the south-west is chiefly associated to-day with the York and Ainsty Hunt.

At Long Marston in this district they show you a room in the Old Hall where Cromwell slept before the battle of Marston Moor. A little tree-topped mound near is still called Cromwell's Gap because his soldiers spent the night there. There are many tales of Cromwell here, but the ghost of Rupert needlessly fleeing to York and his doom seems to haunt the district most.

A mile from Tadcaster, at Jackdaw Crag, is the quarry, formerly known as Thevesdale, which, along with one called Huddlestone Delph, supplied the stone for York Minster. The stone was conveyed in wains to Tadcaster and by boat to York; it was also carried long distances by water for other churches. It has a texture which does not darken with weather, and churches built from it stand out clean and white in contrast with the darker towns and villages. After the fire in 1829 the minster was repaired with the same stone. Now the quarries lie finished and deserted; grass covers the ground, rabbits scutter over it, and little trees grow from its sides; but the walls of the minster remain as its monument.   If you mount a little rise on this otherwise flat land you catch glimpses of the white towers which man wrought so magnificently from this rough stone.

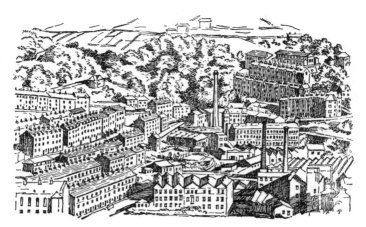

Hebden Bridge

CHAPTER 9

THE STORY OF THE WOOLLEN TRADE

Towns running into one another with never a green field in between; long rows of dreary houses thickening to centres where great factories line the rivers and chimneys pour their smoke over the whole; a conglomeration of humanity dwelling amongst them, and lines of trams and buses to carry it. This is a first impression of the industrial area of the West Riding where towns and villages have expanded to make an unbroken chain from one large city to another. Later you discover the imposing shopping centres, the town halls and parish churches, the open spaces round which the wealthier residents live, and the valleys where the industry spreads out to fields and woods and some rural life. But streets, buildings, and trees all have a coat of black; and rivers and canals passing through the area collect the dirt and filth of the mills.

An outsider may find this a depressing picture, but the average West Riding man in the busier area considers it 'a bit of all right.' Streets and buildings have become his natural element, and he would be dull without them. We remember at a lonely country house the wife of a wealthy woollen manufacturer declaring that she wouldn't live there for ten thousand pounds a year. Decorators going to work in it from the towns would joke about the quietness, and pine for the traffic of the streets before the day was over.

The stretch of country which the woollen industry has enveloped is chiefly lower dale country where becks which have come down from the dark Pennines are flowing towards the Plain of York. It is a sombre, somewhat bleak district, but it has breadth. Hills sweep majestically from the basin in which the town of Huddersfield has grown; a dale runs into the hills near Southowram; and there are moorland hollows above Baildon. But a film of soot covers the most rural corners, and sheep grazing on the surrounding moors are as dark as the heather and rock.

A Cistercian abbey was built in this pleasant land at Kirkstall on the river Aire, and there were priories at Nostell and Kirklees. It was from a window in Kirklees Priory that Robin Hood, as he lay dying, is said to have shot an arrow to mark the spot for his grave. With his memory goes that of George a' Green, Wakefield's Merry Pinder. He reminds us of the mystery plays performed at Wakefield at Whitsuntide and Corpus Christi by members of the local guilds on a wagon with a curtain round the lower part for a dressing-room. Or there comes to mind Christopher Saxton, the first English map maker, born at Tingley, near Leeds, starting out in the sixteenth century with his wheel to map the county.

By the end of the fourteenth century Yorkshire had become a cloth-making district, and it gradually drew the trade from the other centres in Suffolk and Gloucestershire, where the wealthy wool staplers did not encourage its further development lest it should spoil their country. York and Beverley, benefiting from their long - established markets and their position on the river Ouse, were the first Yorkshire centres, but whilst they were becoming famous for fine cloths, a coarser cloth was being made from local wool in the scattered Pennine districts. The monks from the various monasteries at the foots of the dales were then sheep-farming on a large scale, but except for that woven for their own use the wool was largely exported. The cottage weavers, who had no connection with the abbeys, made cloth for their families and the surrounding villages.

The district with its sheep-grazing fells and moors and its many becks and rivers supplying power for the fulling mills and soft water for scouring, was ready set for the staging of the industry, and it gradually spread westward, centred first at Wakefield, then at Halifax, and later at Bradford. The restricting rules of the trade guilds were other reasons for its establishment in the higher Pennine towns where trade was free, but an important factor was that people could live cheaper in the scattered moorland areas, and that the small farmers in the upland districts, unable to wrench more than a bare living from the land, were glad to turn to spinning and weaving in addition. As the trade grew, the nearness of coal and iron helped to keep it here.

It was in the fifteenth century, while Halifax was rising in importance, that the industry began to take the form of which the modern factory is a natural outcome. It started with farmers spinning and weaving on the small high farms, and carrying their pieces of cloth to the nearest market, bringing back two or three stones of wool for the next week's work, which would employ the whole family. From them there developed the clothiers, the forerunners of our modern manufacturers.

The clothier was merely a more go-ahead man than the rest, who began to buy extra wool and to employ a few spinners and weavers outside his own family, himself taking the finished cloth to the market. The majority of the people still worked

in their own cottages, fetching the wool from the clothier and
returning him the finished cloth, but some worked in a shed
attached to the clothier's house.   Many of the houses and
cottages were rebuilt or refaced in the seventeenth century
with long rows of stone-mullioned windows to give light, and
in some cases a third story was added.

Numbers of these clothiers' houses remain in the outlying
districts of Huddersfield and Halifax; particularly fine examples
are seen from the road from Pole Moor to Golcar.   They
perch in easy fashion on the hillside, and seem to express in
their sturdy walls the spirit and vigour of their owners,
working their way to power.   The original dwelling stands in
the centre, with farm-buildings on one side, and the weaving
extension on the other.   So unaltered are they here that passing
them you can almost see the men starting out for the market
in the early morning with the pieces of cloth strapped to
donkeys or ponies, and returning with the new wool, weary
but anxious to hear how the farm work had progressed in their
absence.   The vision fades as you see the line of electric pylons
across the hill, and the masts of the B.B.C. station at Pole
Moor behind.   What would the clothiers have made of these
or the huge mills in the valley, they to whom the hand-loom,
the violin, and the oil lamp were the last achievement?   Or
perhaps there were one or two who, as they added a new
improvement to a spinning-wheel or a loom, visualized
something of the future which is our to-day.

The Yorkshire clothiers were poorer than the Gloucester
and Suffolk wool staplers had been, for they had to contend
with a harsher climate, and at first a prejudice against Yorkshire
cloth.

> Three great evils come out of the North,
> A cold wind, a cunning knave, and a shrinking cloth,

said one of Ray's proverbs of 1687, but the two last slurs were
soon removed.   Some men rose to considerable wealth; as
early as 1747 Samuel Hill of Soyland had an annual trading

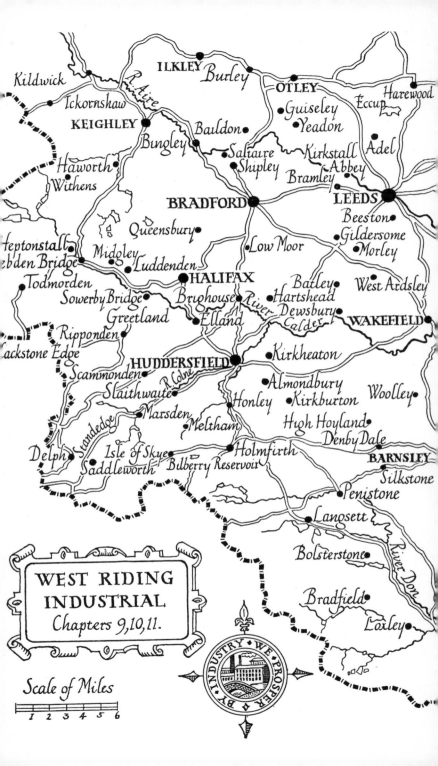

WEST RIDING
INDUSTRIAL
Chapters 9,10,11.

Scale of Miles

1 2 3 4 5 6

INDUSTRY · WE · PROSPER · BY

account of £35,527, and gave out work to people at long distances. He dealt chiefly in very fine quality cloth made from foreign wool, and sold back to foreign merchants. Such men built the larger seventeenth- and eighteenth-century houses with mullioned windows and chamfered doorways, which yet in their greater dignity fit the district perfectly. The gentry also turned to making money out of the industry, for there was not then the lowering of status which was later attached to trade.

But for the most part the clothiers stayed in their original houses, living on familiar terms with those they employed. The period, known as the 'domestic system,' lasted with little change except slight improvements to existing machinery until the arrival of steam power for driving the looms. All along the clothier remained a farmer as much as a manufacturer, interested in the land which supplied him with corn for his family and horses and room for his tenters. The diary of Cornelius Ashworth of Wheatley records: 'A fine warm droughty day. I churned and sized a warp in the morning.' A droughty, pronounced 'drufty,' day was welcomed as good for drying the cloth. Joseph Rogerson of Bramley writes in his diary for 11th August 1808: 'Very throng in our mill. Mowing oats on Swinnow Close. Got part wool dry out-of-doors. A slubber left us. A great many oats ripe. Got a fine Perch out of our dam with line.' The order of the remarks shows how mixed up in Rogerson's mind were the mill and the life of the country. They were connected in other ways, such as the use of seak, the sediment from the scouring tanks, to manure the land.

The first mills were for fulling, and these were generally owned by the lord of the manor, and let to tenants. Until ammonia was used to remove the oil, the cloth was pounded in stale urine, called in old records 'wash' and 'weeting,' and this was collected in troughs in cottage gardens. The fulling mills were generally lower down the valleys where the streams were larger. The clothiers took their cloth down to be scoured and washed, carried it back to dry on their tenters, took it down again to be milled in soap, and again brought it home for the final drying. Defoe tells how he saw cloth drying on tenters round almost every house as he came down to Halifax. The old saying, 'From Hull, Hell, and Halifax, good Lord deliver us,' arose from the severe laws against felons being kept up longer here than in most places because so much cloth was stolen from the tenters. The cloth stretched tightly on them originated the expression 'on tenter-hooks.'

When scribbling machines for carding were introduced, these were run by water power, and buildings were put up for them close to the fulling mills. Later the slubbing billies for winding the carded wool on to cops ready for spinning were also run in the scribbling mills. These mills growing up by the streams made the nucleus of the valley village which we know to-day. As more machinery was introduced spinning mills were built in the valleys, but the weaving was still done in the clothiers' warehouses in those communities high on the hills which were often spoken of as 'towns.'

You can picture the activity of that time, the fetching and carrying for the various processes, and the many workers with their specialized jobs. There were children feeding the scribbling machines; slubbers drawing out the cardings, earning twice as much as the hand-loom weavers in the sheds, and perhaps because of this proving the most awkward of all the workpeople—it was generally the slubbers who stayed away from work to attend the various feasts. After the cloth left the mill there were all the processes connected with finishing. In the croppers' room men pulled up the nap with teazles while the preemer boys squatted on the floor, cleaning the teazles by picking out the fluff. At tables at the other end the croppers smoothed the cloth with their great shears. The croppers earned big wages, which was why they fought so bitterly against the introduction of machinery.

There was a continual coming and going. Besides the short journeys to the mills, there were journeys to places as far

E

distant as Austwick in Craven and Dunsop Bridge in Bowland. As the demand for cloth grew, the clothiers put out some spinning work in these districts, for until machinery was invented it was difficult to keep the spinning up with the weaving. Agents were given a halfpenny a pound to deliver the wool to the farmhouses and collect the yarn. Some old milestones above Settle give the number of miles to Halifax.

The local wool soon proved insufficient, and though chapmen came round selling wool, many clothiers preferred to journey themselves to distant markets, buying Spanish, Irish, and Lincolnshire wool. Tom Priestley of Goodgreave travelled regularly to London in the early eighteenth century with a string of eight or nine packhorses, taking twenty pounds' worth of cloth on each journey, making twenty pounds profit on it, and bringing back wool from Kent and Suffolk.

At first the cloth was sold at the markets and annual fairs of which Bartholomew Fair in London was the most famous. As the trade developed the number of towns holding weekly markets increased; that at Leeds held on the bridge over the river Aire spread a long distance up the street. The local markets were a step forward in the trade, because they supplied the small clothier with ready money. The many covered cloth halls built in the West Riding towns during the eighteenth century were a natural sequence. The towns were eager to have these because they brought extra trade. The Piece Hall opened in Halifax in 1779 still remains, a two-storied building surrounding a paved courtyard, and with a cupola over the entrance. Each manufacturer who subscribed £28 4s. became the owner of a room in this, but the small makers displayed their cloth in the area. The rooms open on to an arcade or gallery round which the merchants walked to view the cloth, conducting their business with the clothiers in whispers. The market opened at ten o'clock and lasted two hours, and packhorses and carts were allowed in from half-past twelve to four to remove the cloth.

The area is now used as a wholesale fruit market, and there

is a morning bustle perhaps as great as the clothiers knew
From the gallery we watched a man going round with a carrot
for each of the horses, and it might have been the shade of a
clothier with his farmer's love for horses. The dust of years
makes a blind to the window panes in the rooms round the
galleries now, and we found only a few occupied, one by an old
man making wire frames for wreaths. The use of the cloth

Milnsbridge in the Colne Valley

halls went with the passing of the domestic system and the
growing tendency to make fancy cloths which demanded more
secret bargaining.

Inventions of and improvements to machinery were introduced chiefly from Lancashire, the cotton area, from about
1780 onwards, but for another half century these were merely
added to existing machines, and made little difference to
the system. Even after steam power was established, a few
mills continued to be built on the higher land where this
was conveniently near to a seam of coal. The more acces-
sible of these remain as the upland manufacturing villages of

to-day.   It is in the remoter valleys such as Deanhead near
Huddersfield that you find the little derelict mills whose
gaping windows and falling roofs are dumb reminders of the
simple beginnings of the industry.   But the general tendency
was to come down to the valleys where as well as the rivers
there were now the canals for power and transport, and the
good turnpike roads.

Many of the new mills in the valleys took every process,
and began to be called factories, and their owners manufacturers.   They are the symbols of what we call the Industrial
Revolution, through which the industry has grown to the
enormous concerns of to-day.   The dark and the bright pages
of its history are in these walls.   In Marsden we are reminded
of the risings of the croppers, who were not able to realize
that the unemployment amongst them was due as much to
bad trade caused by the Napoleonic wars as to the new shearing machines.   The first cropping machines were made in
Marsden in 1812 by two brothers, Enoch and James Taylor.
The motto of the Luddites, 'Enoch 'as made 'em, an' Enoch 'll
break 'em,' arose because they named the hammers with which
they smashed the machines after Enoch Taylor.   It was at
Marsden too, that the Luddites shot and killed William
Horsfall of Ottiwell Mills.   The men's resentment against
the machines was pitted against the mill-owner's realization
that he must install them or drop out.

The worst evils which came with machinery were long
hours, low wages, and the employment of children, who were
taught at that time that rooks said 'Wark, wark,' not 'Caw,
caw.'   It was necessary to be up at five o'clock to get to the
mill in time, and fathers carried the youngest children on
their shoulders.   In busy times women and children worked
until eleven o'clock at night, sometimes seven days a week,
and often they slept in the mill so as to be ready to start
again in the morning.   A mill-owner's diary of 1808 records:
'Slubbers and childer laid in mill all night.'   It was these
hardships which roused the indignation of a few prominent

men and brought Richard Oastler's protest to Parliament, and eventually the Acts limiting working hours and the employment of children. There was bitterness, too, in the adjustments which followed through strikes and trade unions. It was a conflict of natures as well as a fight for better conditions. The masters were hard working themselves, and had personal dealings with the men, and they resented their herding together in unions against them. Where a hard, relentless nature had the power, this had disastrous results.

The tendency for various places to specialize had started in the early days; Halifax was famous for shalloons and kerseys, which were in great demand for troops abroad; Wakefield made tammy cloths; and Leeds broadcloth and northern dozens, which were half the length of a broadcloth. To-day fine worsteds and fancy tweeds are made in Huddersfield and the Colne Valley, dress goods in Bradford, and shoddy in the region between Dewsbury and Leeds, though every place now has supplements of its own, such as cotton, artificial silk, and corduroy.

The making of mungo or shoddy was introduced in 1834 by George Parr, who found that rags torn up by machinery and used with a cotton warp could be made into cheap cloth. Through a curious prejudice, the West Riding has never been very proud of this department of its industry. Thomas Carlyle is said to have had much to do with giving the word 'shoddy' its secondary meaning of cheap and worthless, but the late Sir James Kitson of Leeds explained to him that shoddy had enabled the working classes to have cheap, clean garments instead of those passed down from one generation to another. A southerner wearing grey flannels said superiorly to a northerner in a London hotel: 'Well, what is shoddy, anyway?' and received the answer: 'The stuff your trousers are made of.' The rags come from all over the world, collected by many agencies, including the 'rag and bone' man. Dewsbury is the only place in the world where auction sales of rags are regularly held.

Some mills specialize in spinning, weaving, dyeing, or finishing, but the big mills, as did the first ones in the valleys, take the whole process of turning wool into cloth, except occasionally the first dressing and washing. Once in the mill it is oiled and blended, carded, spun, woven to a design, burled and mended, milled (fulled), washed, dyed, tentered, sheared, pressed, steamed, and finally 'cuttled and rigged up,' that is folded and made ready for delivery.

Along with the mills there grew up the factories connected with them, chiefly engineering ones making machinery and profiting in the beginning from the nearness of the ironstone. As the woollen mills have progressed from the first cottage weavers, so these have expanded in their scope and size from the first card-makers fitting bits of wire into pieces of leather and the joiners making the heavy wooden looms.

Up to the beginning of the Great War, the mill and improvements to it were the chief interests of its owner's life; Joseph Rogerson wondering in his diary of 1813 whether he should adopt the new gas-lighting is typical of the men to whom new inventions mattered in the extent to which they affected the mill. In the country districts the owner still lived in the substantial stone house he had built near it, and which had usually a small farm connected with it. His home was run very much on the lines of a large farmhouse. The owner would speak precisely to his family, but would use dialect and 'thee' and 'thou' in addressing his workpeople.

In the towns he no longer lived as his grandparents had probably done, in a house built actually in the mill yard, nor possibly in the stone house which his parents had built five or ten minutes' walk away; but in a more imposing one, then on the fringe of the town, and now almost a part of it. Characteristic features of these houses were the rubber mats outside the front doors, with the owners' names cut in them, and the conservatories filled with ferns, chrysanthemums, and occasionally orchids. In many, a bust of Gladstone stood in the hall, for these early manufacturers were staunch Liberals. There was an ample, important feeling about their homes, which were generally within sight of the smoke of the mills which had made them.

One of us as a child used to stand for hours at an attic window in one of these houses, watching the smoke from the chimneys. The mills were only allowed to turn out smoke for a prescribed time, and seven or eight sending out dark spirals into the sky would suddenly stop and another lot would begin, and so on through the great mass of chimney-stacks. We would pick out a particular chimney, and see how long it was before its turn came.

The life of the family pivoted round the life of the mill. Spring had come when it was no longer necessary to light up by six o'clock, the closing time. The owner would come home for a meal at that hour, and as often as not would walk down again during the evening to see that all was right. He was still at heart very much like the old clothier, and we think he was a happy man.

The tall mill chimneys were a point of pride with the owner, a symbol of the importance of his mill. Some member of the family would ride in the hoist up to the top of a new one, and place a flag there to announce its completion. Older men tell with admiration of how a textile machine-maker went to the top of his chimney-stack when he was over seventy years old. It had been raised, and before the ladder was taken down he climbed up it, and walked round the parapet at the top.

In those days fires in mills were common, owing to the greasy floors and lack of modern precautions. They seemed every-body's concern. As soon as the buzzer went everything was dropped, and crowds ran to the nearest hill to watch. The fires often broke out at night, and in the darkness the lofty building would be silhouetted in the vivid glare as flames leapt through the empty windows. As a dull boom announced the collapse of the roof on to the red-hot mass below, a gasp would go round the crowd and for a moment their faces would be lit up in the flare. There are few mill fires now, chiefly because automatic sprinklers are installed on every floor of most mills. These are expensive, but pay for themselves in a few years by the reduction on insurance premiums.

Those shrewd, proud manufacturers, with much of the old tradition behind them, gave place to a different generation with more money to spend, and, in varying degrees, more education. Of those who made large fortunes some moved to other parts, some did much for their own towns, and some did little but blatantly spend their money. This last section, whose chief fault was lack of education, helped to create the scorn which the southerner expressed for the people of the industrial north, a scorn which is only now beginning to disappear.

The clogs and shawls of the Yorkshire mill-girl vanished with the Great War, when high wages gave her more money to spend on dress. Shawls always seemed a cosy protection in the wild weather which comes to these parts in winter. There was something individual and characterful about them, with their patterns ranging from dull plain red to fine Paisley. They have become symbols of the past, as have the clogs, whose clattering irons on the granite sets were signals of the opening and closing of the mills. They are part of the evolution of the community which now summons its workers by a buzzer instead of the bell or still earlier horn.

The enormous profits of the War-time gave place to the slump of 1921, when goods dropped suddenly in value, and first the new firms went out, and then many which had been established from the days of the clothiers. It is not only the eighteenth - century mills in the cloughs which lie derelict to-day. The loss of all that had been their life, coming so soon after the loss of sons in the War, brought an atmosphere of tragedy to the district. Luxury shops closed down, cars were sold, and poverty faced many who had thought themselves secure for life.

The woollen district, by dint of hard work, is pulling it-self round from the depression. Once again mills are working overtime, their lighted windows making a magic picture in the darkness, and large cars and new shops have returned to the streets. But the manufacturers have not the same intimate connection with the mill. They tend to move out to country districts to live, or to places like Harrogate and Ilkley. Some are prompted by a genuine love for the country, an inheritance perhaps from their farming ancestors; others have merely a desire to leave an ugly place. One lady urging her husband to move, said: 'We 've got to get out of here, or you 'll be John all your life'; on the other side a lady gave as her reason for refusing to leave her own small manufacturing town: 'I 'd rather be a big bug in a little place, than a little bug in a big place.'

The present-day manufacturer has much more on his shoulders than the earlier clothiers had. If a slack time comes he has the worry not only of tremendous overhead charges but of hundreds of families depending on him for a livelihood. This responsibility has made him careful, for he must have a reserve to carry him over a bad period. Every manufacturer knows how easily the old Yorkshire saying comes true: 'Clogs to clogs in three generations.'

The Headrow, Leeds

CHAPTER 10

THE WEST RIDING TOWNS (1).

'As threng as Throp's wife when she tried to hang hersen wi' t' dish-claat.' 'As slow as haver malt.' 'As bad as a cat in pattens.' 'As queer as Dick hatband which went nine times round and wouldn't tie.'

Where else but in the industrial West Riding would you hear such phrases still in everyday use? Apt similes which would take sentences to explain are a feature of its broad, robust dialect. They linger most in the crowded areas where the classes are more segregated. Whether you like them or not is a guide to whether you will like the homely, somewhat blunt, but kindly people who use them.

This region divides itself roughly into two parts, the larger eastern area centred round Wakefield, Leeds, and Bradford and merging on to the Plain of York, and the more scattered western district round Huddersfield and Halifax, where the valleys dwindle into the moors. There is no particular place where it can be said that one ends and another begins. The difference lies in the hearts of each, and in the contrasting country which surrounds them. Those in the eastern area take their short car rides, cycle runs, and walks to the east and north where hedges line the fields and the villages are rural, country which is followed by the two famous hunts of the Bramham Moor and the York and Ainsty. Those to the west turn to the Pennine moors, and except where they join the two seldom mix, for long miles of dreary, industrialized country lie between.

The eastern area is purely urban. It is here that the smaller towns and villages link up the larger ones in an unbroken mass of buildings. Small towns we call them, and yet the population of one is more than that of several country towns in the North and East Ridings. They owe their growth not only to the woollen trade, but to all the other trades which came with the canals and good roads, and were in some way connected with it, the iron works at Low Moor, the engineering works, the wholesale clothing factories which were a natural result of the invention of shoddy.

These indeterminate-looking towns seem monotonous to outsiders, but the dweller in one considers his own vitally individual. He knows its streets and ginnels, its chapels and churches, and finds the whole satisfying. He reserves the right to grumble about it, but is quick to resent an outsider doing so. Only those who have connections with them live in these places, so that each family has definite roots which in many cases go back through generations and centuries. Members of families have had passed down to them tales of when there were woods where factories now stand, and paths crossed green fields where rows of houses now line a busy street, and it was so lonely where the new housing estates are that the women and girls dared not go past at night. The hundred-year-old story of the clerk of Beeston has a homely country ring about it.

He used to announce the hymns in the church and sing the first few bars, and one night he started on the wrong tune, struggled on for a few lines, and then said: 'Stop, lads, we 've got into a wrong metre. Let 's begin again.' Now a person in that district, not necessarily knowing the story, will add 'like t'clerk o' Beeston' to 'let 's begin again.'

It is not long since bitter feuds existed between the villages. As recently as 1889 the Bramley almanac says: '. . . and our relationships with the neighbouring villages are of a far more friendly nature than they used to be.' Communities would have uncomplimentary sayings about each other. This had its unpleasant side, but it tended to develop a local pride which shows itself to-day in the resentment of a smaller place at being absorbed by a larger. In 1938 when Shipley effectively opposed a plan for its inclusion with Bradford, the jubilation almost amounted to public rejoicing.

Leeds is in the old district of Loidis, which with the neighbouring district of Elmet remained a stronghold of the British for some time after the Anglian and Norse invasions; Paulinus baptised converts at Dewsbury, which became a Saxon parish; there was a Knights Templars' house at Temple Newsam; and the beautiful Norman church at Adel tells its own story. But Dewsbury is now a big manufacturing town, making shoddy and blankets, and here, as in the whole district, the new busy life swamps the interest in the old. Vigorous, noisy, ever covering up the relics of the past, industry has claimed the soul and spirit of the land for its own.

Of all the towns Wakefield has retained most of the ancient spirit. It is difficult to imagine Robin Hood and the Merry Pinder here now, but it has some feeling of a cathedral town, and though there is a modern bridge over the Calder it has retained its old bridge on which a fourteenth-century chapel is built. This, the first great clothing town in the west of Yorkshire, owning for a long period the largest market, and becoming particularly famous for finishing and dressing cloth, was when Daniel Defoe visited it in the early eighteenth century

WASH DAY IN THE WEST RIDING

'a large, handsome, rich clothing town, full of people, and full of trade.'

By the time of the Industrial Revolution Wakefield had an upper class, chiefly drawn from the clothiers and merchants who were anxious that the district should not become commercialized. By refusing applications for factory sites on its canal and river, they stopped its growth for a time, but the coal development crept up to it, factories followed, and it merely remained a smaller place than it would otherwise have been, while the families of those who had opposed its development left. Yet the town in its present state is very suitable for its position as capital of the West Riding. There is dignity about this governing centre with its handsome offices and town hall.

Bradford, at the second corner of the triangle, has now the largest wool market in the world. Journeys to the Bradford wool sales, examining the bales of wool, and bidding in the circular auction room have their place in the life of every mill. It is an inconvenient town with little plan about it. There is no really main road; steep streets lined with shops and warehouses and paved with stone sets branch in all directions, but it has an air of individuality and it inspires pride in its citizens.

In pre-War days the town used to radiate wealth, and seemed to have a greater proportion of Rolls-Royce cars than most places. It was as though with its late beginning it had set itself to make money and little else. Because of its former prosperity the collapse of Bradford in the slump was more noticeable than in many places. It had an empty, haunted air, and to pass through it was to realize how small was the step between prosperity and failure. The revival has come, if slowly, and Bradford begins to look its old prosperous self again, but it is not quite the same. The present Bradford is a more sober place. Its people are becoming citizens. Its art gallery flourishes, it has built a new civic theatre, and it takes a pride in its musical and literary associations.

It has been said that many Scotch lairds and south-country estate owners are Bradford wool merchants heavily disguised, but a great number of men would not be happy to cut themselves off completely from the old life. Some, while still keeping their connection with the wool market, have bought farms in the country. There is a tale of one man who found at the exchange that the price of wool was rising rapidly and wired to his bailiff: 'Start shearing. Wool rising.' The bailiff wired back: 'Sorry, cannot. Lambing.' So the indignant merchant wired again: 'Who's boss? Stop lambing and start shearing.'

Wakefield may be the governing and Bradford the wool centre, but Leeds is the real heart of the industrial area and indeed of the whole West Riding. It is difficult to say just why this city on the eastern verge with its suburbs running out to rural land should be the centre, but the dreary railway entrance through smoke and dirt into Leeds means coming home to a West Riding man. The enormous new Queen's Hotel is a Yorkshire hotel. The city square, designed in the heavy Victorian tradition, has statues whose removal or non-removal for modern improvements has been a subject for the correspondence columns of Yorkshire papers for years.

During this century the fine new street of the Headrow has been built, and now the old street of Briggate is to be remodelled so that it will be left with only one of its first shops. But Leeds's greatest contribution to this era is its housing of the people from demolished slum property in enormous blocks of flats. Those at Quarry Hill near the city centre are like a village, on such a huge scale that they might seem inhuman were it not for the various colours of the curtains dotted on them like a patchwork quilt. The flats are built in a circle surrounding a courtyard where there are children's playgrounds and special drying spaces. Lifts go to the upper stories, and each flat has its bathroom and special contrivance where the rubbish, tipped down a hole in the kitchen sink, is whisked away on the system of a vacuum. The tenants seemed pleased with everything except the rents. 'Tell 'em,' one woman said, 'we can't get any teeth for paying wer rent.'

Growing from an iron and coal mining district, Leeds became for four hundred years a woollen town. During the Industrial Revolution it turned to engineering, and in this century it has become the centre of the wholesale clothing trade, manufacturing ready-made clothing, principally for men. It is a city of many trades, and for that reason it does not suffer from a depression as the other towns do. The cream pottery named from the town is no longer made here, but down its yards and narrow streets many small industries employing two or three people survive from the past. One man carves and paints hobby-horses, another cuts walking-sticks, and another makes clay pipes. Six firms manufacture between them two thousand tons of passover cake a year; this supplies the large Jewish population of the town, and is also sent all over the world.

The principal Yorkshire university was founded here in 1904 from the Yorkshire College of Science which was opened in 1885. The town's triennial musical festival has also infused its culture into the whole county; we know an old man in the dales who, when he was young, used to walk fifteen miles to the nearest railway station to attend the festival. The town draws its shoppers from a large radius, so that manufacturers' families from villages beyond Huddersfield, farmers from the dales and the Plain of York, and shipowners from Goole pass each other in the streets.

In spite of these various interests and outside influences Leeds keeps provincial in spirit largely because it has a distinct life of its own. Lying as it does close to rural country, its well-known families have stayed in or near the town, for it lies close to rural country. Many still live in the houses which their ancestors built during the nineteenth century and which, enclosed in large grounds, can ignore the new building estates which surround them. The immediate suburbs stretch farther and farther out, and even where these have extended to already established villages they spread the influence of the town from which they come.

Leeds is all these things and many more. It is Woodhouse

Moor on an autumn evening with the glaring lights of the feast coming on one after another, and people crowding to the entrances.   It is the statue of Queen Victoria removed here from in front of the town hall because the moor was one of the first open parks of her reign.   It is public dinners in the Great Northern Hotel, and pantomimes at the Grand and Royal Theatres lasting well into March; the flower sellers with their hand-carts in Briggate and the orators outside the town hall on a Sunday night.   It is the skaters on the lake in Roundhay Park; the crowds and decorated wagons on Children's Day in that great open space which will remain when the country just beyond it has been drawn into the town; the tattoo in the park; the flower show which follows; and the snatches of conversation which you hear in the tents.

'Come on, mother.'

'The trouble is, you go away just as they 're coming out.'

' . . . and then a drought comes, and a lovely bloom dies in three days.'

'I said I 'd try some last year, but I didn't.'

In the midst of the dirt and smoke strange agricultural industries flourish, hanging on to their few acres of land because they are peculiarly suitable for their purpose.   There are enormous rhubarb fields in the districts round Leeds, Hunslet, and Morley.   In the spring when the new yellow shoots spring from the earth to become quickly a carpet of green leaves, or in the summer when their great sheathed flowers shoot upwards into a tropical luxuriance, they are a strange sight in their surroundings of grey houses and mills.

The fields are merely the nurseries, for the roots must be three years in them before they are brought into the forcing sheds.   These are long, low, highly heated buildings where the tender pink sticks are produced in six weeks.   The first batches are brought in to the sheds in November, and the season for gathering lasts from January to May.   The long vistas of plants rising with their brilliant pink stems and yellow foliage in the dim light of the sheds, and the men moving up and down

the rows with flickering candles gathering the sticks, make a
bizarre scene. Electricity is not used during the season
because it turns the leaves green, and the market demands
yellow leaves on forced rhubarb. Sixty tons of rhubarb go
from this district every day, most of it to Covent Garden on the
train known as the 'Rhubarb Special.' It is sold in bundles
in England, but Scotland prefers it by weight, and likes the
thicker sticks. At the end of the season the forced roots are
burnt, and next autumn a new lot is brought in from the fields.

Another peculiar plant is the liquorice grown round Pontefract, where again the land is particularly suited for it. This
local product was once used for making confectionery, particularly the round flat sweets known as Pontefract or Pomfret
cakes; but the large confectionery firms established here because of it now import their liquorice, and the small amount
grown in the district is sold to chemists. It is a tall, bushy
plant with small blue flowers, and is left four years in the
fields before the roots are dug up for use.

A different country survival is the fair held at Lee Gap at
West Ardsley. The charter for this was granted by Henry I to
Nostell Priory, and the monks used to perform miracle plays
there. Until the market was held at Wakefield it had a big
trade in woollen cloth, but in 1656 the inhabitants begged that
it should be stopped, for it had become nothing but a meeting
of idle persons with a few horses and peddling goods to sell,
and often lives were lost.

The fair opened on St Bartholomew's Day, and lasted three
weeks and three days. Now it is merely held on the first and
last of these days, and is known as First Lee and Latter Lee.
During the last century and the beginning of this it was a
famous horse fair. A man named Welsh Jimmy used to
come with strings of fifty or sixty unbroken Welsh ponies
which he would race wildly up and down. Tales are told
about the risk of buying horses at Lee Gap. Men were
warned not to take the middle animal of three, as it would
probably not be able to stand, and not to buy one early in the

morning or it might not survive the day. We knew an old man who was sent as a boy by his father to buy a horse at the fair and was taken advantage of by the gipsies and came home with a poor one. His angry parent declared that he must bear the loss when it was sold, but the boy had learnt his lesson, and the next year he sold the horse at a profit. But there were many good horses at the fair, and farmers, mill-owners, and tradesmen came to buy them. We heard an old man saying to another: 'Aye, I bought one off t' hill yonder eighteen year ago, an' I still 'ave 'im.'

Even to-day hawkers of all kinds come with their horses along the roads to Lee Gap. On the fair ground there are caravans, gipsies cooking meals over the fires, cheap-jacks and side-shows; and the horses race up and down between them and in the field below. There are the same greetings: ' 'Ello, Tom, 'ow 's ta goin' on?' 'Tha 's nearly a stranger.' The same kind of crowd gathers round when a bargain is being made, and there are similar jokes to cover up the seriousness. 'Get agate and get 'im bought. Yer can buy 'im i' five minutes if yer put yersen in t' mind for it. 'E 's a good sooart, 'e 'll not knock thi' brains out or owt o' that.' But it is all a little coarse and tawdry, as if the heart had gone out of it.

The early clothiers gave their money freely to build the Perpendicular parish churches of the district. The monuments of the nineteenth-century manufacturers are the enormous chapels, symbols of the great Nonconformist tradition here. The manufacturer with his Liberal ideas found the chapel more to his taste than the church. He liked to be able to take a share in its government; some actually built chapels themselves, and ruled them like autocrats. We are now celebrating the centenaries of many of these Independent chapels; tall buildings with broad galleries and large schoolrooms and vestries underneath, but yet with a warm, furnished look in the interiors. They have names such as Providence, Ebenezer, and Zion. They reached their peak at Heckmondwike in the Upper Independent Chapel which stands on a hill with an imposing front facing the road. A wall and iron railings surround its large graveyard whose tombstones are a sign of the affluence to which the woollen - manufacturing families attained. Tall granite pillars rise one above another, as if each had tried to go a little better than the last. We should call them ostentatious to-day, but their size and solidity matched the mills and substantial houses, and the stability and power which these families felt had come to themselves and their descendants for all time.

Along with the chapels went the parks, those Victorian parks which are in every town of any size, and which were either the grounds of a large house or made from a piece of land given or willed by some wealthy benefactor. They are all much the same, with a drive up the centre, paths branching from it, and seats at intervals, a pond with ducks and swans, and a bandstand with seats ranged in a circle round it. There are sooty laurel and rhododendron bushes round the edges, and flower beds increasing in display to a *chef-d'œuvre* near the bandstand. The weekly band performances made somewhere to go in the days before cinemas. They varied according to the town they were in, but many a happily married woman to-day met her husband at a band performance in a West Riding park.

It is a rough speech you hear in these towns with broad *u*'s, the article 'the' shortened to t', and often the possessive *s* omitted. The last characteristic was noticeable in the fourteenth-century Towneley mystery plays of Wakefield, where we find 'Noe flood,' 'heven king.' Many other words in these plays are still used in the dialect speech: 'lig' for lies; 'lapped,' meaning wrapped; 'threap,' argue; to 'lake,' play; 'nesh,' delicate; 'addle,' earn; 'fettle,' prepare; 'sneck,' latch. The closing lines might have been written to-day:

1st *Shepherd*. What grace we have fun'.
2nd *Shepherd*. Come forth, now are we won.
3rd *Shepherd*. To sing are we bun'.

The West Riding dialect is not so pure as that of the North and East Ridings, because of the early influence coming with industry from the midlands, but good old words such as thoil (bear), jannock (thorough), piggin (lading can), voider (clothes basket), gallock (left-handed), thible (wooden stirrer) survive. It is not so pleasant to hear as many dialects because the voices which speak it are harsher from their struggle to make themselves heard above the roar of machinery. A crowd of mill-girls coming home from work will still keep the strident tone; and the habit spreads, clinging in a milder form to much of the middle-class population. The merest hint of it in a voice betrays the origin of the speaker.

In nine cases out of ten you will find that person humorous and quick-witted, downright and kind-hearted, and not without dignity. He is loyal to his own town, and proud of what has made it. He likes streets and pavements because they have been his whole environment, and he chooses Bridlington and Scarborough for his holidays because there are streets and pavements and crowds there too. Not even in these sophisticated days is he very far removed in spirit from that West Riding man who the first time he went to the seaside was very pleased with it all, but found something, he didn't just know what, wanting, and finally wrote home: 'Send ma an owd shoddy sample or two for ma to smell at, t' air 's fair wauf here, an' hezzan't a bit o' flavour abaht it.'

Halifax

CHAPTER 11

THE WEST RIDING TOWNS (2)

Looking down to Halifax from Beacon Hill on a still winter day, you see the town in the deep valley below through a curtain of smoke, black smoke from the chimneys and white from the water-cooling towers mingling into a thick grey haze. The factories and houses emerge gradually from it, and finally the sooted walls of the parish church, which was there when the weavers worked in the cottages, and has borne the attack of every fresh chimney. As you watch, the smoky veil casts a glamour over it all. You marvel at the brains and ingenuity of the men who planned these factories, and the stoical endurance of those who worked them and their fore-runners. They seem to have conquered nature here. Hill-sides which in many parts would be thought too steep for anything but sheep-grazing are covered with houses and crossed with roads.

The picture of a factory town seen from above either through smoke or in the clarity of a summer evening is a familiar one in this west part of the industrial area, where the development has been chiefly up valleys between hills, and the large towns lie at the junctions of several valleys.   There are tracts of open country in between these towns with farms and rocky becks and bluebell woods, but it is never without signs of the domination of industry.   Tall chimneys start into view; the field and wood paths are trodden bare and hard; and mill workers come home at night to the remotest cottages.   The Pennine moors creep down to villages and towns, and raise their grim barrier against further encroachment, but the roads which cross them are highways made for heavy traffic to and from Lancashire, which is just over the other side.   It is a bleak land where snow lingers long after it is forgotten in the milder country to the east.

The towns of Huddersfield, Halifax, and Keighley at the extreme north dominate this area.   Huddersfield is something of an upstart; Almondbury, a village one and a half miles away, supplies the antiquity.   Here seventeenth-century half-timbered houses cluster round the fifteenth-century church; and the mound of Castle Hill, the site of a British hill fort and a medieval castle, overshadows it.   A coin of Cartimandua, Queen of the Brigantes, found near here, is now in the Ravensknowle Museum.   The citizens of Huddersfield erected a tower on the hill to celebrate the Diamond Jubilee of Queen Victoria, and it gives a native of the district a proprietary kind of pleasure to pick out this tower from long distances.

Huddersfield is a well-planned town, chiefly owing to the regulations of the Ramsden family who were lords of the manor when it was growing.   In 1766 Sir John Ramsden built the oval cloth hall which was pulled down in 1930.   This hall was a late one, and its memories are chiefly of the first manufacturers bringing their worsteds in covered wagons to the market.   The valleys from which they came spread like a fan into the hills, and the villages dotted along them have now grown into each other, but Huddersfield is still a centre for them, as a country town is for a rural district.

On market days the manufacturers' wives wearing their crinolines or bustles would come in from the outlying places to buy calico and buttons, and along with their husbands would end the day with a Yorkshire high tea at a relative's house. To-day these families with their spreading connections present a strong barrier to the outside world. It is made up of the many experiences which they or their forbears have shared, the inventions of machinery, the building of new mills and chimneys, the growth of the town, the ups and downs of trade.

As well as the pulsing life of the outside valleys, Huddersfield has to do with the roads which go beyond them over the moors to Lancashire, many of them hill passes. They are known by the inns on them—the Isle of Skye above Holmfirth, Nont Sarah's (a corruption of My Aunt Sarah's) above Scammonden, the Great Western on the Stanedge Pass, though this road is now usually called by its own name. Bill's o' Jack's Inn, a few miles beyond the Isle of Skye, was pulled down in 1938. Its name is interesting as testifying to the custom in these parts, as in the more northerly dale country, of calling a man by his father's name, sometimes going back two generations, as Bill o' Jack's o' Tom's. The inn had a sinister reputation because a murder is supposed to have taken place there.

These high roads cross fine stretches of moorland, grass-covered in the south, but merging in the north into heather and peat-hags with boulders of dark millstone grit accentuating their fierceness. Many of the valleys are now taken up with reservoirs to supply the towns, and the farms which once lined their hillsides are slipping gradually back to moorland.

Tremendous snowstorms sweep the moors, and though the plough is brought on to the road as soon as a storm begins, even during the night, the drifts generally get the better of it, and next day the papers have pictures and accounts of cars and lorries buried under the snow. For days, sometimes weeks, after a double way has been cut through, high walls of

snow on either side remain to tell of the storm.   The white
covering on the moors and rugged valleys gives them for a time
a gentler aspect, but after a day or two, even on the highest
summits, the snow is sprinkled with soot.

The early system of the woollen trade, necessitating incessant
journeys, is the reason for the many roads round Huddersfield
and Halifax.   Numbers of pack-horse ways have vanished into
enclosed fields or boggy moor, and only an occasional stone
stoop remains to tell of them, but a few are modern routes.
Some of them were made for their purpose, others utilized
older tracks.   The most famous of these is the Roman road
from Ilkley to Manchester over Blackstone Edge.   This was
used as the main way from Halifax to Lancashire until the
turnpike road to Rochdale was made in 1735.   It can still be
followed down a slope below the present road, crossing a
beck by a Roman bridge, a plain little bridge with two square
arches, built about A.D. 125, and turning up the hillside
parallel with the modern road.   It is sunk in bog here and
difficult to find in places, but as it nears the summit the paving
begins to show through.   The finest stretch, just over the
county border, shows the small stone blocks and raised edging
and the groove worn down the centre, probably by the weighted
poles which the Romans dragged behind their wagons to act
as brakes.

The vast black stretches of moor with forest ahead must
have seemed interminable to the Roman builders as step by step
they laid what was to be a main road for sixteen hundred years.
You wonder if they felt the cold of this wind-swept track, and
how many of them died by the way.   Other figures followed
them down the road.   Ralph Thoresby in February 1682 told
of 'trouble and hazard in passing Blackstone-edge where we
had a sore storm of snow on the height of it, when it was fair
sunshine on both sides,' and of how drifts made it difficult to
get through, and patches where the snow had blown off it were
so icy that his horse fell.   Defoe, one of the last travellers, also
crossed it in a storm, and described it as horrible, with water

running down the hollow like a river. Later, when the new turnpike road left it deserted, Chartists from Yorkshire and Lancashire met on the summit to discuss their plans, and perhaps a Halifax coiner came along it; but they and shepherds were then the only users. Archaeologists come down it now, measure the pavement, discuss the groove, and work out theories.

It is easy round Halifax to imagine the trains of pack-horses struggling up and down the hills to reach the town on its ridge, and to realize how the difficulty of approach finally lost it its position as the centre of the woollen trade. The first trams here must have seemed a miracle. Up to the end they ran on a very narrow gauge and swayed and rocked down the hills in an alarming manner. The town flourishes and now has important carpet mills and toffee factories as well as woollen mills.

Wainhouse Tower on an edge of the ridge on which Halifax stands is a monument to the stubborn, sometimes bitter, part of the West Riding character. Originally built as a brick chimney stack for a dye works, it was turned into an observation tower from which its owner could overlook his neighbour's grounds. It now serves to give an individual touch to the distant views of Halifax from the hills round Huddersfield. Seen at night from these hills the town is a fairy place, a huge expanse of twinkling lights with ribbons of light running from it.

Formerly the villages which surround and connect these two towns had a distinct life of their own. At Elland in the early nineteenth century the women were lamenting the removal of the town wells, and declared that if the common mangle went too they would 'nivver know nowt.' The mill hands then wore blue cotton dresses with white spots and made with short sleeves, checked aprons, handkerchiefs on their heads, grey stockings, bright clogs, and as a rule coral necklaces. The post office and general store was kept by Hannah Buckley, who used to carry the letters round to deliver in her apron. Her chief commodities were liquorice root from Pontefract and 'scaarin' stooans.'

There are large stone quarries at Elland, Crosland Moor near Huddersfield, and Midgley near Halifax, for in the high parts houses are still built of stone, but the smaller industries connected with them have gone. One was the making of bakstones for baking oatcakes. About 1825 a man from Saddleworth used to go round hawking these, carrying them edges upwards balanced on each side of a horse. As he went along the street he called out: 'Havercake bakst'ns!' His stock came from the quarry at Delph which had supplied bakstones for hundreds of years. The name Delph actually means a quarry; only this year a roadman, directing us near Hebden Bridge, told us to go past the 'delph 'oile.'

We are told how a century ago donkeys bringing a wedding party to Elland from Blackley wore earthenware hats. The pottery where these were made still exists, but now makes bricks and pipes. The old pottery at Salendine Nook two miles away was closed in 1935. This was started by a family of potters named Morton who fled from Scotland over three hundred years ago to avoid religious persecution, and settled here with a few workmen and soon had a good trade. They made chiefly large earthenware bowls for kneading bread, stew jars, and pie dishes of a rough brown texture on the outside and yellow glaze inside. Ranged on the shelves in the dim interior of the pottery, these were an entrancing sight.

The hillside round Blackley is a forgotten corner, dotted with little wind-swept farmhouses, but always within sight of mills. As children we saw a haystack belonging to one of the farms set on fire by lightning. The fire engine when it came stood helplessly by, for there was scarcely any water at hand, and the fire seemed to laugh at the pitiful bucketfuls thrown on to it. The family watched in mute despair the quick destruction of what was to have fed their cattle through the year. Whispers went round that it would mean their leaving the farm because they were not insured. The storm passed over, leaving behind it a sparkling freshness on land that had needed rain, and tragedy in the smouldering embers of a stack.

The old names for holidays are still used in this part of the West Riding: Halifax Wakes, Honley Feast, Bowling Tide, Pontefract Stattis (a contraction of statutes), Longwood Thump, Meltham and Ripponden Rush-bearings. These holidays are all in different weeks; 'staggered' holidays, which are now being considered, were arranged long ago in the West Riding. The rush-bearings proclaim the religious origin of holidays, but by the seventeenth century these had developed into rowdiness. Horsemen going home took longer journeys to avoid them, and parsons found their churches empty because the people were going round to one after another. The feasts generally ended with a fight. At Longwood Thump a father asked his son: 'Has ta foughten?'

'Noow, fatther.'

'Cum then,' said the father, 'get thee foughten, and let's gooa whomm (home).'

Familiar features of the summer months are the Sings, Sunday afternoon performances by local choirs in fields. Every one in the neighbourhood goes to them, drawn by the music as much as by the meeting of friends. West Riding people are notoriously musical; almost every village has its choral society whose performance of the *Messiah* is one of the events of Christmas time. Weeks of practice go to the preparation of the hymns for a Sunday school anniversary, and the volume of sound when the day comes is enormous. Huddersfield had one of the first competitive musical festivals, originated by Mrs Sunderland, the Yorkshire soprano, who was born at Brighouse. It lasts for a week, and on the two final nights the audience fills the town hall. Particular tunes are often attached to places; *Pratty Flowers* is known as the Holmfirth anthem, and the famous tune, *On Ilkla' Moor baht 'at*, needs no explanation.

Some remnants of old customs are kept up in the remoter districts. The Pace Egg play which used to be performed in many Yorkshire villages has been revived at Midgley near Hebden Bridge, though the players now are children. The head-dresses made of enormous paper hoops of various colours are copies of those worn by early players. The villagers wait outside their houses for ''t' Pace Eggers,' and watch St George, Slasher, and the Doctor enacting a story which is pagan in origin, going back to a belief that the dead spirit of vegetation comes to life again in the spring.

The pretentious buildings of the Victorian mechanics' institutes are features of the villages round Halifax. They look on to seventeenth-century halls and manor houses which were built by the yeomen a few of whom became clothiers, and have survived marvellously to become the homes of modern manufacturers. Sometimes there are two or three in a village. Barkisland Hall, dignified and aloof, has on its doorway the motto, 'Once his, now mine, but I know not whose afterwards.' High Sunderland has the inscription, 'May the Almighty grant that the race of Sunderland may quietly inhabit this seat and maintain the rights of their ancestors, free from strife, until an ant drink up the waters of the sea, and a tortoise walk round the whole world.' Howroyd and Clay House at Greetland retain their panelled rooms and staircases; and the fifteenth-century hall at Shibden has been restored and its grounds made into a public park.

West of Halifax the old weaving villages lie along the hill-sides, situated just above the forest line and below the heather. Modern mills have been built in a few of these, such as Old Town above Hebden Bridge, and mingle strangely with the unaltered cottages and houses, but for the most part a new village in the valley has superseded the old as far as industry is concerned. So you get the manufacturing village near the river, and the old village, now a purely farming community, a mile or half a mile up the hillside. One after another they come—Sowerby and Sowerby Bridge, Luddenden and Ludden-den Foot, Heptonstall and Hebden Bridge. The farmers' families work in the valley mills, but during the last few years an almost entirely new population, much of it Irish, has come to inhabit these farms. Mills still line the river, but now that

Halifax is left behind they appear less frequently and the upland villages and the moors which sweep from them tell of open country ahead. Suddenly where Hebden Bridge lies in a small hollow, the story of the woollen industry seems to be crystallized as in an epilogue.

We came down to Hebden Bridge from the high moor road from Haworth on an early summer evening. At this hour only a few thin wreaths of smoke curled into the sky, and the buildings stood out clear but softened in the mellow light. We could see how beautiful the valley had been before it was invaded by industry, which seemed as much an intruder here as in the smoking towns which you glimpse from the train in the valley of the Rhône. Yet the effect of it was arresting. The tall houses are built in tiers on the hillsides overlooking the mills with their many windows. From this height the figures of mill-girls trudging home up the ginnels appeared shortened. It was market day and in the square below the stalls and the women's dresses made patches of bright colour. On the opposite side the hill jutted out between two valleys, and on its summit the village of Heptonstall clustered round a church tower.

The rows of four-storied buildings which give Hebden Bridge its foreign air, are really rows of two-storied houses built one above the other. The lower half is entered from a street on one level, and the top half from a higher one. The front doors of the top rows often open on to balconies. These houses, running at angles along the hillsides, are reached by steep streets or cobbled ginnels. Their architecture was probably influenced by the hilly country and the fact that the manufacturers would not find it easy to get land for building from the farmers. They make a vivid picture of the old part of Hebden Bridge. The new part of the town is where the valley opens to Halifax, and from here an easy road runs by the river Calder to Todmorden, which has the air of a Lancashire town. Custom has changed in this district and the mills are now mostly cotton and flannel, and its principal trade is wholesale clothing.

The road to Heptonstall climbs steeply out of Hebden Bridge past a large Methodist chapel with a row of cottages built under it after the manner of the houses across the valleys. As you rise to the summit the low houses draw you into an old-world village with cobbled alleys branching from a narrow road. It is a little reminiscent of Pateley Bridge and Dent, but there is something almost frightening as well as attractive about the main street lying north and south so that shadows fill it for most of the day. It seems in keeping with the place that the builders of the large new church should have left the old one as a ruin in the churchyard. One Sunday in the year the villagers hold a service in the roofless building. It has a curious plan with two naves and two aisles, and is a mixture of Perpendicular and Tudor architecture. The old gravestones, many of them seventeenth century, which once paved the aisles are now open to the sky.

Near the churchyard a square of weavers' cottages tell of past activity. The old houses in Heptonstall are all of stone; one down an alley has a doorway decorated with quaint figures of a man and wife and their initials. In the eighteenth century the introduction into Halifax of brick for building brought forth the scorn of the Heptonstall people, who likened it to wax, but can hardly have composed the rhyme:

> Halifax is made of wax,
> Heptonstall of stone.
> There 's pretty girls in Halifax,
> In Heptonstall there 's none.

Now brick has come to Heptonstall in a new housing estate which is to supply the whole neighbourhood, to the annoyance of villages long distances away. One fears that the names of the new streets will not have the same ring as the old ones, The Town, Top o' th' Town, and Town Head. Th' is a common abbreviation. There is a Top o' th' Close Road near Todmorden, and an inn called 'Bird i' th' Hand' with a sign:

> One bird i' th' hand is better far
> Than two which in the bushes are.

You hear the 'th' for 'the' in the speech of the mill-girls who climb the steep hill to Heptonstall when the mills in the valleys close. It has changed here from the t' which we heard round Leeds.

The present road from Hebden Bridge to Haworth goes over the moor, but the old Haworth road runs up the valley below. Hand-loom weaving was carried on in all the farmhouses near the road, and at Crimsworth a chapel tells of the time when the hillside was heavily populated and there were numbers of weavers' cottages. It seems a distant time, but in one of the farmhouses we met an old lady, still active, who remembered two brothers weaving in a cottage lower down the road, and a man from higher up carrying his pieces on his back to Halifax market. She seemed to connect in her person the old and new life. The names of several of these farms have the suffix 'royd,' meaning a clearing, a familiar ending to the names and farms of this district.

No corn is grown on these farms, which are now occupied in rearing sheep and cattle. On many of them a little extra money is made by serving teas for walkers, and almost all of them are surrounded by hen-runs and rather ramshackle hen-houses. This is good land for hens, and further west in the Cowling district the breeding of poultry has become a large and important industry.

A path, now almost lost in places over the moors, goes past the ruined cottage of Withens, the supposed scene of Emily Brontë's *Wuthering Heights*, to Haworth. It is a squat cottage huddled on the hillside, a square chimney its only attempt at architecture. Three trees stand near, and there is a small walled garden, but the land round it has gone back to moor. It is an attractive moorland cottage, but it lacks the spaciousness and dignity of the house described in *Wuthering Heights*.

These moors which the Brontës loved are not so stark and grim as those further south. They are covered with heather and cut by little green valleys, and curlews and grouse call on them. Rushes wave by the footpath as you go down from Withens, and two trees stand sentinel at a stone stile. Hundreds of people have walked this way to see the moors which inspired the Brontës, and hundreds follow them, not quite knowing why they come. Where a branch path joins the main one a man and a woman stopped us to ask the way to the 'Brontë Café.' The woman wore imitation skin shoes whose heels

Withens

turned over as she walked on the rough path. Neither of them knew anything about Withens or much about the Brontës or the moors, and yet it was indirectly because of all three of these that they had come this way.

Modern Haworth with mills in the valley climbs past the park to the old village, which is not very changed from the days when the Brontës knew it. It is probable that much of it would have been swept away now but for their association. There is an exciting air about this corner which has become a literary shrine for pilgrims from all parts of the world. They walk through the old vicarage, which is now a museum, see the family relics, the manuscripts of stories which the sisters wrote as children, the furniture they used, and the rooms in which they sat; look out over the garden to the churchyard where

Emily and Charlotte are buried—that sombre graveyard with its closely packed dark stone memorials; and go into the Black Swan Inn to see the chair in which Bramwell always sat.

The village itself appears to take the fame of the Brontës very calmly. There is a tale of an old man who, asked by a visitor which was the Brontës' house, said he didn't know. Surely, the visitor declared, he must have heard of the celebrated Brontë family who had lived here. 'I 've lived i' Haworth man and lad for sixty year,' said the old man, 'an' there were nivver a Brontë played i' Haworth band 'at ivver I heeard on.' The fact that they will tell such stories against themselves is a proof of the pride of West Riding people in their association with this family whose renown has brought distinction to Haworth.

These moors are surrounded by industry—the Yorkshire cotton town of Keighley yet lies to the north—but they look over country which is leaving it behind for the green pastures of Craven.

Ellerbeck Hall, Slaidburn

CHAPTER 12

THE BORDERS OF CRAVEN

THERE is magic about a place-name with its district attached to
it. Skipton-in-Craven, we say, and we see the old market town,
the 'sheep town,' with its wide main street cobbled at the edges
where the stalls stand, the church looking down on it, and
the mellowed walls of the castle of the Cliffords towering above
it, but we see also the green pastures of Craven with their
dazzling limestone outcrops, and grey towns and villages
clustered under their shadow. Bolton-by-Bowland is mentioned, and the white cottages and flowery gardens round the
green, and the hill running up to the rubble-walled church,
appear before us in their setting of rich agricultural land
merging into heather- and bracken-covered moors. Horton-
in-Ribblesdale brings to mind not only the straggling limestone village, but the fells rising from the narrow valley to the
peaks of Penyghent and Ingleborough. The district of Craven
includes Bowland as well as Malhamdale, Ribblesdale, and the

upper part of Wharfedale; and the town of Skipton, which is its capital, draws the life of all these places to itself.

Skipton is not wholly an agricultural town. The woollen mills which were built along its canals, and were later turned to cotton mills, still flourish, but, owing to the lie of the land and the restrictions on it, these and the houses connected with them all grew at the lower end, and have never been sufficiently numerous to rob the old town of its country atmosphere. Here the dirt and smoke are being left behind. Sheffield people going north say that not until they reach Skipton do they feel to come out of the haze which hangs over the industrial area, and to breathe pure, unpolluted air.

The excitement of holiday making pervades the streets, of people leaving trains and buses to tramp the dale fells and explore the Craven caves and waterfalls, of travellers passing through on their way to the coast, the Lake District, and Scotland. This atmosphere has become an integral part of the town, and its stimulation is infectious as you arrive from the sterner working regions to the country again.

Underlying this the fuller life of the market persists through the year, undeterred by blizzards and east winds, a life in which a spring drought is dreaded because it stops the grass growing and a wet July is only bad because it means a poor hay harvest.

> Skipton-in-Craven
> Is never a haven
> But many a day of foul weather.

Wet or fine, a varied crowd comes week by week to the market: farmers from remote dale villages; lowland farmers looking for mountain sheep to eat their turnips; butchers seeking stock to feed the vast town areas; dealers from long distances. As many as eight thousand sheep change hands in one day at the autumn sales in the auction mart. 'Aye, we tak' 'em to Skipton market,' says a farmer high up Wharfedale. 'Finest market i' England,' says a farmer from a hill farm above Haworth. The eating-houses where a hot meat-and-potato pie and a cup of tea could be had for fourpence have gone with the coffee taverns, but down Hardcastle's Yard there is still an oat-bread baker. He is an old man making the mixture as he was taught by his mother, shaping it on the riddle-board by a deft move-ment of the wrist before he throws it, covered by a piece of flannel, on to the bakstone.

In June the voices of Irishmen waiting to be hired for the hay harvest mingle with the mixed dialects of the district; and one summer day potters and dealers display their horses on the cobbles at the side of the road, keeping feebly alive the Skipton Horse Fair which was once an event in the north.

Skipton owed its market in the first place to the lords of the castle and to the monks of Bolton Priory in Wharfedale. They made good roads to it, and when the Forest of Knaresborough was converted into arable land in 1770 great quantities of corn grown there were brought to Skipton along these roads. From that time the Craven farmers began to put down their arable land to pasture for which it was better suited, and to concen-trate on rearing stock. Seeing the unbroken greenness of this country where meadows and cultivated pastures merge almost imperceptibly into grassy moorland we forget that for centuries the gold of cornfields mingled with the green.

The castle keeps the memory of the Clifford family alive; of Henry, the Shepherd Lord, coming to his estates after the Wars of the Roses; of Eleanor Clifford sheltering from the rebels in the Pilgrimage of Grace; of the castle held for the king in the Civil War. They seem real persons still, but the most human of them is Lady Anne Clifford. Coming to her estates after a thirty years' struggle to obtain them from her uncle, she repaired the damage done to the castle in the Civil War, as she did at her castle at Appleby and smaller ones at Barden Tower and Pendragon in Westmorland. She was happiest when she was here in the country, making journeys to her houses, managing her affairs, and settling disputes in a high-handed manner to her own advantage. When a member of a family who for centuries had annually paid a hen to the

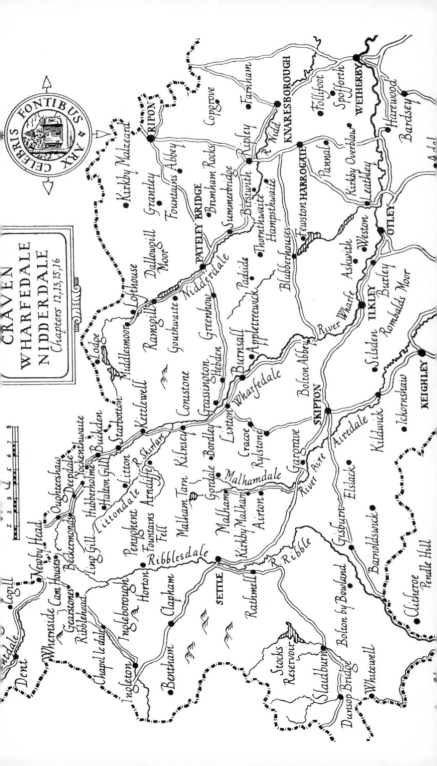

Clifford family for some right refused to pay, she went to court about it, won her case, and afterwards invited her opponent to dinner to help her eat the hen.   She lived in an age when women were allowed to take a part in business, long before the Victorian era turned them into household furniture.   Her diaries reveal a fine heartiness.   Twice she tells of the good meals she has eaten, and only at the end of the day remembered that it was Friday and she should have lived on fish.

West of Skipton, leaving the limestone fells, the gentle district of Bowland seems to sleep its life away.   It is a land of green fields and woods bounded now by stone walls, now by hedges, now by hedges growing on low walls.   Stretches of moorland mix in a friendly manner with them and yet rise to grandeur near the county border.   The country is watered by the now tranquil rivers of the Ribble and Hodder and their tributaries, whose banks almost all the way are arched by fine trees through which are glimpses of moor.   The stretch from Slaidburn to Dunsop Bridge, where the road runs here beside the river, here out of sight of it, is one of those corners of Yorkshire where all types of scenery join to produce an entrancing whole.

For a distance before they meet, gently and inevitably, in rich wooded land at Great Mitton, the rivers form the south and west borders of the county.   The road runs above the Hodder to Whitewell whose large hotel, appearing suddenly on the rolling country, has usually a few fishermen starting out from it or standing in front of it discussing the day's sport.

Northward the border rises to the moorland of Bowland Forest, still with its mixture of wooded lower slopes and heather, and bracken-covered summits, and through this the ravine called the Trough of Bowland cuts a way into Lancashire. The influence of Lancashire is evident along the border and to some extent all over Bowland, not only the Lancashire of the markets and towns whose reservoirs are in these valleys, but also its northern rural end which has much of the spirit of Westmorland.   The peak of Pendle Hill, the Lancashire outpost of the Pennines, peeping through a dip in the fells, rearing its shape above them, or rising across enormous flat stretches of waste, is a part of almost every scene.

The villages scattered sparsely along it are pleasant and easeful like the land. Gisburn's quiet streets lead under the gateway built with its stones to the ruins of Sawley Abbey. Bolton-by-Bowland's ancient cottages with their carved door-heads look across the road to the stocks and part of a stone cross on the green. Opposite the church is the entrance to Bolton Hall where Henry VI was sheltered after the battle of Hexham.

Slaidburn, the largest village, has caught within itself the whole spirit of Bowland. Built in a T shape with the church and early eighteenth-century grammar school at the foot and cottages running in a dwindling line along the top, it lies on a rise above the river and is gently encircled by the rolling blue hills. At the junction of the roads, a focus for the village, as the village is for the district, stands the Hark to Bounty Inn whose curious name was changed from plain 'Dog' after an Pendle Forest hound named Bounty which used to bay on a particular note when it found a scent.

At one end of the building, exterior steps lead to where an ancient studded oak door opens to the hall in which the Swain-mote Courts of the Forest were held. It is a panelled room with wooden seats surrounding a table at one end, and an ante-room where the jury sat leading out of it. There is still the oak chest in which the papers of the forest were kept. In the dim light of this room you picture what was the vital period in this particular country's life, the time when the English squires and yeomen were in their heyday, and when it must have seemed as though the abundant life of the English countryside would never change appreciably.

The yeomen here were of a type common in Lancashire. They were homely, but some possessed considerable wealth, and they had a strong sense of their own dignity and re-sponsibility. You find their houses, such as Ellerbeck Hall near Slaidburn, in snug corners or on commanding sites.   The smaller ones are perhaps the least altered, because they are now homesteads for small farms whose rents do not allow for more than necessary restoration.   But even these, made as they were for the large families of those days, are usually too big for their present tenants.

These houses are distinct from the mansions such as Bolton Hall and Hammerton Hall, whose owners are said at one time to have been able to ride all the way to York on their own land.   This was good country for the sporting knight or squire, though theirs were not the pompous hunts of to-day; many a meet was started by a farmer sighting a fox, and setting off after it with his two hounds, blowing a horn to let his neighbours know.   Sometimes they went far afield over the county border through the dip of the Trough of Bowland.   The yeomen describe the hunts in their diaries along with visits to relatives and attendances at funerals and christenings; they were as familiar a part of their existence as births and deaths.

Knights and yeomen were generous to their own villages. They built the grammar schools which the yeomen's sons attended along with the boys of the village; and they left farms and land to provide annuities for the poor.   The rents from these are still distributed in the neighbourhood, though there are no real poor in Bowland to-day.

There remains here that sense of friendly communication between rich and poor which distinguished the days of the yeomen.   It shows in the attitude of the sexton of the church who, when a new vicar asked him how he had liked his first Sunday morning's service, said: 'Well, sir, there was just one thing.   At the end of the responses you say 'Ahmen' and I say 'Aymen.'   The vicar respected his preference, and in future allowed the sexton to make the responses himself.

Here and there the moor is cut by a little valley with a beck running down it and one or two farmhouses near its head. These 'fell farms' are sheep farms with grazing on the moor, and near the beck a few meadows whose hay harvest is late and not very good. On them sheep shearing is still a communal affair. A farmer sends word that he is clipping on a certain day and any number up to thirty or forty of the neighbouring farmers arrive to help. They come in cars now, and find that the sheep have been driven down from the moors the day before, and that the farmer has collected sufficient wooden stocks on which to rest the sheep. Formerly each man carried his own stock to a clipping, and two or three met at dawn at certain places along the fells and drove the sheep down for the farmer. They did not go if it was wet because soaked fleeces are difficult to clip. There is still a large meal for the helpers at the end of a day's work, but the dance which used to follow is a thing of the past.

A few years ago, in a West Riding town, a suit was made in just over three hours, starting with shearing the fleece, and going through the spinning and weaving of the cloth to sewing the last button on the suit; and one of the five men chosen to clip the sheep was a Bowland shepherd.

We dropped down from this pleasant country to the little town of Bentham on a market day, to a scene of stir and bustle, but not of haste. Bearded farmers were poking cows and sheep with gnarled sticks, and traps and carts of all descriptions reared up at the sides of the streets were a happy sight in this age in which the farmer's trap has almost vanished. Later we met them rumbling along the roads with a farmer and his wife and perhaps a daughter or two packed in between the hampers and baskets.

Eastwards across the valley, Ingleborough towers up beyond long stretches of limestone land. At its foot is the village of Ingleton where the Kingsdale Beck trickles below the houses. The most spectacular of the caves and potholes for which the limestone country is famous are round here: Weathercote Cave where there are miles of underground rivers, Yordas Cave on a slope of Gragreth, Alum Pot on Ingleborough, Victoria Cave at Settle. The pothole of Gaping Ghyll was first descended in 1872 by Mr John Birkbeck, and now visitors are

*F

let down on a seat worked by a pulley. Fresh caves and passages are continually being discovered, and interest in them has brought, in the speleologists armed with ropes and flash-lights, a new section into the community.

The hills are also pierced with small potholes, miniatures of the large hollows worn by the action of water and, like them, lined with ferns and little trees which have rooted on the sides. Not being railed off, these are dangerous for sheep and lambs, which, if they are not killed by a fall down them, may be im-prisoned for days before the shepherd discovers their where-abouts. When he does find them he has to be let down by a rope to rescue them.

Through Clapham, where the houses line the beck, we come to Austwick, yet another of the Craven villages nestling attrac-tively under the lower slopes of Ingleborough. Here the cluster of houses and barns sheltering between fine sycamores looks to the fells for its life. This is a cattle-rearing country, and herds grazing on the pastures bring to mind 'the cattle on a thousand hills.' Sheep are kept on the higher fells, and the farmers join to employ two shepherds to look after them. Each year the men who wish to apply for the job put in a tender, which is usually a shilling for each sheep gait, and the farmers, who have votes allotted according to the number of their gaits, decide on the likeliest applicant.

From long distances the people of these villages round Ingleborough can watch the shepherds coming down from the fells, and sometimes they have welcomed them back from perilous journeys. They remember one man bringing his sheep down in a blizzard, and arriving back with his clothes coated with ice, and his arms frozen stiffly at his sides. When he was brought into the house to thaw in front of the fire, his one desire was to go to sleep, and the farmer's wife who was left to look after him kept him awake by slapping him on the face, saying: 'We mun wakken 'im now or 'e 'll nivver wakken i' t' morn.'

Another shepherd, caught in a blinding snowstorm and

knowing he could not find his way down, turned with a few sheep into a little fold on the fell and kept himself alive by driving them round all night. Searchers found him next morning completely exhausted. These are wild open fells—it would be possible for a sheep to travel from here across un-enclosed moorland to where the shepherds join to clip at Whitendale in Bowland—but there is a soft graciousness about the villages lying under them on the west side, a charm which has the gentleness of lowland country about it, and yet is here among the fells.

Gordale Bridge

CHAPTER 13

MALHAMDALE AND RIBBLESDALE

THE old town of Settle huddling under the tall limestone scar of Castlebergh has its place on the main road north, and also stands as a gateway to the dale country in the east. It lies on the line of the Craven Fault, and its houses and walls are built of limestone which that upheaval threw to the surface.

The main street runs at one side of the market square, in the middle of which are houses whose front doors open on to an overhanging balcony built over a block of shops. When Thomas Gray visited Settle in 1769 most of the houses were like this. The cattle market with its accompanying trade and the postal centre have gone from here to Skipton, but Settle keeps its character as a kind of capital of Ribblesdale, and its flourishing weekly market draws the people from high and lowland farms.

The market crowded into the little square has the feeling of a Flemish market scene. The striped awnings of the stalls, the piles of fruit and vegetables, the neat pattern of the drapery stalls, the bright new buckets and milk cans, make vivid patches of colour against the more sober ropes and harness and the grey background of houses and hill.

The people lean over and watch from the balconies, while down below little groups gather to discuss the topic of the moment; who has been snowed up, how lambing is proceeding, how the grass is growing, how much hay is cut or gathered.

'Has ta finished?' a pleasant-faced woman greets another on a late August morning.

'Aye, this week, and that's three weeks ower late.'

'We've twea meadows to cut yet,' says the first woman, who seems to be from a high farm.

'We've naught but a couple o' pikes out.'

Settle market used to be famous for leather for which buyers came regularly from as far as Barnsley and Sheffield; and it had its own tanneries. There were also several small cotton mills where children, many of whom were brought from Keighley and boarded in the villages, were employed. Earlier than that, hemp was grown here and spun into linen in such quantities that the bye-laws of Settle and Giggleswick restricted the washing of it in the water-courses and prohibited the drying and beating of flax in the houses.

The wealth of the district in the late eighteenth and early nineteenth centuries is reflected in the importance of the Craven Bank. This was founded in 1791 by a Quaker family named Birkbeck, and it soon had several branches. Large houses which are now hotels and cafés in the main street were built by the banking families. The first notes were engraved with a view of Castlebergh, but in 1817 this was changed to the Craven heifer, a remarkable beast which was born at Bolton Abbey in 1807 and eventually won first prize at Smithfield Show. When the bank lost the privilege of issuing notes, the farmers were at first reluctant to accept the new Bank of England notes, and asked for those 'wi' a coo on 'em.'

Until 1838, when it built a church of its own, Settle joined

with the church in the neighbouring village of Giggleswick.
Here also is the grammar school, founded in 1512. This
is to-day one of the largest public schools in the north, and is
interesting as being one of the early grammar schools which
have survived and expanded. The yeomen farmers sent their
sons to it, and some of these went out into the world to become
doctors and lawyers, and to take a prominent part in English
life. The community gathered here in dignified houses, in such
villages as Stackhouse, Stainforth, and Malham Tarn, kept their
connection with these people, and created in the district a
circle of culture which persists to-day.

Flashes of the story of this corner of Craven pass before you
as you stand in Giggleswick churchyard. Families come to
the church service from the village of Langcliffe, built in 1315
a mile to the south of an older one which was destroyed in
a Scots raid. Samuel Watson of Stainforth is moved to speak
in the church in 1659, and 'some of yᵉ rudest sort pulled him
down and brok his head upon yᵉ seates and having haled him
out threw him down upon yᵉ ice.' At the end of the eighteenth
century men are busy making the cottages opposite the church
into a weaving shed, and as early as 1836, when the industry
has passed from here, other men are turning them into cottages
again. Once more a story of the verger of the church shows us
the independence of the people. He was about to take up the
collection as usual before the sermon when the visiting parson
stopped him, saying: 'We 'll have the collection after the sermon.'
'Just as you like, sir,' the verger called out, 'but it won't mak'
a harpoth o' difference.'

Come back into Settle again on a summer evening, rather
a cold evening with a suspicion of drizzle in the air, so that the
houses take on a more sombre tone. It has not daunted the
folk dancers who are giving a display in the square. There is
nothing ghostly about these figures. They hop, skip, and
prance, now to a fiddle, now to a concertina, out of one dance
into another with scarcely a break, young and not so young,
dalespeople and visitors, joining together to revive folk dances

many of which originated in the Yorkshire dales. Now and again the watching children are caught in, then all stand back to see a sword dance by four men. They end with a few modern dances, and every one, including the spectators on the balcony and the old houses themselves, has enjoyed the evening.

Between that evening and the early ghosts in the churchyard come the people who made Settle and all this district into a holiday area. They appeared first in the eighteenth century when it had become the custom for well-to-do families to make a northern tour to the Lake District. They would leave the coaches and stay for a few days at such places as Settle and Ingleton which supplied them amply with the unusual sights they demanded. There were the Ingleton waterfalls—these travellers rarely missed a waterfall—the limestone caves which, though they had not yet been explored, were there to excite awe and wonder, the phenomenon of the ebbing and flowing well on Buckhaw Brow outside Giggleswick. Old descriptions of this well would lead one to imagine it as a kind of tidal lake. Early writers and artists were also tremendously impressed by Castlebergh Hill behind Settle, describing and engraving it as an awesome precipice two or three times higher than it is. Some of them tell of a natural sundial formed by rocks jutting from the hill, and how these rocks had numbers painted on them.

The visitors took excursions to Gordale Scar near Malham, and marvelled at the glories of the fine rocky ravine formed aeons ago by the collapse of a cave. Thomas Hurtley in 1786 described this as a 'Stupendous Pavilion of Sable Rock apparently rent asunder by some dreadful although inscrutable elementary convulsion.'

They went to Malham Tarn, from which the river Aire rises and almost immediately drops underground, and three miles lower down they saw it reappear beneath the rocks of Malham Cove, where they were lost in wonder at this great limestone amphitheatre. We thought of them and the enthusiasms which have left their mark on these places as we watched the setting sun touch the white stone with fire and then slowly leave it in deepening shadow. On a narrow shelf of rock half-way up the cove a procession of goats leisurely picked their way to the other side. It seemed as though the limestone ledge would not hold them, but they walked unconcernedly across, stopping now and again to look round or down into the chasm where the river bubbled out of its prison. Thousands have followed the early tourists, from the Victorian poets and sightseers coming by railway train to the rucksacked walkers of to-day, and though we may smile at the visitor who, on seeing Gordale Scar, declared that 'the idea for personal safety excited some awful sensations accompanied with a tremor,' yet each generation in its way has marvelled at the wonders of this limestone land.

The village of Malham a mile below the cove reflects the broad moorland in its open green and low straggling houses; Kirkby Malham, a mile below it, reflects the soft, wooded valley which is now merging into Airedale. Passing below the church, where you can see the lay marriage register signed by Oliver Cromwell when he was visiting General Lambert here, the river seems to linger in this gentle country as if it knew what degradation lay before it.

But when we think of Malhamdale we think most of the windy uplands, those extensive grassy fells whose limestone scars and clowders, and the dry walls made from them, catch the glint of sunshine or the lowering frown of storms. This pasture land was owned by the monks of Fountains Abbey, but the priors of Bolton also had rights of grazing on it, and both monasteries had granges at Malham where there were great annual sheep fairs. The monks made many of the tracks over the moors; monastic crosses which it was their custom to place at intervals along their roads have been found built into the enclosure walls of the road which comes up from Kilnsey in Wharfedale and goes westward to Ingleton and the Lake District where at Watendlath in Borrowdale the abbey sheep were pastured in winter. Another track

DALES CHILDREN

went from Malham Tarn, in which the monks had fishing rights, to Arncliffe in Littondale, and tradition says that fish was taken along this road to the abbey on the backs of mules.

Other routes across the fells are prehistoric tracks leading to Bronze and Iron Age settlements where the shapes of the round dwelling-huts, the square fields, and the burial barrows are visible; near the track to Bordley there is a Bronze Age 'Druids' circle.' The bridle ways and posting tracks which followed them are slipping back with them into the moor. Even when the bridle ways were in use it was easy to get lost on the moors, and guides to accompany travellers over the pastures to Wharfedale were as much in demand as guides to show the caves or the way up the fell peaks.

Here and there, as at Bordley where the Eshton beck starts on its journey to the river Aire, a valley opens out of the moor, and a few farmhouses and perhaps an old hall survive from a more populous age; but on the whole this is an enormous stretch of open pasture, and the farms dotted surprisingly over it are moorland farms. One or two join each other, but the majority stand in their own patch of cultivation and look over unbroken fell. Some of them are on the sites of shepherds' huts and farmsteads of the monastic days, larger houses being built as the land was improved, so that for centuries men have lived here defying the watching moor. It was a man from one of them who, describing it to us, said: 'If there's another Noah's flood, there won't be manny houses left i' England when t' watter comes blashin' doon oor chimney pots.'

Middle House, in a bend just out of sight of Malham Tarn, is one of the highest. It stands like a sentinel on the hillside —a plain, unlovely house which seems to resist instead of sink into its position. Walking here one cold spring day we met the two children from the house climbing the field path on their way from the school at Malham Tarn. Their faces glowed with the wind, and they were not tired, for they eagerly offered to show us the old farmhouse on the hill behind; and after they had fetched large pieces of jam tart and parkin from the dairy we started out.

The old house, a low building with mullioned windows, lies. in a sheltered hollow, an indescribably peaceful place, surrounded by trees which grow more luxuriantly than trees will ever grow round the new and more exposed home. The children's father remembered living here, and, though it is now used as a barn, they explained to us that all the windows had glass in them until the hikers broke it. 'Here's t' tups,' the little girl said as she opened one door; and there were hens in another room. The house was not so remote when the old road which went over the hill behind was used, and drovers coming to Malham Fair left their sheep near it while they went down to an inn which has vanished with the road.

A man must have a mixture of the moors and farming in his blood to live happily and make a living on these farms. Farmers retiring from them and going down to live in Settle enjoy the sense of freedom for a few months; then time begins to hang heavily on their hands, and they look round for a bit of land to run hens on. Next they rent a field and buy a cow, and in no time they have got another farm together, and are happy again.

Malhamdale never really gathers itself into a narrow valley, but Ribblesdale is a dale from the moment it cuts through the hills out of Settle. Its river may forsake the country at its end, but its beginnings are on Yorkshire fells. It seems fantastic that man who is as it were on sufferance in this wild, formidable valley, ever overcame it so far as to build a railway here, but in winter storms when snowdrifts pile up in the hollows, the dale still gets the better of the railway.

The river ripples in the bottom, and grey villages stand high above it or straggle along its banks, but the fell peaks and the stretches leading to them predominate in this valley: Penyghent tiptoeing up from the village of Horton, beckoning you to its summit for a view reaching beyond the fells and dales and the golden sands of Morecambe Bay to the hills of the Lake

District; Ingleborough and Whernside grim and majestic at
the head of the dale—a triangle of peaks which lift Ribblesdale
into grandeur. Their nearness to each other enables en-
thusiastic walkers to climb all three of these hills in one day.

Horton-in-Ribblesdale

The road starts past the Settle Lime Works, a modern out·
come of the lime workers once congregated at Buckhaw Brow,
through the villages of Langcliffe and Stainforth. The old
buildings beside it are of limestone which has been preserved
by brushing over with plaster, as whitewash has preserved the
old barns. They are clustered in the hoary village of Horton
which stretches for nearly a mile under the fells. The Norman
church stands out in rugged relief from them, outlined against
the green of Penyghent. It is reached by a lych gate, which
also leads the way to a cottage which was once a grammar school
in the churchyard. The village has been enlarged to house the
workers in the limeworks and the alien population arriving in
such numbers has wrought a change from the time when the
coming of a stranger was an event here.

We met an old woman who when she was fourteen years old was hired at the Lancaster hirings to be a servant girl at Horton. She told us that when she arrived it seemed to her a very wild country. Eventually she married, and, except for her voice, might be a daleswoman now. As she told her story, looking out over her cottage garden to Penyghent, we could see the rather pathetic child coming here far from every one she knew, to a life which was to be hard work in the house and on the farm for little wage.

Near the head of the valley on the east side, the fells are cut by the narrow wooded ravine of Ling Gill. You reach it through the hamlet of New Houses, past Horton Tarn, which is said to have been formed by a sheep falling into a pot-hole and blocking up the outlet, and near high lonely farms. The beck is crossed by a bridge which was repaired in 1765 'At the cost or the whole West Riding.' A little beyond this the track joins the Roman road from Ingleton to Bainbridge. This also is a green track now, but it joins the main road at Ribblehead again. Lord Torrington travelling this way in 1792 found the inn at Gearstones, now a shooting lodge, 'the seat of misery in a desert' and the scenery 'black and frightful.' A sheep fair was being held on the moor and the ground was crowded with Scotch cattle and drovers, and he tells how the Scotsmen were wrapped in plaids which they threw off to run after straying cattle.

The railway crosses the open moor, but it has not robbed the flat land between Ingleborough and Whernside of its curious fascination. This is high moorland, and yet in the stretch between the peaks there is a strip of cultivated land with walled meadows and pastures and farmhouses built along it. The farms resting under the shadow of the fells show their Norse origin in names like Gunner Fleet and Winterscales.

The farms under Whernside face the sun and there is good meadow land on either side of the little river Greta, but the hay harvest is quite three weeks later than lower down the dale, and fine weather has to be taken advantage of. The family were working hard as we came to Gunner Fleet, for the clouds which for us made shadows over the hillsides were for them enemies which in a few minutes might undo a day's work. Now and again a boy would clamber down to drink from a spring at the side of the beck. Three young sheep dogs raced up and down the banks. ''Is fayther were a terble good setter,' said the farmer, pointing to one of them. Marsh marigolds grew by the stream and there were harebells up the banks. It was a good meadow, but a grassy knoll had heather on its summit, and it was obvious that heather would slowly cover the meadow again if the farmer's work relaxed.

Ingleborough lay ahead, at first deep blue as clouds rolled over the sun, then turning to a warm brown showing every detail as the sun sank and long shadows began to creep up it. We met a woman who had lived for years on a farm on the lower slopes of Ingleborough. It was fine up there, she said, showing in her voice some realization of the majesty of a mountain farm, but it was winter for nine months of the year, and at all seasons sudden hail or snow storms which never reached the land below would sweep round the house.

Ingleborough stands imperturbable, unchanging, yet not altogether aloof. Prehistoric men made a settlement on its summit; it watched the Romans build their road; saw farms enclosed on its flanks; suffered an annual horse race to be run on its flat top; and to-day its first thin covering of snow warns the dalespeople for miles round that it is time to put on their winter clothing. In this upper region where winter never seems very far away, the brief summer is especially beautiful. The farmer summed it up well. 'Aye, it's all reet when t' weather's good,' he said, 'but we get all soarts i' winter.'

Dent

CHAPTER 14

DENTDALE

OUR first view of Dentdale was from the north shoulder of Whernside. We had climbed past the farms at Ribblehead, made our way over the limestone clints below the Whernside tarns, and suddenly the dale appeared below, a vivid green basin in the fells, crossed and recrossed with the darker lines of stone walls and field hedges. Here and there the river Dee glimmered between trees, and narrow strips of road led to farms or ran by clusters of cottages. Moor birds called round us on the fell, but there was no sound from the valley. It was like a toy country sparkling with the radiance and brightness of new paint.

Many people's first view of Dentdale is from the Settle to Carlisle railway line. The train runs along the side of the fell below a fence made of old railway sleepers set on end, in places three deep, to prevent the snow from drifting on to the track; and then suddenly in the immense loneliness the grey moors open for a space, and from the viaduct which crosses it there is a fleeting view of the grassy valley. Such glimpses often prove disappointing if you come to explore them, but Dentdale more than fulfils its promise.

The fairy, Hob, is said to have haunted the moors at the head of the dale. The story passed down from people who claim to have seen him is that he was a little man who wore a green coat and used to jump on the backs of their horses. One day a farmer walking over Blea Moor found three rings, and slipping these down his walking-stick, twirled it round so that one flew off and was lost. He sold the others for a shilling to a gamekeeper who, discovering that they were made of silver and enamel, resold them in Kirkby Lonsdale; and little Hob has never been seen since the disappearance of the rings.

The legend of the dwarf seems fitting at the head of Dentdale, which itself is a miniature valley possessing only one large village besides its few scattered hamlets and farms. It lies on a narrow strip of Yorkshire jutting into Westmorland. The County Stone on Crag Hill between the branch valleys of Deepdale and Barbondale marks the meeting of Yorkshire, Lancashire, and Westmorland, and standing by this you can see across the dale to where Westmorland curls round to enclose it again. It has little affinity with the other Pennine dales and is in character more like the Kendal hill country and the Lake District whose dialect its own resembles.

The river Dee, flowing first over a bed of solid rock, smoothed like marble by the action of the water, now disappears underground, now goes through a rocky gorge to swirl as a whirlpool in a hollow called Hell Cauldron, and with each mile becomes more thickly lined with trees.

A kingfisher searching for trout adds his vivid plumage to the colour which the seasons bring to the valley—bluebells carpeting the hillsides, wild flowers covering the banks which enclose the narrow roads, bracken blazing on the fells, purple blackberries decorating the hedges. The largest and most luscious blackberries we have ever picked in the north we found at the roadside in Dentdale. We could have stopped and filled a basket.

The farmhouses lie for the most part a field's length from the road. A few of these are L-shaped, and most of them have chimneys jutting from the wall on corbels or ending in circular stone stacks, a Westmorland type of architecture seldom found in Yorkshire. An unusually old example is Gibb's Hall, whose tiny round-headed windows seem to blink at passers-by, and which even in ruin has an elegant air. It was the home of William and Mary Howitt, the Quaker authors of many country books.

The dale gradually lulls you into its restful peace, and makes the surprise of Dent Town the greater. From this side you approach it up a slight hill and see the clustered houses with the sober church standing out from them in rough relief. Suddenly the main road becomes a cobbled way and the white irregular houses opening straight on to it draw together as if to close themselves in from the rest of the world. As the road twists and curls between them, other cobbled ways lead into it, and caught in them you feel to have stepped out of Yorkshire, out of England even. Originally the houses had narrow outside galleries under the projecting roofs, and the women dried their clothes there, and sat gossiping with their neighbours as they knitted. Hartley Coleridge, describing, the town, said: 'Where cart with cart in cumbrous conflict meets.' It was impossible for anything unusually tall to pass, and it is told how a caravan from a visiting circus got wedged and could not be moved until the wheels were taken off. Shorn of the galleries Dent is still unbelievably quaint, something left over from a more individual era.

At a bend in the road a huge granite slab, out of which the village water pours, is a memorial to Adam Sedgwick, the geologist, who was born at the parsonage here in 1785. He has left a record of what he remembered of Dent, and what his father told him of an earlier period

After farming, knitting was the main industry of the valley. Men, women, and children knitted in their leisure time and as they walked beside their wagons or shepherded on the moors; Southey calls them 'the terrible knitters of Dent.' There were schools where children were taught to knit as part of their lessons, and at night older people met at each other's houses—'gaeing a sitting' they called it—and sang and told legends and ghost stories as they knitted by the light of a peat fire, calling out, 'Turn a peeat,' if they wanted more light to pick up a dropped stitch. Stories of these days are only hearsay now, and no one knits as the old knitters did, swaying as they worked with curved needles kept firm in a wooden knitting sheath. But old men can remember being made to wind the wool for their parents, and how they disliked doing it because the tightly bound cops in which it came took so long to undo. One man told us that his mother could knit a man's coat in a day, and another that his mother knitted a jersey every week, working only at night, and earned six shillings, which reckoned out at twopence an hour.

Originally the work was mostly stockings made of fine yarn, but this declined as long trousers came into fashion, and the people then turned to knitting coarse worsted, called 'bump,' into leg coverings and jackets. It was brought from Kendal one week and the knitted garments were taken back the next. There was also a market at Dent, and again old men remember going down to this as boys to fetch yarn for their parents.

Another industry which came and declined was the mining and dressing of marble in the ravine of Arten Gill, up which until 1805 the main road to Hawes ran. The saw mill which in 1780 was converted from a spinning mill has vanished, but the polishing shop and show-room remain, and models and moulds lying about give the impression that work stopped abruptly and without warning. The deeds of the mill show that it had the right to gather sand, used in marble and stone sawing, from the tarns on Whernside and Widdale Fells; this was brought down the hillsides in panniers on donkeys. Many of the fireplaces in railway-station waiting-rooms were made here from black marble quarried from the hill behind. Finer Italian marble was made into staircases for town halls and fireplaces for the Inns of Court, London, and the Royal Palace at St Petersburg. The quarry closed when the railway came, and as a last gesture the black marble was used to make the railway viaduct.

The story of decline in Dent includes what were a vital section in its life, the yeomen, who were here called by the Westmorland name of 'statesmen.' These statesmen, many of whose families had owned their farms since the Civil War, augmented their incomes in various ways: they were wig-makers, coopers, spinners, carders, one mined the hard coal on the hills and took it on pack-horses to Kendal, and all of them knitted. Their farms, with the small pieces of cultivated land eked out by pasturage on the fells, provided them with only a bare living, and as the industries declined they were faced with poverty. Some emigrated, and many sold their farms and moved to the towns. Practically all the farmers to-day are tenant farmers, and the whole texture of the life of the valley has changed. To us who never knew the independent states-men, the old oak pews in the church, with dates and initials carved on them or picked out with brass-headed nails, reveal them as real persons. Adam Sedgwick tells how they came on horseback to church, the wife riding pillion behind her husband, and their daughters walking beside them in long scarlet cloaks with silk hoods which had been handed down from mother to daughter. For years after the going of the statesmen men were wearing up their elaborate coats and waistcoats made by Thomas Archer, a famous tailor of Dent. The old grammar school in the churchyard, where they came as boys and later sent their sons to be taught by the vicar, is empty now, a silent witness to them as are the tombstones which surround it.

Dent still hold its sports, which originated in a horse race held on a course which has now disappeared. That first time we came down from Whernside a man driving a trap along the road to Deepdale told us that the sports were to be held the next day, and that there would be 'a terble lot o' folk i' Dent.' His words echoed through a silent valley, but a 'terble lot o' folk' did come into Dent the next day. A bellman rounded up the competitors for the local races, which ended with a fell race, and then came horse-trotting, bringing bookies with their raucous voices to destroy the feeling of a country event.

The troubled past of this now placid farming community has resulted in a philosophic calm in the people. The old times lie in an aura of romance, even the hard days not very far back when a good farm man did not earn more than £20 a year. They say that people were happier then, and all they themselves ask is for a quiet life and just to keep going gently along. 'We were reared on the land, and we belong there,' a man in the valley said. But it was on a high narrow road climbing out of Dent that we met the middle-aged farmer who could give clear reasons for his philosophy. There was nothing like farming for him; he found quite enough excitement in it to feel no need to go to the pictures or even to bet on horses.

'There's your sheep an' stock,' he said, 'and t' breeding of 'em. You wonder what they'll do, and how they'll turn out. You gan to market and buy your males and females, and wonder what they'll do for you, and how many of 'em 'll dee. You ken every yan of your sheep, and can pick 'em out of another man's flock. Marks are only for neighbours' sheep, so that you'll ken 'em when they git amang yours. Then there's growing grass. You nivver know how it'll turn. It might rain and spoil it, or you might just get it in afore a storm comes. There's always change; it's nivver dull. There's all t' walls to keep i' order. It's a kind of art, if you like. It's t' young uns that won't go on t' farms to-day; they must have amusement and shorter hours. It's funny.'

He remembered his father telling him of these fells being enclosed, and how building the walls round the enclosures gave work for years to the farmers' sons. The fell 'fences' have a proprietary fascination for Dent people. Their forefathers earned two and ninepence to three shillings a rood for building them, and during that time lived chiefly on raw bacon, havercake, and skimmed milk when tea was dear. It was healthy work, but it was cold and exposed, and men would not do it to-day when they could earn as much as twelve shillings to fourteen shillings a rood at it.

The farmer preferred enclosed moor to common land because it made for better neighbours. 'You see,' he said, 'if a man's mair thrifty, and makes mair money na his neighbours, he can buy mair sheep to put on t' common land, and then there's trouble. There's bin queer things happened on these hills ower sheep—murder even. But that's how you are, that's farming. An' money means a lot to some folks, whether a man's got eddication or not.'

Our friend put much of the trouble of to-day down to education. He did not think much to it, nor of the way 't' schules' had killed the dialect. When he was a boy they had a schoolmaster who used to punish them when they spoke at school as they were obliged to speak to their parents at home.

Below Dent the dale narrows almost into a ravine before the Dee joins the river Rawthey near Sedbergh, where the humpy shapes, like elephant backs, of the Howgill Fells shut it in at the foot. This dramatic line of hills broken by sombre hollows was given to Yorkshire from Westmorland by Henry VIII. The breezy open town of Sedbergh nestles under them, centred round its large public school. School buildings and houses are everywhere, shops and hotels are run for it, and in term time there are always boys about the streets. Seeing them, one is amazed to hear from a man of eighty-eight that he remembers when there were only ten boys and one master at Sedbergh School. It was founded in 1525 but, having become almost defunct with the confiscation of the chantry endowments, it was reopened in 1552, and is thus counted as one of the fifty-three grammar schools founded by Edward VI.

George Fox in his journal records how he preached outside the steeple house at Sedbergh, and was roughly treated. A cutting from the yew-tree under which he spoke now grows in the graveyard of the meeting house at Brigflatts a mile away. This is a simple whitewashed building with unstained wood panelling in the interior, little changed from when the Quakers established it here. You can almost see the earnest congregation arriving down the narrow lane, and taking their places inside, the men at one end, and the women at the other.

The intensely rural quality of Westmorland penetrates this corner, the border line of Yorkshire. You feel it in the sunken village of Howgill and the common land beyond it where butterworts and forget-me-nots brighten the boggy patches, but chiefly round the farms, whose methods are often those of the other county. It is evident in the hedging and walling competition held in February. The fact that these two arts could be carried on close to each other shows the mixture of upland and lowland; at one time there were sections for ploughing, but there is no arable land here now. Many of the competitors were young, and the older farmers walked backwards and forwards giving advice, particularly to those who were layering the hedges. These are a mixture of hazel, ash, and thorn planted on the top of an earth bank called a dyke. Every six or seven years the old wood is cut out and the newer branches are shaped to run horizontally in a short thick hedge. As each competitor worked at his particular stretch he would step back occasionally with his advisers and view it at a distance as an artist does a painting.

'Tha wants a lile branch to lig in t' boddom,' an old man called out.

'Tha doesn't want a thick spot an' then a thin spot,' said another.

There was no time limit; as one man put it: 'If it was speed, you could gan all round Sedbergh in a day.' As it was, it took each competitor most of a wet day to finish his ten yards, and we agreed as the one who summed it up with, 'Aye, it's a critical job, it is.'

The Westmorland influence remains along the road which runs under the Howgill Fells past whitewashed cottages to Cautley, where the waterfall of Cautley Spout drops serpent-like down a gloomy hollow on the fell; but immediately the road turns east to Garsdale the Yorkshire feeling sweeps back again.

A small woollen mill, almost hidden in a hollow near this road, shows in its story the ups and downs and changes of the industries established in the dales.   It was originally started by a Mr Robert Foster, a Quaker of Hebblethwaite Hall, who as a boy longed for travel and adventure and ran away to sea and became a midshipman.   At intervals he came home, and is said to have shocked the Quakers by appearing at Lancaster meeting house with his laced cocked hat on his head and a cutlass at his side.   On one of his visits he fell in love with a Quaker lady and immediately settled down as a good statesman and started the mill near his home.   This was first a spinning mill supplying Sedbergh weavers who made cloth which was taken by pack-horse to Newcastle for miners' clothing.   It also acted as a factor for the hand knitters.   The present mill, built in 1837, made horse cloths, rugs, and cloth for lining horse collars.

In Garsdale the memory of John Dawson, the famous self-taught mathematician, reminds one of the mathematicians whom the mountain country of the Lake District produced. At the head of it the road turns into the hidden valley of Grise-dale, a cheerful little dale which seems to catch all the sun-shine.   Standing at one end of this green hollow in the fells you can see all of Grisedale, a circle of cultivated land with farmhouses scattered over it, a small Wesleyan chapel at one end, and at the other the burial ground of a vanished Quaker meeting house.   There are only a few low mounds to indicate that this was ever anything but a little walled pasture, and the farmer's wife rears chickens in it as a farmer's wife rears

CAUTLEY

ducklings in a Quaker burial ground in Langstrothdale.   There
are fewer farms than there used to be and some of the old
houses are falling into ruin, but those which remain have
entrancing names like Fea Fow, Aldershaw, High Ing, Flust,
High Flust.

A road runs up the valley, but the children walk over the
fell to the little school at Lunds at the head of Wensleydale.
On the night of the Jubilee of King George V, we stood on
the summit of this fell, which divides Grisedale from Lunds.
The two districts were joining at the bonfire, which had been
lit by torches carried in a procession from Lunds.   The little
crowd gathered round until the fire burnt low, and then they
all sang *God save the King*, and the Grisedale folk wended
their way back to their farms in this hollow and the Lunds
people turned to their own valley.

Beckermonds

CHAPTER 15

WHARFEDALE

Now we are in the dales which belong wholly to Yorkshire, whose rivers, joining to flow as the Ouse into the Humber, have no life outside the county. Wharfedale and Nidderdale are in the West Riding but their rivers turn to skirt the industrial areas. In its upper parts this is still the limestone district of Craven with its subtle harmony of green fells and grey walls, but here the limestone is more related to the whole, and the villages in the valley seem to be merely a concentration of the scars and grey walls running over the fells and bounding the roadways. The walls gleaming white in the sunshine give an austere decoration to the Wharfedale scene.

Like Ribblesdale, Wharfedale starts under the shadow of

Ingleborough and Whernside, and the two great hills giving their dignity and calm to its beginning are a remembered background as we journey down the valley. Looking across to them from the Fleet Moss pass at the head of the dale, we recollect them as misty shapes folded in autumn mist, as lowering forms breaking the wind, or as snow-covered peaks over which the afternoon light casts a pink glow while men cut a narrow way through the snowdrifts on this high road. But as we watch to-day it is summer, and a haze of heat lies over the boggy valley in which the Wharfe rises.

A green patch on the hillside marks the hamlet of Cam Houses which grew up here when the Roman road on the hillside above was more generally used. Once there were thirteen livings, one occupied by a schoolmaster; now two solitary farmhouses stand bravely in their circle of cultivation, kept company by two ghosts, a dog called Jerry which haunts the path to the road, and a Hob-like spirit known as T' Owd Joiner, because he can be heard hammering in a room in the farmhouse. The inhabitants of this remote hamlet need to be resourceful to keep life running smoothly. An old man who lived here in his younger days told us how once the grandfather clock stopped, and no amount of shaking would make it go. It was too far to fetch a clockmaker to it or to carry it to one, and in desperation the farmer took out the works, put them 'intiv t' pan for t' cauf meeat,' and boiled them well. The dalesmade clock reacted to this drastic treatment, and has gone ever since, though the farmer confessed that he dared not have tried it on a newer-fangled clock.

In Oughtershaw, the first hamlet, the tiny school is closed for the summer holidays, which begin early here so that the children can help with the hay. The scent of newly cut grass is in the air as we drop down from it to Beckermonds. A meadow by the roadside is gay with the aprons and caps of women and girls strewing the hay and raking in into rows. The sun pours down on them, and a woman stops to wipe her forehead with her apron; in the hamlet below a girl carrying

G

a basket full of bottles crosses the bridge on her way to the meadow.

Soon only a strip of grass divides the road from the river, and the lively stream seems to call greetings to the hamlets of Deepdale and Oughtershaw and the farmhouses nestling into the hillsides as it drops through trees to Hubberholme. The trees are full and green now, but in the autumn they will fill this hollow with a blaze of scarlet, yellow, rust, and orange, each day surpassing the glory of the one before.

We stay for a while at the little hamlet of Hubberholme by the rugged church, which in this remote place managed to keep its rood-loft, made in 1558 by William Jake. The voices of the haymakers far up on the hillside seem to mingle here with the voices of haymakers long since gathered into this quiet church-yard in a cleft between the fells.

Faintly there come too the voices of others who, though not actually belonging to it, made their mark on the valley, travellers who used this fell pass on their journeys from Scotland to Lancashire and the West Riding—packmen, pedlars, drovers, tramps. Many of them turned at Raisgill to take the road, which is now only a path, over the fells to Littondale, and so on to Settle. You wonder whether on that rough, hard journey they felt any appreciation of the grandeur of the way. But a few continued past this church at Hubberholme and the inn which belongs to it, and so to Buckden, where they were met by more travellers coming down the Kidstones Pass from Bishopdale or the Stake Pass which is the Roman road from Bainbridge. At Kettlewell, four miles farther down the valley, they were joined by others who had come over the Park Rash pass from Coverdale. These and routes farther down the dale, distinct from the local paths over the fells, have for centuries carried wayfarers into it, strangers bringing not only the excitement of their arrival, but tales of the outside world. Villages standing where they join the dale grew into important places, and until recent days many of them held markets and annual fairs.

The monks of Coverham journeying over the Park Rash pass to Kettlewell, half of which was their property, passed the stone monastic cross which had been erected near the summit to mark the road. At that time it went farther over the hill, and dropped steeply down to Kettlewell, and this route is now a green walled track, tempting you to turn up it for the fells.

Lower down the dale the monks of Fountains Abbey, and still lower those of Bolton Priory, made constant journeys in connection with their sheep pastures and wool. Later the roads were used by carriers bringing wool to be spun and woven in cottages or little mills by the becks, and taking back the cloth on pack-horses to the West Riding.

The large amount of spinning and hand-loom weaving, as well as its market and its position at the junction of roads, made Kettlewell the large village we find to-day with milestones directing the way to it from many parts of the other dales, When the introduction of steam power brought the decline of the woollen industry in the dales, one of the last mills to keep running was the spinning mill at Arncliffe in the branch dale of Littondale, and people used to go over from Kettlewell to work at it.

We climb the fell along the path they took, turning back to see Kettlewell in its hollow with the limestone walls making a pattern round it, white scars breaking from the hills above, and clowders paving the terraces on them. This part of Wharfedale resembles the limestone country of Palestine, and we are not far wrong if we imagine our Bible stories in it. A mile over the open summit, and then the path drops down into Littondale.

Many people who have known and loved Wharfedale for years are unfamiliar with this one branch dale lying along a road which seems merely to lead into the fells. It is a wistful, fascinating valley with lonely wooded becks running down to the river Skirfare, and its three villages mirroring the stages of the dale. Arncliffe, standing stately round its green where blackbirds sing in lofty trees, guards the road which creeps out of one corner of it to the magic valley forking to Darnbrook. It tells the tale of the yeomen families who were once the heart of its life and whose fine old houses remain as a memorial of the prosperity and status to which they attained. Litton, lining the present road, watches the decline of the old tracks which come down to it over the fells. Halton Gill huddles under the hills and keeps its air of expectancy from the time when the path from Raisgill was a pack-horse road, and travellers to Settle halted here as a stage on their journey which for the rest of their way over the shoulder of Penyghent is now a motorists' road.

Penyghent dominates the upper valley, and seems nearer to the village than it does to Horton on the Ribblesdale side. The ascent from Halton is so easy that you reach the summit scarcely feeling to have had the exertion of climbing. We remember Penyghent best in its spring covering of cloud-berries and golden clumps of bilberry plants, but most re-collections of Littondale are brightened by flowers—mealy primroses sprinkling the marshy hillsides with their delicate pink blooms, lilies of the valley carpeting the woods, showy meadow blossoms, and alpine rock plants. They are perhaps intensified here, but all Wharfedale is a wonderland of flowers which flourish in limestone country. Oxlips push through amongst the meeker cowslips on the hillsides, and the frail petals of grass of Parnassus spangle the pastures.

Near Grassington, where at the Ghaistrills the Wharfe has cut a narrow channel through the solid rock, and now forced into this surges down in an angry torrent, wild thyme and rock roses have rooted on the limestone and made a natural rock garden.

The limestone reaches its climax just below the entrance to Littondale in the great overhanging crag at Kilnsey. The village huddling under the crag grew from a grange owned by Fountains Abbey in connection with its great tracts of land in Craven. The monks' road to Borrowdale started here, and at one time they had a hospice, but so many people used this that it was found to be more than the abbey could support.

Strangely enough, the tradition of the great landowning monastery lingers most in the tiny hamlet of Thorpe, where it is said there lived a little group of shoemakers who made and mended shoes for the abbey. After the monasteries were dissolved these men stayed here, and until recent days the village was famous for its shoes. Directories of 1823 show two shoemakers and two cobblers, and only fifty or sixty years ago people came long distances to be measured for shoes in Thorpe. It is a tiny hidden village surrounded by bumpy hills which would echo to the noise of the cobblers' hammers. Passing through it you seem to see faint figures in leather aprons bending over the benches in what were their workshops.

Across the valley, bracing itself to meet the west winds which sweep down the opening from Skipton, is the town of Grassington. Grassington's main street is one of those few corners which have survived surprisingly in their original quaintness through a ruthless age, and should be safe to-day. It runs as a narrow road out of a cobbled market square with little alleys opening from it, owing its crowded plan to the need to house lead miners in a small space.

On quiet winter days the market place seems to catch echoes of its once vigorous life. There sounds the clatter of miners' clogs as they come down from the moors, catching the smell of their bacon cooking as they arrive at the top of the last hill; women fetch water from the pump put up by Stephen Eddy, a famous mine manager; a man goes round the streets announcing in rhyme that Thomas Airey's company are performing a play in the barn that night; Thomas Airey's son blows his horn as he guides the mail coach into the market-place; farmers drive in in traps for the market.

The scene swings forward to the present day with crowds pouring in to the square from the buses and hikers turning in to the Youth Hostel, taking the place of the miners and the coach passengers. Still the life of the dale goes on much as of old; farmers bring down the sheep from the fells; old men gather in the blacksmith's shop; and there are busy preparations for haytime. Then the pendulum swings the other way to Roger de Plumpton building Grassington Hall in the thirteenth century, and further back still to prehistoric men making their settlements on the hill pastures.

The hillsides and terraces of Wharfedale have been thickly inhabited in prehistoric times. Faint shapes, covered now with grass, show what were small ploughed fields and beehive dwellings; on the hills above Deepdale there is a group of these circular dwellings, some of them several feet high. There are Bronze and Iron Age village sites in Littondale and round Linton and other places. Behind Grassington the plan of an important Celtic village can be traced, with square fields, beehive dwellings, dewponds scattered on the pastures, and a large stone circle where the Iron Age people held their meetings. A sunken green road goes through it and along the hillside to another site above Coniston.

In Wharfedale many of the villages in the valley have been built immediately below prehistoric sites. At Coniston a line of Saxon cultivation terraces, made so that corn could be grown on the hillsides, comes between the two. You feel the continuity of life in this upland region where in mole heaps and rabbit scrapes you may pick up pieces of flint which were worked by men living here two thousand years ago. They were not a particularly backward or wholly unrecorded race, for it is thought that the site was used during the Roman occupation.

Below Grassington the Craven Fault dies out on the moors towards Nidderdale, and the limestone country ends abruptly. The walls and houses are a warm brown now, the trees grow thicker round the river, and you feel to be suddenly in another country. The grammar school at Burnsall with its mullioned windows and projecting porch recalls those other buildings which we have seen and admired as we came down the dale: cottages with dated doorways in Langstrothdale, the yeomen's

houses at Starbotton, Kilnsey, and in Littondale, the old hall
at Grassington, the barns with their projecting wings and
open porches. They are part of our memory of the upper
dale as we cross the bridge over the river and take the road
to Appletreewick.

Approaching Appletreewick down the dale, the village faces
you in a long line up a hill which has for background the
craggy peaks of Simon's Seat and Earl's Seat. The hills of the
upper dale rise steeply behind so that the little village seems
tossed between fells on either side and gives a feeling of arrival
at a foreign place. Later you discover the wooded paths by
the river only a field's length away, but for the present the
upland street with the fells wrapping it round is enough. It is
an irregular street; now a cottage comes close to the road; now a
solid farmhouse stands back behind a garden; now a barn
wedges between them. At the top and the bottom are more
yeomen's houses. Low and High Hall they are called at
Appletreewick, and whereas you heard of the Wades, Symond-
sons, Knowleses, and Dawsons higher up the dale, here you
have the Prestons, Cravens, and Youngs.

Low Hall has been largely rebuilt, but High Hall stands as a
fine type of a prosperous yeoman's house. It is a farmhouse
now with only a small part in use, but the musicians' gallery
remains above the main hall. You can picture one of the
owners listening with his guests to the music here, wearing his
'best doublet and stockings of straw colour' or his 'cloke and
green breeches with lace,' mentioned in wills of the Youngs.
Whereas the yeomen of Bowland were connected chiefly with
agriculture, and the statesmen of Dent were never more than
small farmers, these landowners worked lead mines on their
land or rented them to others, and made considerable sums of
money. Lead mines are referred to along with corn mills in
their wills.

Appletreewick Fair, held in the flat field by the river, would
be in full swing in their time. The hill behind the village is
still called Sheep Fair Hill, because the black-faced sheep

were turned on to it along with the Highland cattle and Scotch ponies. Onion Lane which leads down to the river was named from the onions hung for sale over the walls. Onions were a great feature of the fair and their sale persisted to the end of its existence, after the cattle and horses ceased to come.

The priors of Bolton obtained the charter for Appletreewick Fair. Monks' Hall in the centre of the village is on the site of an abbey grange, and it is their influence, not that of the monks of Fountains, which sways the valley now. We come down over the old bridge at Barden, past the tower which Lady Anne restored, to the priory in its gentle wooded site on the river Wharfe with purple fells stretching dark and mysterious above it. There is always colour here, for after the spring and summer flowers have left the woods and meadows, and the purple of the heather has faded to brown, a golden carpet of bracken covers the hills the winter through, blazing into fresh splendour after every shower of rain, making a vivid background for the abbey ruins.

This Augustinian monastery had considerable property, but the priors left the work and management of their sheep farms and iron and lead mines chiefly to laymen. They themselves were all ordained and served in their appropriated churches. They made the priory a centre of culture and learning. Henry, Lord Clifford, the Shepherd Lord, when he settled at Barden after his estates were restored to him at the end of the Wars of the Roses, studied astronomy with the monks of Bolton. Except for occasional Scots raids, their records show a fairly peaceful life. You can imagine them in these grounds crossing the river by the stepping-stones to meditate in the woods, and seldom far away from the sound of running water.

The priors had much communication with Skipton Castle; one of their monastic crosses remains by the side of the road near Halton East. They continued this road eastwards over Blubberhouses Moor to Harrogate, and monks and laymen came along it on their way to Brough where they crossed the Humber for the Lincolnshire fair at Boston.

Under the shadow of Beamsley Beacon the road down the valley comes to Ilkley. Antiquarians think of Ilkley as the Roman town of Olicana, and trace the Roman road from it up the dale to the Stake Pass above Buckden; they study the Anglian crosses in the churchyard, the swastika stone on the moor, and the cup and ring markings on Baildon Moor. Walkers think of crossing the moor from the towns and of the many disputes about rights of way.

To the old, Ilkley is the Victorian resort which spread from a little village partly because of its spa waters, partly because of the growing love for moors and wild scenery, and partly because it could be easily reached from the towns. They remember how they used to walk past White Wells House and the tarn, and home by Heber's Ghyll; and how they stood on the famous Cow and Calf rocks on the moors behind the town, and saw the dale twisting up into the purple fells. Many of them cut their names and the date on the rock, and though one disagrees with such disfigurements, there is something almost historical now about those initials cut so deeply and painstakingly, as if their carvers had some suspicion of the hundreds who would come after them, their feet wearing the rocks smooth again.

Modern Ilkley with red-roofed villas has spread to the hillside at Middleton across the river, and the town has become a little self-conscious about its beauty. If future conditions should condemn it to oblivion again, its memory would survive in the song, *On Ilkla' Moor baht 'at*, which is almost a Yorkshire anthem.

The pleasant rolling country beyond Ilkley has arable fields between its trim meadows and pastures, and is broken by patches of woodland, and great parks such as Weston and Farnley. Down secluded roads there are the unspoilt villages of Leathley, whose church has a Saxon tower, Askwith, Denton, and Weston. The gritstone outcrop of Almscliffe Crag, where

* G

many rock climbers take their first lessons, towers above it in superb isolation.   In the prosperous days of the railways town dwellers built large houses in this open land, and smaller ones followed round the railway stations, so that you pass suddenly from the old part of a rural village into one which, although time has softened its newness, is yet suburban.

For a small space the commercial town of Otley obtrudes its mills and printing works by the river, but still remains half a country town, with its agricultural show one of the first in the

Wetherby Show

season.   'Are you showing at Otley?' is a stock question in the district when April comes in.   Clustered immediately under the high hill of Otley Chevin, the town might have been an Innsbruck or an Edinburgh had it developed in a different way.

From the high land outside Kirkby Overblow you look back on a view as expansive and grand as many higher up the dale. All the way Wharfedale gives these particularly beautiful stretches which, lovely in themselves, yet beckon you on to explore the rest.   At Wetherby you are on the Great North

Road again, catching through the circle of new houses which surrounds it some feeling of the old coaching town, where drovers bringing sheep and cattle from Scotland put up for the night. The river is crossed by a bridge to which there still clings a faint memory of a chapel overlooked by a Norman castle which stood for only a few years on a nearby hill. Like Skipton, this is the 'sheep town,' and sheep and cattle are still brought into its market, and farmers' wives sell butter, eggs, and chickens in the old shambles. Country and town meet in the Grange Park on Whit Tuesday for Wetherby Show.

Past Boston Spa with its gracious Georgian air, and its hotel built for spa visitors but now turned into houses, through the brewery town of Tadcaster, the river comes on its last stretch into low-lying country, whose villages, out of the line of traffic, seem to belong to a past age. Ryther, whose simple Norman church built by Saxon workers is reached by a raised path across the marshy land, typifies the still, drowsy country where willows line the river and pink balsam spreads over its banks. Cawood, at whose castle Wolsey stayed before his last journey, sleeps on it, and only seems to rise to activity when the salmon fishers come with their boats and nets up the river Ouse.

In this warm, humid land trees are green when there is no sign of life in those of the upper dale; and lambs are almost sheep before the first black-faced lambs appear on the fells round Cam. It is a strange country to see the end of a river born under the shadow of Ingleborough and Whernside; and yet, when the soft muddy banks of the Wharfe fail to hold the volume of water and floods spread out over the low land, you know that there have been storms in Langstrothdale, and that this expanse of water has rushed down the gills which cut the high fells.

Packhorse Bridge at Birstwith

CHAPTER 16

NIDDERDALE

SMOLLETT, writing about Harrogate in the middle of the eighteenth century, said: 'Harrowgate is a wild common, bare, bleak, without tree or shrub, or the least kinds of cultivation.' Sydney Smith, more than half a century later, wrote: 'Harrogate is the most heaven-forsaken country under the sun. When I saw it, there were only nine mangy fir trees there, and even they all leaned away from it.'

Yet Harrogate grew, and the wild, treeless common is now its greatest asset. When the Forest of Knaresborough, on whose eastern edge the town lies, was enclosed in 1770, a special clause in the award set apart the Stray as common land with fifty cattle gaits. The place was established as a spa then—one of the stipulations of the enclosure was that all people were to have free access to the wells without payment—but those who signed the clause could not realize how important the Stray would be to a future Harrogate, and how its rights would be so jealously guarded that flower-beds cut on it a hundred and sixty-eight years later would raise a storm of protest until they were laid with grass again.

Harrogate to-day is one of Yorkshire's achievements. Its great hotels and hydros, its shops and schools, medicinal baths and Valley Gardens, are a tangible proof that it has arrived. It was prophesied that it would never compete with Scarborough as a spa, yet Scarborough has one little kiosk to compare with the vast amenities here. As an inland spa it gained by having fewer distractions, and the solemn business of taking the cure could be treated with the importance it deserved.

About 1596 Captain William Slingsby of High Harrogate discovered the first chalybeate spring, but for a hundred years after this, visitors coming to take the water had to lodge in farmhouses or cottages. It was patronized largely by people from the neighbourhood to whom it was known as 'The Spaws.' The first inn, afterwards called the Queen's Head, was built in 1687. At this time the waters were all free, but women used to press round the wells, anxious to serve it or carry it to visitors' lodgings. Buildings were erected round the first spring in High Harrogate, but as sulphur wells were discovered in Low Harrogate the town spread in that direction, and the baths and most of the pump rooms are there now. Round about 1700 numbers of houses for accommodation were built, and Thoresby tells of his astonishment at its growth in little more than ten years.

At the beginning of the nineteenth century the season lasted from July to September, and a report says: 'The three principal houses, the Granby, Dragon and Crown, are frequented by well-bred people (the two former especially, for the latter is said to have a plebeian mixture).' In 1835 an action for sinking a well on his premises, only eighty-two feet from the main sulphur well, was brought against a Joseph Thackwray of the Crown Hotel.

Women still gathered round the wells for custom; Betty Lupton, who for fifty-six years served water from the spring now covered by the Pump Room, was known as the 'Queen of the Wells.' In 1842 an Improvement Act caused the land to be drained and cultivated, more large hotels were built, and Harrogate of to-day was evolved.

To realize into what it has grown you must visit the town on a Saturday morning when the streets are crowded with well-dressed people; or one of the large hotels for a dinner or a cabaret show, of which southerners say they do not see so many smartly dressed women at a London gathering; or the lobby of the Opera House on a Friday night when the White Rose Players are presenting a popular play. See the Valley Gardens on a summer afternoon when the orchestra is playing, and tea is served on the balcony of the café and on the grass. The brilliant colours of the flower-beds vie with the gay umbrellas and the dresses of the women; and there is an air of importance, as if lolling on camp chairs and sipping tea in these gardens were the only thing worth doing on a sunny day.

Harrogate's position has helped its growth. It is well outside the industrial area, yet near enough to share its wealth. West Riding people, along with people from all over the world, visit it, live in it, retire to it. The population, the majority of whom have no roots here, largely reflect the atmosphere given to it by visitors. They unite in its sophistication, which even extends to that once wild common, where you can cross the grass on paths as neat as pavements.

Harrogate's sophistication is largely a relic from the old spa, yet there are faint survivals or reminders of simple pleasures which were for a long time a familiar part of that life. An occasional Punch and Judy show on the Stray at the bottom of Montpellier Parade gives a hint of the time when minstrels and shows were common here in the season. There is much horse riding now, but herds of donkeys no longer gallop their

WHIT-MONDAY IN THE VALLEY GARDENS, HARROGATE

riders along the grass, and the goats which pulled children in tiny carts have vanished.

A few men still stand with Bath chairs for hire, but one or two of these remember when there were as many as seventy, and besides journeys round the town they would push their patrons for miles over the surrounding country. Favourite afternoon walks were to Follifoot or Pannal, where they would have tea and a rest at one of the inns before returning home.

There are no more the long ranks of landaus waiting to take people further afield, but in our quicker fashion we can visit those places to which they went. If some of them are busier, most of them and the roads which lead to them are still beautiful. One day they would make a tour of Knaresborough and visit Mother Shipton's Cave, the Dropping Well with its array of petrified objects, the Chapel of St Robert the Hermit hewn out of the solid rock, the cave where Eugene Aram hid the man he had murdered, the castle where in the dungeon the keeper still points out the slab of limestone licked hollow for its moisture by prisoners. Morbid sights many of them are, and even in the early nineteenth century people were complaining that they brought trippers. But, as with the crowds who visit it to-day, the beauty of the town itself was the chief attraction, the wooded banks sloping up from the river Nidd, and the cottages climbing haphazardly past the church to the castle on its rocky hill. Perhaps they would drive home from Knaresborough through Plumpton, and see the lake overhung with rocks and trees; or through the quiet country of the Nidd to where Ribston pippins originated.

One excursion would be over Blubberhouses Moor when the fields were white with cotton blossom and grouse and plovers called overhead. Another would be to Ripley, where there is a kneeling cross in the churchyard and stories of Oliver Cromwell are told, and on to Burnt Yates. Perhaps they stopped a while here as we once did to watch a village cricket match, and felt the tense atmosphere of the game. A member of the local team had fallen out, and a twelve-year-old boy who had been put in at the last minute batted to a low monotone of 'Steady, Eddy! Steady, Eddy!' from an oldish man much more nervous than he was. A few miles further on they would be admiring the queer fantastic shapes of Brimham Rocks; and then down steep, peaceful little roads they would come to the ruins of Fountains Abbey in the valley of the Skell.

When Thoresby visited Fountains he found a hundred workmen making the gardens and waterworks which he said would become the wonder of later generations. In these spacious grounds, looking on to the magnificence of the ruins, it is not easy to imagine the humble beginnings of this abbey. The twelve monks who came from St Mary's Abbey at York because they disliked the laxity of the rule there, spent their first night under an elm-tree, and for two years until fortune changed suffered poverty and hunger. The site of the ruins, though so lovely, is perhaps not so entrancing as that of Bolton or Rievaulx, but neither of these ruins has the majesty and grandeur of Fountains. Even in decay you feel the tremendous importance to which this monastery attained, and the wealth of possessions behind it, the many churches, the granges whose sites are now farms and villages in Nidderdale and in the country far beyond it, the lead and iron mines which the monks worked. So many guests and travellers received lavish hospitality here that often the rich resources of the monastery were taxed to keep it up.

Leaving the early travellers you take the road through Hampsthwaite, and at Birstwith turn to where a slender pack-horse bridge crosses the Nidd. Looking over the parapet you come under the spell of this valley. Nidderdale, wandering leisurely and pleasantly to the moors, has a wild, vagrant beauty. She is the small, winsome sister of the family of the dales, and insinuates herself quietly into your affections. Some of her loveliest corners are where old stone bridges such as this cross the river and the becks to reach the hamlets and farms on the hillsides. At Thornthwaite a tiny pack-horse bridge across a beck tells of an ancient road and vanished traffic. Mimulus

blooms under the bridge at Wath, which used to be so narrow
that, when carts were first brought into the dale, farmers wishing
to cross it took one wheel off and ran the axle along the parapet.

In 1818 there were forty mills between Ramsgill and Knaresborough on the river Nidd, sixteen for corn, sixteen for flax,
seven for lead, and one for cotton. The whole of Nidderdale
was once famous for linen weaving and bleaching; in 1834
eight hundred flax dressers, called 'hecklers,' and thirteen
hundred linen weavers were employed in Knaresborough.
The flax was brought up the river Ure to Boroughbridge and
the linen taken back that way. The Castle Mills at Knaresborough still make glass cloths for the royal households, as
they nave done for nearly a hundred years. When the weaving
was done on hand-looms in the cottages this firm supplied the
warp and woof, and employed an overseer nicknamed 'the Spy'
to listen at the doors to make sure that the weavers were using
the correct method of throwing the shuttle. The villages had
then a much larger population, and each would be surrounded
by a fringe of bleaching linen. Those were the days when
cotton had not ousted linen for so many uses, when, as an old
man explained to us, 'every one, not only the betterly folk,
had lin' sheets and lin' shirts.'

The hamlet of West End in a hollow of Blubberhouses Moor
was another centre of the industry. There were several mills
here, but its remote position made transport difficult, and
gradually they were closed and the weavers left. Now only
one or two cottages and a few ruined walls remain from what
was a busy community. Some of its trade came for a time to
Nidderdale, and then that also declined.

A few of the Nidderdale mills have been turned into rope
and twine mills, and these with their accompanying rope-walks
are dotted up the valley. One above Pateley is still run by a
water-wheel; another at Summer Bridge is owned by a family
whose ancestor, Charles Gill, born in 1774, invented the tow-
card used in spinning tow.

We took the high way above the valley into Pateley Bridge

on the day of Nidderdale Show, and looked down on to its busy scene. Cars, people, horses, cattle, and sheep were moving over the bridge, and presently the band, playing loudly, marched down the street and turned into the show-field. Marquees, stalls, and rings stood out between the trees, and away at one end we could see the slow, deliberate movements of the players in a cricket match.

The show is held in September at the time of the old feast called Pateley Rant, which survives in a few roundabouts and stalls. It is the great annual meeting-place for the dalespeople. You hear greetings on all sides:

'Noo, Walter, how ista?'

'How's ta gaein on?'

'An' there'll nut be nowt deuin' at West End noo?'

'Aye, nowt.'

There are visitors from the Harrogate side, but it is from the dalesmen standing in little groups that you hear opinions of the stock:

''E's got a grand 'eead on 'im.'

'Yond in's a bit flat i' t' orns.'

Or they discuss the hay harvest:

'Aye, I kept clappin' a bit in. Some on it's guid, and some on it's bad.'

'Aye, that were it. It were warr if yer left it.'

'I got threu wi' a struggle.'

'I 'ad a trouble wi' ma peeats. I got a few o' t' fust lot, but I nivver got t' others.'

It is the ambition of a Nidderdale farmer on a high moor farm to make enough money to be able to move down to one of the lower, richer ones.

Pateley Bridge is the centre of this agricultural district, but it was also a lead mining town. It resembles Grassington in the way that its houses are crowded together on either side of the narrow road where space was precious. Much of the main street was rebuilt at the end of the nineteenth century, but it is still a quaint little place, running up to the fells which seem to overhang it at the top. It became a favourite excursion from Harrogate after the railway was brought up to it, and a starting point from which to visit the gorge at Howstean or the river disappearing into the pothole of Goyden Pot. A notice in a shop in the main street proclaiming it as a 'Post Card Emporium,' and a card hanging there saying simply 'CIGARS,' are relics of that period.

Until the first reservoir was made in 1893 and the lead mines failed, Pateley Bridge had an interesting life of its own. Mr Thomas Thorpe, who owned the Nidderdale Press and lived in the main street, published books and a calendar called *T' Nidderdill Olminac* in which we read, in the broad dialect of the people, of wild scenes at the feast and the Pateley Bridge horse races. These people could turn a phrase and bring a picture before you, like the Nidderdale man who a few years ago told a friend of ours that he always bought the kind of boots 'that leuked up at yer.'

Lead mines were scattered along the hills immediately enclosing the dale, but by far the most numerous and important ones were on the moors to the west, on either side of the main road over Bewerley and Appletreewick Moors into Wharfedale. The veins here were rich and very profitable to work. The many large houses such as Castleshaw, Grassfield House, Eagle Hall, lying within a radius of little more than a mile from Pateley Bridge, were built directly or indirectly from fortunes made in these mines. Greenhow, the highest village in Yorkshire, grew to its present size to house the miners. The great extent of tippings, so that the moors seem to have been upheaved by a cataclysm, have been accumulated through hundreds, probably thousands of years. We know that the Romans worked the mines, for two pigs of lead with Roman inscriptions have been found; a level named Sam Oon was worked either by the Romans or the Brigantes. Later miners coming upon traces of these older workings called them 't' owd man.' Near the entrance to Sam Oon a large square gritstone block with a deep round hole in it is known as the 'Panty Oon,' and there is a tradition that hot embers were placed in this hole and then raked out and dough baked in it for the miners working near. It resembles in shape the hearths still used in Norwegian seters.

The monks of Fountains, Bolton, and Byland got the lead by means of bell pits, and smelted it on baal hills; for a long period an animal poisoned by lead fumes on the moors was said to be 'baaloned.' So profitable was the lead to the abbeys that some of the Foresters became annoyed and opened mines themselves, but the Prior of Bolton employed people to take their ore and do damage and a final dispute ended in his favour.

You can imagine the scene of activity on the moor in the nineteenth century. In Cockhill Mine alone two hundred men, women, and boys were employed, and workers were brought from Swaledàle, Alston, and Derbyshire. Smoke rose from the large ground chimneys which carried the fumes to the summits of the moors. At first the men were paid for the weight of lead, later they received so much a fathom. A few adventurous ones worked levels with their own savings, and often lost them in the venture. One such man, named Lee, took a final pound of candles into the level, and said that when these were finished he would be done with the mine, and that day he cut into a vein which made his fortune. Much money was made in good times, and then a girl in the district thought she was doing much better to marry a miner than a farmer. But in the bad times when trade was poor and veins proved disappointing there was much hardship and poverty. One man took off his shirt before going into a particularly rough place, remarking: 'Ah can git another skin, but ah canna git another shirt.'

The importing of Spanish lead brought the end suddenly, and there are few of the old miners left to bring back the days when 't' Hill,' as Greenhow was called, had a vigorous life, and mining experiences were the topic in the Miners' Arms. Some of the cottages which remain are occupied now by small farmers wresting a precarious living from the high land and finding it difficult to prevent their hens from getting lead poisoned.

Superstition was common in the mines. Witch stones were placed at the entrances, and men carried small ones on their watch chains to ward away bad luck. The commonest superstition had to do with knockings. These weird sounds which the miners believed were the ghosts of dead miners warning them of approaching accidents were probably caused by air pockets above old shafts, but not all the strange happenings in mines can be explained so easily. Mr James Backhouse, who collected much old mining lore, tells how one Sunday about 1905 he went into Blayshaw level, leaving his companion outside. After going about half a mile he turned back, and as he did so he heard a sound as though an iron wagon coming rapidly towards him were bumping over the rails, but when he stopped to listen there was no sound; he met nothing on the way out, and found his companion still waiting at the entrance. He discovered later that miners had often heard these rumblings overhead, and called them the 'Blayshaw Boggle.'

It was whilst a 'flatting bed' was being sunk for the mines that the Stump Cross Caverns were discovered in 1860 near the cross which marked the boundary between the Forest of Knaresborough and the district of Craven. An early advertisement for these is worded: 'These subterranean grottoes are paved with stalagmites, having the appearance of petrified moss and fossils. The walls are hung with stalactites, and spar of every diversity of shape and imaginable variety of colour and prismatic hues, which together with the sweet aeolian sounds produce over the minds of those who visit these unique and magnificent caverns such delightful sensations of sublimity and awe as cannot be adequately expressed.'

Whilst this activity proceeded on the moors, the farming life was going on in the valley which turns northwards at Pateley Bridge. It was influenced to some extent by the mining, but not so far as to suffer ruination when the mines closed, and not nearly so much as later it was to be influenced by the building

of reservoirs.   Upper Nidderdale to-day is shorn of much of
its character by the filling up of parts of it with reservoirs.
The sheets of water have a certain beauty, but they dwarf this
valley which nature watered with a narrow river.   Some of
its heart has gone with the houses, such as the Elizabethan
Gouthwaite Hall, whose sites they have swamped, and with the
deserted farms which, because they would have drained into
the water, are abandoned.

Lofthouse stands on a little hill from which green tracks
start over the moors to Colsterdale.   Beyond it the river valley
narrows and only a few scattered farms lie on the hillsides.
The people living up it are known as the East Grainers, from
'grain,' meaning a fork or branch.   A waterworks road runs
by the river, but the main road climbs the hill, on the top
of which is the village of Middlesmoor.   The church and inn
and little group of cottages, many reached by outside steps,
perch here as if to defy man to venture to them.

The fells sweep down to the village, and the track over them,
the old pack-horse way into Coverdale, has often a covering of
snow in May and sometimes in June.   We saw little stacks of
peat drying on the heather and thought of the man at Pateley
Show who had only got one lot of peat that year.   From the
ridge of the moor we looked down to the head of the valley and
the two great new reservoirs of Scar Head and Angram.   The
Angram reservoir was just completed, and workmen were
pulling down the wooden village of houses, shops, hostels, and
a village hall which had existed temporarily here.   The grey
moors were already drawing back to themselves the deserted
farms above the dam, and the houses stood derelict; one of
these is Lodge, where Maggie Thompson murdered the packmen travelling from Scotland to the West Riding, and buried
them on the moor behind.

The old track disappears into the reservoir now, but you
see it on the other side climbing up the quiet moor to drop
between the hills of Great Whernside and Little Whernside
into Coverdale.

Castle Bolton

CHAPTER 17

WENSLEYDALE

'I ALWAYS think it's such a nice broad dale,' said a Wensleydale lady, explaining to us her preference for her own valley.

A few weeks later a farmer friend, viewing it from an agricultural standpoint, said: 'If I had to live in the dales I'd choose Wensleydale.'

It is true that the farms here, except at the extreme head of the dale, have not the same struggle for existence as those in the narrower dales. The broad valley, stretching in an easy slope far up the fells, gives room for more meadows and cultivated pastures, and the grass makes excellent fodder for cows and sheep.

These rich acres, which are ideally 'England's green and pleasant land,' yet lie between fells and moors which rise to considerable heights. The breadth of the dale makes it possible to get far enough away from the fells to realize them not only as barriers but as individual shapes, each with its own peculiar throne-like summit, and each running down to the valley in a series of terraces which mark the layers of hard and soft rock.

The river Ure cuts a comparatively tame way down the valley, accumulating all its magnificence into three miles between Aysgarth and Redmire, where its waterfalls surpass those of other dale rivers in grandeur. Like them it receives hundreds of little becks from the fells, and storms which flood the lowland and make some of the roads impassable turn the falls into superb torrents.

There is nothing more quietly satisfying than to wander up this dale of the Ure, feeling its peace and repose; to turn now and again to explore the branch dales; to rest on a village green surrounded by grey cottages, or on a hillside looking down to a village clustered below; to check the journey by the fells, Witton Fell, Penhill, Addleborough, Wether Fell, Cotter End, and finally to climb above the valley to their lonely wind-swept heights.

The dale runs from west to east, parallel, not with the valleys, but with the watersheds of Nidderdale and Wharfedale, and divided from them by immense stretches of moorland. These are also the watersheds of many small becks which cut through the moor and run into Wensleydale on the south. The branch dales have their own completeness, their rivers or becks, hamlets, villages, churches, but their life mingles with that of the larger dale. They have been one factor in helping to keep the markets in Wensleydale—Hawes in the upper dale, and Leyburn in the lower—markets which have now absorbed the trade from Swaledale and Upper Wharfedale.

Their unexpectedness makes these valleys fascinating. High up the dale the ravine of Mossdale turns past its two farms into a cosy hollow where there are waterfalls and fine trees. At West Burton below Aysgarth, two roads fork, one to go into the wooded basin of Bishopdale where hedges line the lower meadows, and another to climb into the wild errant valley of

Waldendale. Colsterdale, which joins Wensleydale at its lower end, has all the remote inaccessibility of upland country.

We came down to Colsterdale one autumn day over Masham Moor, arriving through paths brushed by tall, thick heather, and over a little bridge at the first farmhouse. There was no sign of life here, and we felt to have wandered into a deserted valley until we met the farmer himself. He was standing near a field of oats which grew on the hill slope, surrounded on three sides by heather. It was the highest corn field we had seen in the Pennines, but the farmer told us he had grown oats there for several years. It gave a slight idea of how the dales would look when every farm grew its own corn.

Ling thatches on two of the farmhouses presented another picture of former days. At one time all the dale houses were roofed in this way, but the work is hard and tedious, and few men can do it now. The ling, gathered from the moors, dried and shaped, is put on in layers from side to side, and topped with a coping of turf. A house thatched with it takes on a look of immense age. The wandering road brought us past these through the unspoilt villages of Healey and Fearby to the country town of Masham.

The road twists round one corner of the market-place at Masham, skirting the cobbled square and leaving it to its dreams of the past. The spired church, the stone houses and the market cross, the river flowing below, and the vista of green fields and grey fells, have all the promise of the dale in them. A man fishing near the bridge, standing up to his thighs in water, is the forerunner of many such figures which we shall meet in our journey up the dale. In the autumn flocks of sheep are driven along the roads to the great autumn fair at Masham; and in the uncovered mart, packed so closely that they make a grey moving carpet, are all the breeds which you come across in the dale. There are black-faced Swaledales, mountain sheep which live on the fells; large Wensleydales with blue faces and long curly fleeces, a breed which was perfected at Carperby higher up the valley; and, most frequent of all, the Mashams which are cross-breds between these two.

Here where the dale is opening out there are a few corn and root fields, and the trees are larger, the villages on the north side —Thornton Watlass round its square green, Thornton Steward on a ridge with its Norman church half a mile away in a quiet pasture, Spennithorne which you pick out by its fine church tower—look over lowland country; but away on the south side the forgotten little village of Ellingstring is hidden in heathy land, and an old man tells you that this is 'good country i' summer, but hard i' winter,' just as another might at the head of the dale.

This rolling country radiates round the ruins of Jervaulx Abbey. Only a few slender piers of the chapter-house and the walls of the laymen's frater rise to any size at Jervaulx now, but even from these you can imagine what Sir Arthur Darcy at the Dissolution described as 'one of the fairest churches I have ever seen.' The few ruins are memorials of four hundred years of power and influence which began when the monks settled here after eleven years of hardship at a bleaker site at Fors, near Askrigg, and ended with the hanging of its abbot at Tyburn in 1537.

The monks built the bridge over the river Ure at Kilgram. A record telling of this bridge being jealously guarded during an epidemic of the plague so as not to spread infection is one of many showing how the plague affected the life of the district. At East Witton, where houses run in enchanting demureness round three sides of a green, the market was removed to Ulshaw Bridge and it never returned. At Wensley, from which the valley is named, the village which after several years took up its life again was never so large or important as the old one. An entry in later parish registers explains a gap in them at this time as 'the plague was then most hote and fearfull.'

The monks of Jervaulx are said to have invented the recipe for Wensleydale cheese, which they called Cover Bridge cheese, and tradition has it that they gave this to a member of the

Towler family whose descendants kept the inn at Cover Bridge for centuries. This white cheese is still very popular with those who like a mild cheese. Swaledale and Teesdale are inclined to give their own names to it, but here and in the rest of England it is all known as Wensleydale. At one time the cheese was made in almost every farmhouse, which had its special room for drying and storing it. Every day from May to September the milk was heated, curded, kneaded into moulds, and put into the press for the night, and the older cheeses had to be turned. Now, winter and summer, lorries fetch the milk to cheese factories which are scattered up and down the dale, and to the works in Leyburn and Appleby in Westmorland, where it is pasteurized by the Express Dairy Company and sent in special tanks for consumption in London. Wooden stands to hold the milk cans are erected at the entrances to most farms.

The monks of Jervaulx were also famous for horse breeding, and the origin of the famous racing stables at Middleham can probably be traced to their influence.

The towns of Leyburn and Middleham face each other across the river. Leyburn, though old in origin, stands in its breezy open position for the new and progressive, the life of to-day. It has the market for the lower dale, and busy spring and autumn fairs are held here. Middleham mirrors the medieval days of pomp and ceremony, when the Nevilles kept up royal state in the castles, and its grey houses climb the steep main road and gather round the ruined walls of the castle as if to hear of them.

For centuries a great sheep and cattle fair, known as Middleham Moor Fair, flourished on the hill behind the town. Such events were held in other dales, but they reached the greatest size and importance in Wensleydale. Middleham was the largest of them, though Askrigg Hill Fair, held on the fells behind Askrigg, was a famous one. They were more after the character of the Westmorland fairs which still survive as horse fairs at Appleby and Brough. Old men in distant parts of Wharfedale, Nidderdale, and Swaledale, as well as from all corners of Wensleydale, tell how they came walking, riding on horseback, or driving in carts to Middleham Moor Fair.

The town itself was crowded, and house and shop doors were barricaded against stampeding herds of cattle. Bankers erected huts in the market-place, the Hawes bank always using a hen place, and there were other booths. On the moor there were Scotch drovers herding up their cattle, gipsies racing their horses wildly backwards and forwards, perhaps two or three lead miners joining to buy a cow to salt for their winter meat, and women and children buying 'fairings' from the cheap-jacks. Now the moor is as silent on November 5th as on any other day.

At one corner of Middleham a road turns into the valley of Coverdale, and to follow it is to lose yourself in a country which seems to have stood still for perhaps a hundred years. It is the most self-contained of all the branch dales. Joining in the castle at its foot, it has at Coverham the ruin of its own abbey, which was founded by the Nevilles. Part of the abbot's house is incorporated in a later building, but only fragments are left of the abbey, which used to be famous for its singing. You feel that any one living by the river Cover should sing, for it ripples and warbles down the whole of its course, and the birds in the trees which overhang it seem to be inspired by its music. It is a river to be reckoned with; when it joins the Ure near East Witton it is almost as large as the mother stream.

Coverdale is a narrow valley—you could stand on the road on one side of the river, and hear voices in the villages on the other—and it is almost unbelievably quiet. The stillness is probably due to the fact that it has no through road for motorists except for the intrepid ones who venture over the Park Rash Pass into Kettlewell in Wharfedale. This is a comparatively recent state; the road was feasible for horse transport, and for a short time the London to Richmond coach came this way. There was also the traffic for the pack-horse and drovers' path which turned at Arkleside near the head of the valley to go between the hills of Great and Little Whernside into

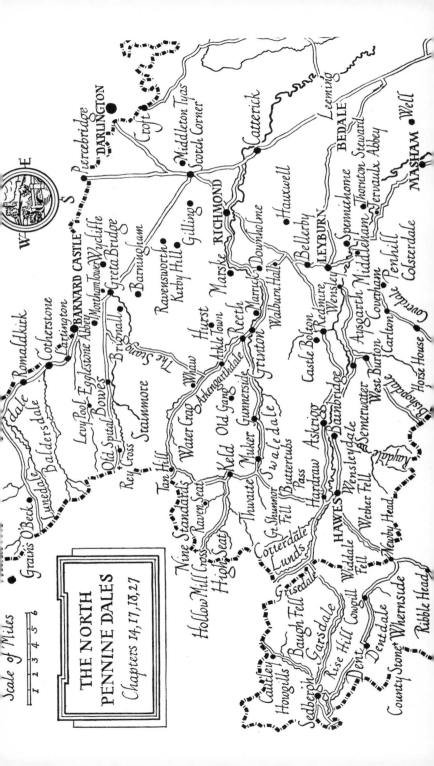

Nidderdale.   Perhaps its time of quietness is almost ended, for there has lately been talk of making the Park Rash Pass into a tarred road.

There lingers in this valley some faint memory from a time when there was life on the fells, echoes of pagan customs existing when the Norsemen came and added to them their own beliefs.   The superstitions of these people have not completely died out here.   The hamlets and villages dotted up it have Scandinavian names such as Scrafton, Gammersgill, Woodale, Arkleside, and Carlton.   Penhill on the north has one of the few British names in the dales.   For an old ceremony which may have originated in these times we must take the track over it to West Witton in Wensleydale again.   Every year on the August Saturday night which ends Witton Feast, a man followed by a procession of villagers carries up the street a straw effigy known as 'Old Bartle.'   At intervals the procession stops, and another man recites:

> 'In Penhill Crags he tore his rags;
> At Hunter's Thorn he blew his horn;
> At Capplebank Stee he brake his knee;
> At Grisgill Beck he brake his neck;
> At Wadham's End he couldn't fend;
> At Grisgill End he made his end,'

ending each recital with 'Shout, lads, shout,' which the crowd obeys.   The effigy is finally burnt in a lane near the village. West Witton church is dedicated to St Bartholomew, and Bartle, a shortening of this name, has become attached to the custom, but it seems probable that it is a survival of a rite connected with the harvest, dating from a time when the last sheaf, which was supposed to hold the corn-spirit, was either burnt or preserved.   There is a legend of a wicked giant on Penhill who, finding his swine dead, rushed out in anger to slay the people, but was turned on by his dog, and the two of them fell to their death over a precipice.   The story and the rhyme seem to indicate that many traditions have intermingled to bring about the custom of the 'Burning of Bartle' which we see to-day.

There is an intimate feeling about the fells of Wensleydale, connected as they are with the legends and history of the valley. On Witton Fell an ancient well with a stone face for a spout is known locally as 'Slavering Sal'; there are remains of a Knights Templars' chapel and stone coffins on the southern slopes of Penhill; Iron Age settlements are plain on the summit and southern slopes of Addleborough; the Roman road goes over Wether Fell; and the old road to the head of the valley mounts Cotter End. The ordinary life of the people was wrapped up with them, sheep were grazed on them, peat was cut from, and lead dug out of them.

Here at West Witton we are in the centre of the lead mining belt going across Wensleydale. The mines near Preston-under-Scar across the valley were some of the last to be worked, but they are silent now and no miners trudge to them over the fells. The old peat roads, too, are fast sinking back into the boggy moor.

On the north ridge of the fell the square bulk of the ruins of Bolton Castle stands out in light relief, dwarfing the little church and the straggling village at its foot. The castle has achieved fame as one of those in which Mary Queen of Scots spent her long years of imprisonment. In the summer of 1938 we saw a play based on one phase of the queen's imprisonment performed in her sitting-room. It brought the story vividly to life, yet Mary Queen of Scots, strong as her personality was, only ruffled the life of the castle for six and a half months, and as we made our way out in the dusk, lit down the narrow stairway by storm lanterns, it was the ghosts of the Scrope family, who built and inhabited the castle, which seemed to follow us.

The castle walls appear to have laid a restraining hand on this district, keeping the rural customs alive. The pastures above Castle Bolton, Redmire, and Preston-under-Scar are all open, and any one with land round the village may graze his cows there. At milking time in the summer months you meet men wearing back-cans and carrying pails, and boys leading donkeys with milk cans strapped to their sides, making their way to the pastures where they milk in the open.

When you think of Wensleydale you think of cows—cows being milked like this in the field, standing in the thick fog grass in the autumn, ambling along the roads to the barns, young stock feeding on the fells, all adding their rich brown colour to the surrounding green, and bringing a sense of the full life of the farm.

Higher up the dale the influence is strong of one or two families who for centuries made themselves felt in its life, and also took a part in that of the country: Thorntons of Askrigg, Robinsons of Raydale, Metcalfes of Nappa. Askrigg Old Hall was burnt down in 1935, but their homes remain in the hall at Colby, in Bear Park, which was once used as a resting place for the nuns of Marrick Abbey in Swaledale, and in houses at Bainbridge, Raydale, and Gayle. The finest example, as the family which inhabited it is the most interesting, is Nappa Hall, a fifteenth-century building with battlemented towers.

The first Metcalfe appeared in Wensleydale in the twelfth century, and from then the family rose to power. They built Nappa Hall, and gradually branches of the family settled in mansions round and married with wealthy families in other dales. They had their own chapel in Askrigg church. The story of Sir Christopher Metcalfe when he was Sheriff of Yorkshire riding to attend the judges at York with a retinue of three hundred of his own kinsmen, all on white horses, shows the power to which they had attained.

Some were arrogant and overbearing. For a generation they carried on a feud with the Thorntons of Askrigg Hall, and whilst the Metcalfes were magistrates the friends and servants of the Thorntons were continually being convicted for petty crimes. Their fortunes changed with Thomas Metcalfe, the 'Black Knight of Nappa.' He mortgaged parts of his estates and besieged the Robinsons at Raydale House above Semerwater when they seized the property on his refusal to pay the mortgage.

The family died out in 1756 in a poverty-stricken bachelor, whom one of the family described as 'the last hopeful heir of the old ruinous house of Nappa.' But those other branches had spread, many of them gradually dropping from their high place; and to-day there are Metcalfes from one end of Wensleydale to the other, and in many parts of Wharfedale and Swaledale. 'I'm one of the Metcalfes,' a little girl said to us a few weeks ago, and she held her head high, for Metcalfe is a name to be proud of still in Wensleydale.

Other notable families occupied the tall Georgian houses which are a feature of Askrigg's main street; a member of one of them, John Pratt, was a famous breeder of racehorses, and kept a fox in a hole in the stables at the back of his house so as to be always ready for a hunt. These men owned land, and had shares in lead mines, and some of them in the three mills on the beck. These were a corn mill, a flax mill, and a later woollen mill which made chiefly checked cloth for lining horse collars. A local man had a suit made of this cloth, which ran out to 'just tweea checks i' each leg.'

Bainbridge, standing round its green, is a gayer place. It displays its local pride in keeping up the old custom of blowing the forest horn at nine o'clock during the winter months, as was done when this was the centre of the Forest of Wensleydale. The dalespeople used to time their clocks by it; now it is just 'summat to listen for of a Sunday night.' This happy community lives under the shelter of Brough Hill, where eighteen hundred years ago the Romans built a fort.

You see the Roman road striking out between walls over Wether Fell as you climb the hill from Bainbridge to Raydale. At Countersett you pass the house where George Fox stayed when he was in this district. Prehistoric man lived on these hills; and flints and a spear-head which have been found since the level of Lake Semerwater was lowered are evidence that there were lake dwellings on it. But the charm of this peaceful hidden valley is outside these things. It is pleasant here to watch the moorhens swimming sturdily across the water and

H

cows wading amongst the rushes, to see the villages and farms and the little ruined church of Stalling Busk perched on the hillside out of the reach of floods, and to glimpse the village of Marsett spread on the open common.

Going up the valley you pass, near Burtersett, a derelict mill, a tall, narrow building standing beside a beck. Here a man used to make candles, using fat from dead sheep for the tallow, and the pith of rushes for wicks. These were tied on a

Hawes

string and repeatedly dipped in the fat and allowed to set, until they were the right thickness. It was a crude method, but the candles suited the people, who for a long time refused to buy wax ones because they dripped, and declared that there were 'no candles like Candle Willie's candles.'

Hawes, T' Haas, as it is called locally, is the market town for the district, and the life of the upper dale revolves round it. The market draws its stock from the high fells of Wensleydale, Wharfedale, and Swaledale; and pedigree Swaledale sheep predominate at the autumn sales. We think of the town on late December afternoons when the shop windows, decorated for Christmas, are lit up, and children press their faces against the glass, changing their wants with every fresh find. It is an amazingly large place to be so near the head of the valley. A family coming from lower down the dale to what seemed a much lonelier farm near Hawes felt themselves more in the world because they were only two miles from the town, and could come down to the shops and the pictures.

Beyond Gayle, whose quaint alleys hold the tradition of knitters, through Appersett, turning from its village green to live its life hidden from passers-by, the fells begin to close in, wrapping one into the other towards the distance. Past the road which leads into the hidden valley of Cotterdale, the old highway along which Lady Anne Clifford went on her way to Pendragon Castle turns up Cotter End. It starts now as a indistinct path, but once on the top there is a hard grassy road. The scattered houses which form the hamlet of Lunds below are lonely since the new road was made on the other side of the river, and the church bell calls few people to its services.

The river Ure trickles down from its source on these hills, and Wild Boar Fell makes a majestic background to the valley. A flock of golden plovers rises in alarm as you turn up the track to Shaw Paddock. It is evening and the family sit round the fire waiting for the butter-man who will exchange groceries for their produce. Presently he knocks and enters and joins the group by the fire.

'Is there aught stirring down t' dale, Tom?' asks the farmer's wife, and you settle down to hear the week's news.

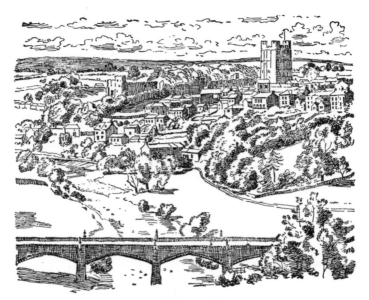

Richmond

CHAPTER 18

SWALEDALE

ALMOST our first recollection of Swaledale is of sitting on the hillside behind Keld, looking down to where the grey houses of the village cluster round the old chapel. On our left was the rocky ravine down which the river Swale cuts a magnificent way between Rogan's Seat and the rounded, heather-covered hill of Kisdon to Muker. Above the relics of ancient forest which line the hillsides stood the farmhouse of Crackpot Hall. We pictured the treeless ravine of Swinnergill running behind it to end in a waterfall which makes a sheltering curtain for a cave. And all round us lay the fells, great sweeping stretches covered with wiry grass and rushes, wrapping over each other to enclose this high corner.

A farmer stopped as he came up the hillside on the way to his farmhouse, and said: 'Are you painting t' faells?' He was a tall, spare man with fair hair, an obvious descendant of the Vikings who, finding in this hilly country some resemblance to their own, settled in it; and he pronounced the word fells as a Norwegian or an Icelander would pronounce it to-day. Norse words are still in general use for features on the landscape, such as beck, wath, grain (a fork or branch), tarn; and they survive in place-names, as in Keld, which means a spring.

One of the most interesting of these is the use of the suffix 'seat,' which, like 'side' and 'sett,' is from the Old Norse word *sætr*. When used for the fell peaks such as High Seat, Lovely Seat, Rogan's Seat, Pinseat, it means 'hill pastures,' but where there was a definite cultivation the word generally means 'a shieling.' Satron, 'a shieling by the pasture in the wood,' and Gunnerside, 'Gunnar's shieling,' are examples of this, but one of the most interesting, because it is easiest to imagine it as it was, is Raven Seat. Now only two farmhouses remain among tall trees by the beck here, and these are reached by moorland paths along which heavy goods have to be carried on sledges, but in the early nineteenth century the shieling had grown into a community of eleven houses and a chapel, and counted two gentlemen and one yeoman amongst its inhabitants.

Crooked Seat, a barn which has been a house on the Kirkby Stephen road, and Robert's Seat House, on the moor between Raven Seat and Tan Hill, are probably early sites. Robert's Seat House was used as a sleeping hut for a keeper watching for poachers before the twelfth of August, but its thick walls and an indefinable feeling of the presence of man haunting it suggest that it was an early habitation. Summer Lodge, lower down the dale, gets its name from having been a hill farm which, like the Norwegian seters of to-day, was only occupied in summer.

It is said that up to the sixteenth century a Norse speech

lingered in the remoter corners of Upper Swaledale and Wensleydale, strongly enough for a dalesman to have made himself understood to a Norwegian. The word laithe for a barn comes from the Old Norse *hlatha;* skellbuse, a partition in the cow shippon, from *skilja,* to divide; balk, a hayloft, from *bjalki,* a beam; and coup, a small cart, from *kupa,* a bowl. To-day a Norwegian would recognize many words in general use. He would know what the shepherd meant when he spoke of a 'bield' for a sheltered place, called himself a 'hind' and his two-year-old sheep a 'gimmer,' or remarked that 't' hogs lig doon on t' brant grund.'

Swaledale is the grandest of all the Yorkshire dales. Its meadows and pastures form a narrow strip of cultivation tossed between fells, and each mile reveals new and lovely vistas on its winding course. Its river rises far from human habitation on High Seat, one of the loftiest and wildest of the Pennine fells, and comes by scattered windswept farms to brown villages: Keld standing high above the river; Muker on a terrace above the beck; Gunnerside drawing together in its narrow street; Low Row sprawled along the hillside; Marske in a sheltered tree-filled hollow. Brown walls enclose and join them, their pattern broken by the stone barns studding the hillsides, one to every two or three meadows. Many stand at the foot of wooded ravines which run up into the fells; at Reeth the Arkle beck comes down another peopled valley with its own villages and hamlets. It is solemn, untamed country, which some people find bleak and bare, but for those to whom its gravity appeals it is wholly satisfying. Churches and a few abbey ruins are dotted down it, but there is little preparation for the sudden burst of architectural splendour which meets you in the old town of Richmond at its foot.

A track behind the hill on which we sat leads to Tan Hill and the road to Brough in Westmorland. Some of the houses along this way are derelict, but the last two are occupied. Of these, Low Frith has been there for centuries, but an old man still living remembers High Frith being built about sixty years

ago, and that even then it was considered quite natural for a man
to build his house on a remote exposed hillside.

Out on the open moorland you may come upon men silently
cutting peat on a ridge of the fell, an uncommon sight in these
dales nowadays when coal can be brought to the door. In
Swaledale, peat was formerly burnt along with hard coal dug
from the fells. The road passes the entrance to the Tan Hill
pit, which was the largest of several dotted on the moor here.
For centuries it supplied this district and many parts of Westmorland with coal, and every morning processions of carts and
donkeys waited their turn for a load. When it was closed
in 1936 the levels ran a mile and a quarter into the hill.

On the lonely moor behind it, at a height of one thousand
seven hundred and thirty-two feet, the sturdy building of
Tan Hill Inn, the highest inn in England, stands on the
Reeth to Westmorland road, facing the moors towards Swaledale and backing on the great tract of Stainmore. The inn
was built to supply packmen and drovers, and flourished with
the traffic of the coal pit. Sixty years ago there were three
cottages here, but a barn is all that remains of them, and
the inn now stands isolated on the moor. It had a famous
landlady in Mrs Susan Peacock, who before she died in 1938
became known to hundreds of people through her wireless
broadcasting. One of our last memories of Mrs Peacock is of
her standing at her porch to wave good-bye to us down a
snow-covered road, while a goat looked up to her begging for
titbits.

From Tan Hill you see across miles of moorland the nine
stone pillars which give their name to Nine Standards Rigg.
They are part of a boundary continued on one side by the Rey
Cross on Stainmore, and on the other by Hollow Mill Cross
which once stood at the head of Swaledale on the road to Westmorland. Old Yorkshire maps call this 'Holomill Crosse,'
and print a cross on a mound, but now only two plain stones
mark the county boundary known as Tail Brig.

Here at the head of Swaledale the fells rise abruptly from

the Westmorland vale of the Eden. From the edge of the ridge there is a view of that broad, rich country, cut with hedgerows and dotted with villages and farms, stretching to the Kendal hills and the higher peaks of the Lake District beyond. Then as you turn eastward with the road, the peaceful vale vanishes, and apparently endless moors stretch on all sides, great sweeping tracts covered with grass and rushes, and rising to lordly peaks.

This is grim, fierce country when the wind lashes across it or mist rolls over and accentuates its vastness, relentless when the sun blazes on it and the only shade is a small round sheepfold, but always exhilarating. Cold grey days, bringing mystery to the dark ravines and hollows, and exaggerating the bulk and solidity of the hills, suit it best. A mile or two further down it is broken by the moorland lake of Birkdale Tarn, an eerie, silent stretch of water where melancholy waves lap on the shores. In the spring plovers swoop in ecstatic flight over it, curlews burble their joyful notes, wheatears dart from rocks and crevices, and grouse shake their winter-ruffled feathers. In summer the dalespeople dig peat here and gather sand for sharpening their scythes, but for most of the year it lies deserted except for sheep and an occasional shepherd. Moors roll round the tarn, but behind the ridges on either side are the first weather-beaten farms of the dale and of the hamlet of Raven Seat, and beyond it the road slips quickly down to the village of Keld.

Through all its changes the dale has remained a community engaged in grazing sheep on the fells. The breed of black-faced horned sheep which have been brought to perfection as Swaledales have ousted the Scottish mountain sheep in this and many other districts. They are hardy sheep, able to live healthily on the fells from the age of four weeks. They are described as having:

> Back like a brig,
> Tail like a lonk,
> Horns like a sickle,
> Eyes like a weasel.

Those reared at the head of Swaledale are pedigree stock, and are bought principally by farmers from other parts to improve their own flocks and to cross with lowland sheep.

Sheep are a part of every picture in the dale; huddled in folds waiting to be dipped; held by their owners to be judged at the shows; moving in flocks over the Buttertubs Pass on their way to the autumn sales at Hawes in Wensleydale; looking light and small beside their lambs as, newly clipped, they are driven by the shepherd and his dog on to the fells again; overblown sheep being rescued from snowdrifts. To an outsider they appear identical, but the shepherd recognizes each sheep individually, and knows if one is missing from the flock.

Let us take the main road down the valley in June when the grass is growing for hay, and the meadows under Kisdon are vivid patches of yellow marsh marigolds and buttercups running up to the heather. It makes an unforgettable Alpine-like picture, and once you have seen it no amount of grey weather can efface it from your mind. But even as it moves to its summer luxuriance the dale remains neat, for although the rich herbage grows thick, it does not reach a great height. Going down to lower country after a month here one June, it was several days before we could rid ourselves of a feeling of untidiness in the overgrown gardens and hedges and the high grass on the roadsides.

Their meadows mean life to the dalespeople, for hay is the one harvest of the year, and they depend on it for winter feed for sheep and cattle. The growth of the grass is noted daily, and from May until it is gathered and led on sledges into the barns it is the chief concern.

Probably of all the villages Muker has best caught the spirit of the dale, with its mixed influence of sheep farming and lead mining, for though time is covering up the signs of mining on the fells, it has left its mark on the people. The first church down the valley is here. Its agricultural show is still kept up in a field which seems a basin in the fells, but its sheep fair is no longer held, and only a concert celebrates the

*H

fair of Muker Old Roy. This took place on the Wednesday before 6th January, and the date and the fact that a stot dance was performed at it suggest that it may have originated in an ancient celebration when the spring sowing began, corresponding with Plough Monday customs in other parts. 'Stot' means a bullock, which animal originally pulled the plough. It was an interesting survival in a district where corn was no longer grown.

See the miners and farmers coming down to the fair, having saved their money for the event, and badgers and tradespeople waiting to collect their accounts before they spend it. There are stalls of toys and drapery, one presided over by 'Spice Mary' from Reeth, who sells cake and sweets, and calls out, 'Here's a twopenny lump of spice for three ha'pence.' The night ends with dancing at the inns in long upstairs rooms lit by candles, the stot dance being performed by the men. There are songs too, and no doubt among them:

> I love Jock Willy Betty,
> And Jock Willy Betty loves me.

This song also illustrates the dale custom of attaching his parent's and grandparent's name to a man instead of a surname.

Below Muker the great lead mining area is concentrated over the moors from above Gunnerside to below Reeth. Here as in Nidderdale there are the extensive devastation on the fells, the tippings from various periods slowly being covered by vegetation, and the tracks winding in all directions to them, but in Swaledale the havoc lies far from the road out of sight of the villages. You must go along the miners' tracks to find them and the ruined buildings, and to discover the romance of this industry which flourished so long, and declined before it became the ugly thing which modern conditions would have made it.

The closing of the lead mines came as a tragedy to the dale. There had been bad times before—a depression at the beginning of the nineteenth century resulted in so many emigrants to America that an office was opened in Hawes to arrange their

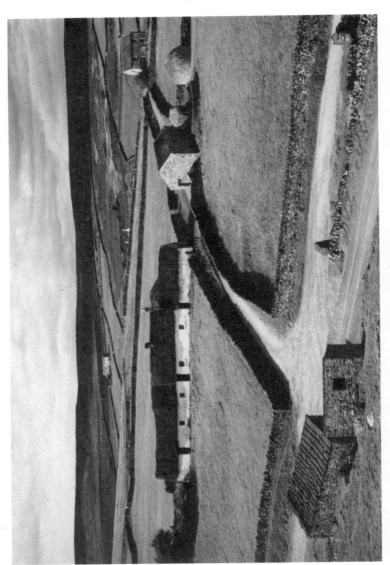

HURST IN SWALEDALE

passages across the 'gert dub,' as they called the Atlantic—but periods of prosperity followed these. In the last depression there was no hope; it was a gradual closing down of one mine after another, continuing to the early years of the present century. Coming as it did at a time of expansion in the woollen and cotton industries, the people were not left destitute; indeed Lancashire cotton manufacturers sent horses and carts to convey families and their furniture free if they would work for them, but that meant leaving a country where their families had been rooted for generations to go to a town where they were to be part of a crowd.

Each ruined mine with its pathetic group of buildings emphasizes one part of the story of the industry. At Old Gang behind Gunnerside you realize the long journeys to the workings, and picture the miners going up in little groups, many of them knitting as they walked. 'Let's sit doon for sex needles,' a man would say if he wanted a rest. We are told of an archer employed in building the levels who many a time ran the three miles home so that his wet clothes should not freeze on him, and yet later if there was a chance of a mine reopening was one of the first there. Old people in Swaledale remember seeing long rows of lights moving in the dark up the fells as the miners went to work.

Some of the buildings were 'shops' where men from long distances lodged during the week, bringing enough food with them on the Monday morning to last them until Saturday night. There are remains of the smelt mill here, the long ground chimney, and the peat house with pillars down the centre to support the roof, which was thatched with ling, but an infinite silence reigns over them now. Once as we passed them an oyster-catcher rose from the heather, and swooped over the track to settle on a rock below. It was a strange, unfamiliar bird to find on this moor so far from its usual sandy shores.

The C. B. mines in Arkengarthdale speak more of the magnitude of the industry to which the whole valley was given up. You think here of the levels running for miles underground and of the huge smelt mills—when the interior of an old one was taken down there was enough stone to build a row of houses. The Arkengarthdale mines are nearer the road, and are more evident in the valley than those of Swaledale. In the early days of mining lead was transported to the market at Barnard Castle over the Stang Pass on the line of a Roman road which crosses the dale.

Hurst, on the moors beyond Fremington, displays more than either of them the desolation both of the mines themselves and of their going. These are some of the oldest mines; it is known that the Romans worked them, and tradition has it that they employed British prisoners. The village grew to house the workers, and except for a few farmhouses there was no need for it when the mines stopped. The few houses which remain gaze with the derelict ones over the tossed moor which once brought them prosperity. At Hurst nothing has come as compensation, yet its site is charming. The cultivated land merging into rolling moors has the character of Scottish low-land scenery, and the older cottages, single-storied white-washed buildings, in their simplicity resemble Scottish crofts.

One of the few legends which survive in Swaledale is set on the moors near Hurst, at the Roan Well whose water is tinged with red from an iron deposit. The story goes that one day a traveller passing by the well was seized by its guardian fiend and drowned, and from that day the water ran red with his blood. Every year the people of the district went to the well and chanted a prayer, until one day the Virgin Mary appeared in a cloud of fire and dipped her foot into the water, and from that time the well had healing power. The Red Hursters, as the people came to be called, still went to the well every year, but now to render thanks for its blessings. The story probably originated from a time when wells were considered sacred, and it was later grafted on to the Roman Catholic belief. In later years, the Methodists revived the legend, and used the water from the well for their love-feasts.

Reeth at the foot of Arkengarthdale was a great centre of

the lead mining area, though looking at it now, standing peacefully round its spacious green, it is difficult to realize that it was ever anything more than a rural village. We are told that when the industry stopped at the end of the nineteenth century it was as though some plague had visited it, for most of the houses stood deserted and forlorn. It was also a great centre for hand knitting, and thousands of pairs of knitted stockings were sold here every year. Its annual fair was held in the autumn, and the miners used to buy their shirts and often their whole winter clothing at the stalls.

> 'But it's rake-time seea I mun away,
> For my partners are all g'yan to wark.'
> Seea I loup'd up an' bid him gud day,
> An' wrowt at t' Awd Gang tell 'twas dark.

ends the old poem of *Reeth Bartle Fair*, but it is years now since miners 'wrowt' at Old Gang, and the tracks leading to it are smooth and grass-grown, nibbled short by sheep.

The upper dale ends abruptly at Reeth. The hills have more colour here than the loftier ones to the north, and at Grinton a mile further down there is softer, wooded country, and a feeling of an easier existence. Swale Hall and Blackburn Hall were the homes of families who took a part in English life as well as that of the dale. The church also brought outside connections, for it was owned by Bridlington Priory, whose charter describes it as 'The church of St Andrew of Swaldale.' Woodman tenants of the Priory lived on Whitaside pasture.

Going up the dale, the road on the north side of the valley, running under the British fort of Maiden Castle, comes to Melbecks on the Haverdale beck. Haver is from the Norse word *hafri*, meaning oats. These were once grown in the valley, and ground at the mill which eventually became a cloth mill on the beck. Havercake and bacon used to be the chief food of the people, and emigrants to America generally took a sack or barrel of home-made oatcake with them.

More echoes of the upper dale reach Grinton. Its church was once the last up the valley, and people wishing to bury their dead in consecrated ground made the long journey down to it. The track they used is known as the Corpse Way. It starts up the valley as two routes, one going through Reeth and along the hillside above Low Row, and the other keeping on the old road past the church and crossing the river at Ivelet by a beautiful pack-horse bridge. A stone here is said to have been used for resting the coffin. The tracks join above Ivelet, and end as one over the summit of Kisdon on its way to Keld. It is long since processions took their melancholy journeys along it, but for us to-day it makes one of the finest walks in the dales.

An old stile below Grinton was supposed to mark the end of the dale. A rhyme referring to this says:

> From Hollow Mill Cross to Stollerston Stile
> The extent of Swaledale is twenty long mile.

Many years ago a pony was disqualified in a local class at Muker Show because of this ancient division, but it hardly fits the country itself, which is still between fells.

Presently along the road there appear the modest ruins of two nunneries standing a mile apart beside the river. At Marrick there is a mutilated church and parts of the monastic building have been taken into a farmhouse. At Ellerton only a plain tower and a few tombstones remain. The gentle spirit of the nuns seems to brood over this area. You imagine them crossing the stepping-stones over the river to visit each other, or climbing the stone causeway which was made from Marrick Abbey to the village above. We have noticed on our journey how the nunneries were usually in remote parts of the country and often very humble buildings, and have felt that life would not go easily for them. We know that the Marrick nuns had disputes with the prior of Bridlington, who claimed the right to grind corn at their mill because the dam was on his land.

The villages now lie chiefly on old roads on either side. Downholme is on a road which goes through Hudswell over the moors to Richmond. All that remains of its ancient hall is a crumbling wall with a lancet window in it, but a mile away on the Leyburn road Walburn Hall, a fine example of a sixteenth-century fortified manor house, is still occupied. Across the valley the village of Marske lies sunk among trees by the beck. At Applegarth, under Whitcliffe Scar, there is an Iron Age settlement, a series of beehive dwellings and little fields under the rocks. In spring primroses cover the hillside in pale yellow sheets, and you wonder whether prehistoric men trod over such flowers, and whether their children came out from the crude little houses to pick bunches of them.

Suddenly a gate seems to close behind you, and you are in Richmond, the loveliest town in the north. From whichever side it is approached Richmond makes an arresting picture. From the Terrace it appears spread on the hillside, its grey houses merging into the castle on its rocky site above the river, and the dark moors stretching behind it up the dale. The Norman keep stands high above the rest, and the curtain wall extends from it, so that it appears as a medieval town centred round this castle. Looking down to it from the west, seeing its many towers rising up above the town, you realize the strong religious life which grew up here under its influence. Coming down to it from the moorland on the south, the grim castle walls standing immediately below display it first as a fortress guarding against attack from the dale country, and then as a protection to the clustered community whose cottages climb up to them.

All these aspects are still felt in the town itself, though here the castle is out of sight. You enter into a large cobbled market-place with shops ranged in an uneven line round it and a market cross at one end. Buses and cars park at random on the cobbles, crowding them sometimes, but only slightly disturbing the atmosphere of the past. In the centre the old building of Trinity Church has had shops fitted under it, and more buildings divide it from its tower. After the new and larger parish church was built, Trinity Church was put to many strange uses before it became the chapel for the grammar school. A curfew bell is still rung from its tower every night.

Narrow alleys called 'wynds' open from the square. Friars' Wynd leads to the Perpendicular tower of Grey Friars' which is all that was built of a new church at the time of the dissolution of the monasteries. Others go to broad quiet streets or run between overhanging cottages under the shadow of the castle. Even when eighteenth-century builders lined the wider streets such as Newbiggin and Frenchgate with tall Georgian houses, the plan of the town remained that of the one which first grew up round the castle. The later life, like that of to-day, must always have been coloured a little by the castle which first made Richmond into a town, and by those religious communities which were for so long a part of it. The men and women who went from the tall houses in Frenchgate to see Edmund Kean act in the eighteenth-century theatre in Friars' Wynd looked from their homes to where a mile further down the river the ruins of Easby Abbey stand as a memorial to the white-robed Premonstratentian monks who farmed and worshipped there, or nearer still to the scanty ruins of the little priory of St Martin.

During the early prosperity of the lead industry in the dales some of the ore was brought to Richmond to sell, and there were many lead-merchants among its citizens. It was also a large market for the knitting industry in the dale. To-day, although it has a market, and military camps surround it, it is a town belonging partly to the dale country, partly to the softer land below it, but chiefly enclosed in itself and its own past history. It is a precious relic still in its lovely setting.

Market Day, Northallerton

CHAPTER 19

THE PLAIN OF YORK

THE thought of a plain seldom moves one to ecstasy; it brings no prospect of narrow valleys and ravines, sweeping moors and hidden villages; it is prosaic. Yet the plain is not without majesty if it has extent, and if there are view-points from which that extent can be seen. The roads and villages on it may be ordinary and all very similar, but seen from a distance and as a whole there is a kind of enchantment about them.

From Garrowby Hill on the Yorkshire Wolds or Sutton Bank on the Hambleton Hills you can look across the vast area of the Plain of York to where it rises towards the Pennines; or on the eastern flanks of the Pennines see across its agricultural land to where the moors and the Wolds fade away into a blue distance. Railway trains move across it, there are mansions in wooded parks, church spires and towers mark the villages, and

larger clusters the towns.   There are many of these, for since
man learnt the art of draining he has been attracted to the rich
land and mild climate of the plain.   It is a reasonable land in
which to live and farm.   On many winter days, passing in
sunshine through its green open country, you see snow lying
thickly on the hills on either side.

The accessibility of the plain has made it a route for travellers
and armies.   It was inevitable that the Great North Road should
go through it from Roman times and probably earlier.   Kings
have waited on it while their forces collected; battles have been
fought round its bridges and over its level fields.   The hills
have their sudden bursts of drama and romance, but the plain
makes steady history through the ages.

The story of the town of Boroughbridge has been one of the
road from the time when the route north was made through
here instead of the Roman town of Aldborough a mile to
the east.   For centuries its bridge was the only public one
between York and Ripon.   It was one of the halting-places for
Scotch drovers, and during the season blacksmiths made as
much as £6 a day shoeing footsore cattle; the present smith
keeps a few cattle shoes in the shop which his family has
owned for two hundred years.

Some of the drovers came for the great annual fair which
was held here in June.   William Metcalfe of Sessay, near
Thirsk, visiting Barnaby Fair in 1797, records in his diary:
'A good sheep fair, though several small sheep unsold.
Showers.'   He also tells of seeing a show 'where was a fine
majestic lion, also a she-lion, a ferocious tiger, a young elephant,
a leopard, hyena, two panthers, etc.,' recording the excitement
of this side-show amongst the more serious business of the
fair.

The town's supreme activity came in the coaching and
posting days, for the meeting here of the Great North Road and
the road to Thirsk brought double traffic.   As early as 1672 the
home of the Tancreds in the main street had been turned into
a hotel, and later a house of the Mauleverers became The

Three Greyhounds. They grew with the increasing trade, until the Crown Hotel could accommodate over a hundred horses. An aura of the coaching days hangs about the yards whose stables are garages now, but it is change, not the sadness of decline, that you feel here, for Boroughbridge is again one of the popular halting-places on the Great North Road. It is a town of hotels, large ones in the main street or their own grounds, a row of modern hotel cottages, one of which you can have for yourself for the night, and a large lorryman's café where through day and night drivers from all parts meet over their hot tea or coffee.

Between the present era and that of the coaches, Borough-bridge suffered a period of neglect when traffic had gone to the railways and only a few pedestrians passed through the town. Grass grew between the cobbles of the streets and many inns closed their doors, until at last a few cyclists came as harbingers of the streams of traffic of to-day. Boroughbridge remembers this with dismay when it is proposed to by-pass the town. Should the life of the road fail there is little now to take its place. A few boats come up the river and canal, but goods are no longer unloaded for the dales nor their produce shipped here.

The Devil's Arrows, three large Bronze Age standing stones just outside the town, were connected with a prehistoric settle-ment. The later Brigantine village east of Boroughbridge gave way to the town of Isurium, the Roman centre of civil life in Yorkshire, as York was the military centre. The village of Aldborough now stands on the site, and through centuries Roman pavements and remains have been discovered here. During excavations by the Yorkshire Archaeological Society in 1938 we saw at the bottom of a trench sections of the town wall and a slab of stone with a raised rectangular centre, and held in our hands bits of jewellery and pottery which the Romans had worn and used. These personal possessions seemed to bring their owners near, until we looked at the six feet of solid soil which had been cut through before the wall was reached. They sank still further into the past as we went into the village, and saw Roman stones built into the Decorated church, and a continuance of what seemed an old charity in the loaves of bread ready to be distributed to the poor.

In the town of Ripon, lying west of the Great North Road, there is little atmosphere of travel. It is a market for the district which includes the lower parts of Nidderdale and Wensleydale. There is a dale feeling in the villages clustering round it; West Tanfield with its houses along the banks of the Ure, and Marmion Tower, the gatehouse of the Marmions and the FitzHughs, standing by the church; Well, whose curious cross marked a stage in the journey from Wensleydale to York; Snape, at whose castle Catherine Parr lived with her first husband.

To Ripon's importance as a market there is added the dignity and tradition of a cathedral city. A distant view of it, as the grey towers of the minster rise above the darker buildings and the green surrounding country, has the quality of an old print. The atmosphere of a picturesque past haunts the walls of Ripon strongly enough to impose itself on the modern progressive town. The people cherish the memory of St Wilfrid who rebuilt the first cathedral in 669 and was later canonized. Every year a ceremony is held to commemorate his return from exile. A local man, impersonating the saint, declares the fair in the market-place open, and then rides round the town on a white horse.

It was a scene of bustle as we came to it on a hot June afternoon in 1938. The town itself hems in the market-place, and the roundabouts and shows were overwhelming in the small and slightly raised space. The waiting crowd arranged itself along the pavements and between the shows as best it could, watching the town hall. The ceremony was broadcast that year, and at intervals the commentator came out on to the balcony and described us through a microphone. Presently an attendant led a white horse to the door, St Wilfrid emerged and mounted it, declared the fair open, and to its jangling music started his journey round the town, followed by the band.

The present minster was built in the twelfth and early thirteenth centuries and enlarged in the sixteenth century, but the crypt is part of St Wilfrid's church. It is a miniature church under the high altar, and the relics of the saint were later enshrined in it. In the north wall a slit something like a squint, probably made to enable the relics to be seen without going into the crypt, is known as St Wilfrid's Needle. From the top of the west tower of the minister we saw the figure of the saint riding on his white horse through the streets, and he seemed to connect the old and the new life.

Another link is the blowing of the wakeman's horn every night in the market-place, a survival from the time when one of the duties of the wakeman was to blow a horn at nine o'clock as a signal that from then until three or four o'clock in the morning he was watching the town. A householder with one door to his house paid twopence and one with two doors fourpence to the wakeman, who had to make good any loss if a house was robbed. The wakeman's house, a thirteenth-century building with a seventeenth-century front, remains, though there has been no wakeman since Ripon became a mayoralty in 1604. Inscribed over the Town Hall are the words which are still the motto of the city: 'Except ye Lord keep ye cittie ye Wakeman waketh in vain.' Ripon can claim another good saying in 'As true a steel as Ripon rowels,' which became a general expression to describe an honest man, and originated from the very fine spurs which were made here and in the neighbourhood.

It was owing to an act of kindness on the part of one of the inhabitants that this was the first place in England to manufacture varnish. A refugee from the French Revolution wandering through England came to Ripon, where he was befriended by Mr David Williamson, a banker who had travelled in France. In return for his kindness the Frenchman told him the secret of varnish making. Mr Williamson started to make it in his leisure time, but finally deserted banking for it, and the business grew so that travellers were sent to all parts. The varnish was delivered in copper vessels which had to be returned. To-day varnish and paint made by three or four firms in Ripon are sent all over the world. The strong stifling smell of it greets you on entering the town from the south.

Topcliffe

Ripon is on the river Ure, but it is the river Swale which divides the plain naturally into two and, largely because of its barrier, turns the villages east of it to the Hambletons and west of it to the Pennines. Topcliffe on its east bank, though only seven miles from Ripon, belongs in spirit to the eastern moorlands. At the time of Topcliffe Fair gipsies camp on the flat land near the river here, and their caravans add to the beauty of the scene as their smoke curls up to where the village and the church stand on a hill above the bridge. After announcing at the village cross a poll tax levied by Henry VII, Henry

Percy, fourth Earl of Northumberland, was slain here by an enraged mob. The corn mill, which is still working, once had a miller so miserly that he used to press his face into the flour bin before going out, so that he should know if his wife had used any flour while he was away.

Thirsk under the Hambleton Hills is the market town for this district. Though the earth and timber castle of the Mowbrays stood here only from 1135 to 1176, the brick-built town owes something of its plan to it. Its market-place has an attractive air of rural activity, and is remarkable for the number of old-established shops. Their customers come from rural villages under the Hambleton and Howardian Hills: Kirkby Wiske, standing on the twining river Wiske whose name means 'damp meadow,' Sutton-under-Whitestonecliff where an old stone crab mill stands in the centre of the village.

From Boroughbridge to Catterick these towns and what were Anglian villages lie a mile or so off the Great North Road, which itself cuts a lonely way through the country. This stretch was a favourite haunt of highwaymen in the coaching days. Coaches were often attacked, and private travellers carrying money and valuables dared not venture along it until a party had been formed. A man never knew when he was safe, for many of the innkeepers were in league with the highwaymen, with whom they shared the spoils. In 1812 the landlord of the King's Head at Kirklington just off the main road turned highwayman himself.

To-day as we start along the road we are confronted by the new aerodrome at Dishforth, where the enormous hangars and the houses for the airmen have brought a new village, and bombers fly night and day over the once quiet land. South of Leeming the road takes the name of Leeming Lane. This part of the plain is known as the Vale of Mowbray, and is famous for its nursery gardens. The rich soil produces an unusual depth of colour in blue flowers, particularly lupins and delphiniums, which with the roses brighten the fields by the roadside in summer.

The old town of Bedale lies west of the road here. Its wide main street, which is also the market-place, leads up to the church, whose tower was fortified against Scots raids. It is a thriving little place, the centre of a famous hunt, and it supports a flourishing rope - making industry. This was established in Bedale at a time when the bulk of the work was done by 'tramp spinners' who made nets at seaports in the fishing seasons and afterwards travelled about the country from one rope-making firm to another.

Coming down to the town on a late winter afternoon when the lighted shop windows gleam and sparkle, you might be in a town high up between the fells to which it leads, but red brick mingles with the stone in its buildings and some feeling of the road going north spreads to it.

The market towns which are the life of the plain lie east of the river Swale now. Northallerton, the capital of the North Riding, gives its name to the old district of Allertonshire. It runs in a dignified line on either side of a wide main street, narrowing where the market hall juts into it and widening again where the church stands beyond a green. Camden called Northallerton Fair 'The greatest faire of kine and oxen and of most resort that ever I saw in all my life.' This would be held in the main street, which still presents a busy scene on market days. Stalls are ranged on the cobbles at the side of the street, farmers' wives sell eggs and butter outside the tolbooth, and cars and carts unload crates of dead rabbits and live hens.

The people whom you meet here are chiefly from the villages of the plain. You imagine them journeying home to Brompton, famous for its hog-back coffins, past the site of the Battle of the Standard to Danby Wiske with its moated rectory, and perhaps further still to Ellerton and Bolton-on-Swale where Henry Jenkins was born and lived through nine reigns to the age of one hundred and sixty-nine. The parish registers describe Henry Jenkins merely as 'a very old poor man,' and in modern times we have come to think that he may have magnified his age through forgetfulness, but he is said to have told of being sent to Northallerton at the age of ten or twelve with a cartload of arrows to be used at Flodden Field. In these days he would have been asked his recipe for long life, and from an old book of his mother's which he treasured he would have recommended tar water, nettle tea, a raw new-laid egg every morning, or to be electrified daily. Certainly it was not luxury which prolonged his days, for he described the house in which he was born as 'chiefly composed of large tree branches, clay or road dirt, thatched with straw, and divided into compartments.' At the age of a hundred, if his tale is true, he swam across the Swale and walked to London.

Yarm, the last town on the plain, lies on the northern edge of Yorkshire. The river Tees, still uncontaminated by industry, sweeps round the northern end of it and often floods the low-lying houses. The town, with its Georgian brick houses and tolbooth, resembles Northallerton; and its straggling main street forms the longest market-place in Yorkshire.

For a few days during the annual fair in October it bursts into a strange and furious life. Roundabouts, stalls, and gipsies' caravans are ranged in a close line on either side of the street, and dealers race their horses wildly between them, yelling as they run with them or drive them from low flat carts, careless of the traffic on this main road from Thirsk to Stockton. Others bargain where the horses stand in rows by the pavement. There is now an auction mart at which the farmers sell their horses, but the gipsy dealers still prefer to display their stock and bargain in the main street.

Gipsies make their fires on the cobbles, and sit round them in family groups, many of the women smoking pipes, while lurcher dogs prowl about, and a smell of onions and burning wood hangs in the air. Swarthy gipsies move along the streets in tawdry tinsel dresses or beckon from the caravans: 'Come in, and I'll tell you the future, lady. You've got a lucky face.' 'Come in and have your hands read, ladies. I tell you names.'

YARM FAIR

They come from all parts, Lincolnshire, the midlands, Scotland, to this almost the last of the year's fairs. One old man has brought horses to Yarm since he was a boy, and the local people know they are safe in dealing with him. Many of the caravans are occupied by his married family, who form a gipsy clan.

On the second day of the fair, cattle are sold on the grass verges of the roads outside the town; and on the third day sheep are sold both in and out of the town. Yarm Fair was formerly noted for cheese, which was sold in great quantities and shipped down the river Tees to London. William Metcalfe of Thirsk records each year in his diary that he has weighed his cheese and set the draught off for Yarm. In 1796 he arrived about half-past five on the day before the fair, and put up at the sign of the Ship. Whilst he was delivering his cheese the next morning his wagon stuck fast in the entry to Green Tree Yard, and had difficulty in getting back, and he writes that 'Ewbank, the landlord, behaved not very well.' In 1820, three hundred and eighty-three wagons and carts, each wagon holding one and a half tons, came laden with cheese into Yarm market. In 1938 we saw no cheese, only the gipsies clinging tenaciously to a way of life which modern conditions are fast destroying.

Crayke

CHAPTER 20

THE HOWARDIAN HILLS

WE first met the travelling circus on the narrow leafy road which runs from Brandsby to Hovingham. It was a simple procession, the larger motor traffic having gone a longer way round by the main road. A troupe of Shetland ponies led it; next came a van pulled by two piebald ponies and a white one, and driven by a woman with a bright handkerchief tied round her head; a light cart and a few straggling Shetland ponies brought up the rear. They moved carefully but steadily down the hill, anxious not to be late for the afternoon performance at Hovingham.

The marquee was already up on the green when we arrived, and more ponies grazed quietly on the grass. In an hour the circus people had contrived to look as though they had been there a week; women were cleaning the caravans, and men who

WASHINGTON ON A MULE AT MT. VERNON

would presently appear as riders and clowns were working in their shirt sleeves. They seemed so settled that it was difficult to realize that early next morning they would be moving on to another village far enough away to tempt a fresh audience.

The modest little company fitted into the rural country round the Howardian Hills with its quiet charm and harmony. This is a corner of Yorkshire which most resembles southern scenery; its gracious wooded country might be in some parts of Gloucestershire or Somerset. It has their look of luxuriant fertility, of a land where life is not a continual struggle against weather and hard conditions. The low-lying hills into which the rolling country north of the Forest of Galtres merges are little more than risings in the land, making sheltered or open sites for the villages. A network of roads crosses them, and trees cover the highest places. It is significant that this line of hills which ends at the foot of the higher ridge of the Hamble-tons should have come a century and a half ago to be called after the Howards, one of the large land - owning families of the district.

Even the cottages here have a richer architecture than in many parts, as though an easier existence had given time and energy for some adornment. They are principally of light stone, harmonizing with the ancient churches, but a few are half-timbered, and almost all have mellowed red-tiled roofs whose colour gives warmth to the scene. Riotous little gardens separate them from the cobble-lined roads, and borders of stone mushrooms brought from some stack-yard are reminiscent of Cotswold gardens.

All the villages take on the gentle aspect of the country, but they vary in plan and each leaves a distinct little picture in the mind. Hovingham, at which we have arrived with the circus, is a pleasant example, standing round a green with the church and hall on one side and pantiled cottages and the inn on the other. It is one of the high northern line of villages situated on or near the course of the Roman road from Malton to Aldborough. These places lie close together; Barton-le-

Street and Appleton-le-Street proclaim by their names their position on the road; Slingsby is built of stone from the ruins of its castle which was never completed because of the Civil War; Stonegrave stretches along a ridge of hill looking down to the castle of Gilling in the woods; Oswaldkirk is the only place in Yorkshire named after St Oswald; Ampleforth has a Roman Catholic college built into a Benedictine monastery.

Much of the charm of these villages is that they are unspoilt. Coxwold with all the ingredients of a show village yet remains natural and unself-conscious. It is situated on a hill at the top of which is the church with its elaborate octagonal tower. A stretch of grass borders the road, and behind it new and old houses mingle with the seventeenth-century grammar school and almshouses. Fruit trees pruned and trained into precise patterns on the walls of the houses add to the neat well-kept air, but this usual characteristic of a village connected with a manor house is not strained or exaggerated here.

The village ends at the house where Laurence Sterne lived when he came to be vicar of Coxwold in 1760. It is chiefly remarkable for the enormous chimney which stretches so far across the gable that there is room for a window in it. You can still see Sterne's study and the bedroom with a well opening into it. Sterne gave the house the name of Shandy Hall, and he wrote *A Sentimental Journey* and a large part of *Tristram Shandy* here. He liked Coxwold, finding he could live in it cheaply on the good things of the land. You imagine him going across the road to take the services in the church, passing up the chancel between the massive monuments to the Belasyse and Wombwell families of Newburgh Priory, those tombs which are such a feature at Coxwold. We know a man who sheltered from a thunderstorm in this church and found it an eerie sight when the lightning caught the marble figures and seemed to bring them to life.

Husthwaite a mile away has its air of being well tended accentuated by fine clipped yew-trees, but its charm is of a more solid kind. It seems to have grown in spirit as it has gathered round its simple early Norman church with its aisleless nave and low chancel arch.

The flatter region to the south, retaining some memory of the forest where King James I had a shooting lodge, centres now round the town of Easingwold where the Swainmote Courts of the Forest were held. The town, which is long and straggling, divides into three parts with the market-place in the middle. It seems to have been almost completely rebuilt in the Georgian period, but to-day an air of decay hangs over it, and it appears much too large for itself. It is one of those places which modern conditions have left to sleep on the countryside; and you wonder how the number of people who inhabit them live, so little now does their influence seem to affect the surrounding land.

Perhaps the vanishing life of this southern area is best expressed at Tollerton on the western fringe of it. Its windmill, restored in 1937 by the Yorkshire Archaeological Society, is still working, and its whitewashed walls and the miller's cottage below make a pleasant picture on the land, but it suffers from the nearness of the steam mill at Brandsby, which is not dependent on the weather.

'Nay,' an old man told us, 'it 'll never be used much again, it's just a landmark. They 're out o' date, them things, they 're like folks, when they gets owd they gets owd-fashioned.'

He was drawn two ways, remaining faithful to the old mill which had helped to form the pattern of his life, but admiring the new one which 'ground oats like flour, you couldn't tell what it was.'

Of the castles which have guarded this desirable land, the only considerable remains are the stark ruins of Sheriff Hutton of which Leland declared that he 'saw no House in the North so like a Princely Logginges.' It had many royal connections, for, like Middleham, the castle passed to the Neville family by marriage, and through them to Richard III. The tomb of Richard's son Edward is in Sheriff Hutton church. Elizabeth, sister of the princes murdered in the tower, was imprisoned here, and released after the battle of Bosworth to become the wife of Henry VII.

Sheriff Hutton is an empty shell, but a mansion has been built on to Gilling Castle, and another on to the fifteenth-century tower at Crayke. Crayke castle has a remarkable site on an isolated hill which can be seen from long distances. The village climbs up one side of it, and beyond the church the castle stands on the summit, commanding a vast extent of the Plain of York with a distant view of the minster in its midst. Recent excavations have revealed that the hill has been continually occupied from early times. Egfrid, King of Northumbria, gave it and the land for three miles round it to St Cuthbert, and it was one of the places where the saint's body rested on the long, sad journey from Lindisfarne. Until 1844 the hill remained an island belonging to Durham in the midst of Yorkshire.

Wandering about the Howardian country you discover amongst the number of large houses a proportion which can only be called mansions. They stand, generally on the sites of older castles or of monasteries, in enormous grounds or wooded parks. Unwieldy and expensive to keep up though they may be for the generations which have inherited them, they yet stand as substantial signs of particular phases of English social life. They show the growing pride of the landowner in his estate, and his desire to beautify it, and show also the wealth which allowed such homes to be built. You imagine the great houses rising on their historic sites in a size and magnificence which could not be contemplated to-day; and yet the builders appear as human beings when you see the furnished rooms and the treasures in pictures and china which they collected from all parts of the world to ornament them. In their ambitious plan the houses fit the district almost as well as the old villages do, or perhaps it is rather that they and their influence have given to this piece of Yorkshire the look and feeling of a well-loved garden.

Castle Howard is the supreme example. Like Blenheim,

it is one of the English mansions designed by Sir John Vanbrugh at the beginning of the eighteenth century. Standing in its enormous park, it resembles a royal palace in its conception and achievement. Its domes and many windows can be seen from across a lake on the north and from temples in the grounds, which were laid out at a period when English landscape gardening was being established. Southward the view extends over lawns and park to the distant Wolds which, seen from this great estate, almost lose their identity to become a background to it. The whole is a monument to the lordly ideas of its creators and the century which produced them.

The splendour of the exterior is more than matched by the interior. The state rooms are hung with pictures by Van Dyck, Rubens, Canaletto, Lely, and Domenichino; even the bedrooms have their share and go by the name of the artist whose pictures predominate. The four-post beds and the furniture in the state rooms show faithfully the periods in which they were assembled, just as the treasures of china and wood, brought from many countries at a time when only the wealthy travelled, bring a personal picture of successive heads of the family adding to the richness of a house which was to become one of the show places of England.

Newburgh Priory, near Coxwold, is another type of mansion. It retains about its walls some of the sanctity of the Augustinian priory on the site of which it was built about 1600. It lies nearer to the road, its entrance marked by magnificent clipped yew-trees. Motorists stopping to admire these are accosted by two peacocks which fly over from the stable wall across the road to beg for crumbs. Peacocks and clipped yews prepare you for the dignity of this house, which has often welcomed royal guests.

After the Dissolution Newburgh Priory was granted to the Belasye family, a member of which, Thomas Belasye, married Mary, daughter of Oliver Cromwell. She is supposed to have brought her father's body here, and had it buried in a sarcophagus at the top of the house. The Wombwell family

I

inherited with the estate the tradition that to tamper with the
sarcophagus would bring disaster. When King Edward VII
stayed here he was anxious to test the truth of the story, but
he was not allowed, and the memorial keeps its secret. Through
all these later legends the memory lingers here of William of
Newburgh, the twelfth-century historian prior, who regarded
his task as would a modern historian.

The river Derwent borders the district on the east, and flows
through sylvan scenery which its British name, meaning 'river
where oaks are common,' suggests. In one of its loveliest
corners, where the river is crossed by a medieval bridge, are the
ruins of Kirkham Priory. This, another Augustinian priory,
was founded by Walter Espec in 1121. It was not one of the
wealthiest monasteries, for the new church which the canons
began in the middle of the thirteenth century was never completed beyond the aisled choir. Amongst the scanty ruins are
a Norman doorway, a twelfth-century gatehouse rebuilt in the
thirteenth century of Tadcaster stone, and a beautiful lava-
torium in the cloister. It was unique amongst monasteries in
that, though it stood so near the river, its water for draining
was brought from springs on the hillside to the east. To-day
it fits its hilly site so well that you cannot imagine its ever having
been anything but a lovely ruin.

Beyond it the river winds to Malton, where the church at
Old Malton is a fragment of another priory by the Derwent.
Old Malton seems to complete the peaceful story of life by the
river. It was once a fuller one, for the river Derwent was made
navigable in the reign of Queen Anne and ships were built here.
The new town which we know to-day as Malton is more related
to the continuous life of the road. For many people it is merely
a place on the route from the West Riding to the coast, and
they remember it chiefly because its narrow streets curb
the traffic for a time. They have come to it from York
along a great new highway which goes relentlessly over
the country, cutting out corners and by-passing villages,
and have glimpsed here and there a deserted bend of the old

road, telling of the days when this was a pleasant winding way to the coast.

Malton the touring place lies along the main roads through it, but Malton the rural centre lies in the market square which branches from it. Here is the town which followed that built by Eustace Fitz-John after the Battle of the Standard to replace the one burnt by the Scots. Two churches stand in it, St Michael's, which is one of a group, rare in England, standing with no burial ground round them in the centre of a town, and St Leonard's, which has a timber spire covered with lead.

Malton has now an important market to which the trade from smaller markets has come. The buses which start out from the square on market days stop for the first few miles at almost every road end to drop a red-faced, prosperous-looking farmer or a farmer's wife with her empty baskets hung on her arms.

The autumn sheep fair is still opened here by a proclamation requiring all to keep the peace, and representatives of the lord of the manor, the auctioneers, and the town crier parade the market and fair ground. It is remarkable for the variety of sheep: Lincolns and Leicesters from the Wolds, Mashams from the Pennine dales, 'Jocks' from the moors, Cheviots from the Border, and cross-breds from everywhere. It is held at a time for a changing stock, when summer pasturage is over and the flocks are ready to be folded on the turnips. A great many rams are sold, but their fleeces are not dyed various colours as they used to be. A feature of the fair is the amount of cheap clothing sold to the farm men.

There are well-known racing stables in the surrounding country, for the town has long been a racing centre; sixteen times in thirty-five years the St Leger was won by horses from Malton. Drake, writing in 1736, was surprised at the amount of horse racing in the district, 'where scarce a village so mean but raises a bit of plate once a year for the purpose.'

Standing on the Pickering road are a lodge and three gateways, all that remains of a Jacobean mansion built by Ralph, Lord Eure, in 1600 on the site of a Norman castle. His estate came eventually to his two great-granddaughters who could not agree about shares, and after much negotiation the house was pulled down in 1674 and the materials divided between them. Through all these incidents of country life, the tradition of the road is strongest in Malton. It is on the site of the Roman camp, Derventio, which had six roads converging on it, so that the old spirit of the town is not entirely antagonistic to the great new highway.

Byland   Abbey

CHAPTER 21

THE HAMBLETON HILLS

THERE is a certain significance about country approaching hills. It gains a reflection of their importance, and the new land to which they lead. This is evident in the villages which nestle under the foot of the Hambleton Hills, for though they look over the gentle country of the Howardians, heather and bracken creep down towards them and the breath of the moor blows on them.

Kilburn with its mellow rural air expresses perfectly the mingled atmosphere of these villages. A little beck runs beside the road and is crossed by narrow bridges to reach the cottages which lie over it behind long gardens—a new-comer is not considered a real inhabitant until at some time or other he has slipped from one of these bridges into the beck. A few half-timbered cottages amongst the rest give it an old-world air. Piles of oak weathering in the open behind one of these tell of a flourishing local industry revived in this peaceful

village.   In his workshop here Mr Thompson and the joiners
he has trained make the seasoned oak into church and house
furniture which is becoming famous all over the country.
Some of the men are skilled carvers, turning out work which
competes with that of early church carvers.   You are reminded
of the group of craftsmen who in the fifteenth and sixteenth
centuries worked not very far away across the plain at Ripon
carving for the abbey churches at Ripon, Beverley, Easby
Jervaulx, and Bridlington, and for the smaller parish churches.
To-day the dignified work of the Kilburn craftsmen is found in
many churches and public buildings, and as the Ripon carvers
can be recognized by a particular pattern of a vine scroll, the
Kilburn craftsmen carve on all their work the figure of a mouse,
which signifies industry in quiet places.   It is probable that
in two or three hundred years collectors will be treasuring
pieces of Kilburn household furniture as now they treasure
the work of Sheraton or Hepplewhite.

The industry employs about thirty joiners, and gives to
the community that liveliness which was in all English villages
before the heart went out of them with the loss of their crafts.
Kilburn's feast and sports survive as an occasion in the year,
not as a pathetic relic.   The feast itself is set in the main
street, and for weeks beforehand the children save up for the
event.   On the last evening the custom is kept up of electing a
Lord Mayor and Lady Mayoress, who ride on a cart heading
a procession through the village.   The Lord Mayor visits
every house, criticizing something about it or the garden and
demanding a fine.   The Lady Mayoress, impersonated by a
man, is allowed to kiss every lady 'she' meets that night.

Kilburn has an unusual background in the figure of the
White Horse cut on the cliffs behind.   This can be picked out
for long distances across the plain, whether it is distinguishable
or not being a test of the clarity of the day.   It extends over
two acres, and we have seen twenty people standing together on
its eye.

The horse is not a relic of prehistoric times like some similar figures in the south. It was cut as recently as 1857 at the expense of a man named Thomas Taylor, who as a child had been a 'town lad' at Kilburn, that is an orphan apprenticed at the expense of the village. He was sent to a drysalter in London and eventually became a master. When he expressed a wish to do something for the village in appreciation of the help he had received, an old farmer suggested cutting the horse, and offered to give the land. Plans were made by the schoolmaster, the shape was cut, and everybody helped to pare the turf and ling and clear the space around. The horse was then whitewashed and there were great celebrations, two bullocks being roasted above it and a hundred and twelve gallons of beer drunk. At times since then the figure has almost faded from the hillside, but has always been restored, and recently a sum of money was raised, the interest to be used to cover it with lime at certain intervals, and to give it an annual grooming, that is weeding, at Kilburn feast time.

The road running out of Kilburn through Oldstead is a meandering lane between hedges, and for much of the year the rolling ground on either side is decked with flowers creeping to the dim woods above. It is a peaceful lane which seems to close the silence into itself. Suddenly round a bend it is spanned by an ancient gateway which makes a frame for the ruins of Byland Abbey beyond.

Byland is chiefly memorable for its lovely Early English west front, whose trefoil-headed doorway, tall lancets, and part of a circular window have an ethereal beauty. But some of Byland's fairest memories are of simple things which connect it with the countryside of to-day; brick fireplaces giving the interior a homely look; a suggestion of new glaze left on the green and yellow tile pavements by a shower of rain; the hillside seen through the nave windows like a blue amphitheatre as the smoke from the chimneys of Wass hangs over it; gnarled fruit-trees in the enclosure telling of the long period when the ruins were open to the road, and cottage gardens were made amongst them.

You think of how the monks came to this place after much wandering, moving first because of Scots invaders from Calder in Cumberland to Hood, and in a little while from there to a site near the present village of Old Byland—it was whilst they were here that they built the church at Scawton. The position proved impracticable because the bells clashed with those of Rievaulx Abbey across the river, and again they moved to build a church and cloister at a place called Stocking, where they stayed until they were given this site near Wass.

It is a pleasant thought that some of the joy at a rest from wandering went into the building of Byland Abbey of which, twenty years after they had moved into it, Abbot Philip wrote, 'and there, God willing, they shall prosperously remain for ever.' One wonders which would have surprised him most, to know that four hundred years later his monastery and all that it stood for would be ruthlessly swept away, or that in another four hundred years a generation would rise to lavish tender care on its ruins.

The country in which the abbey stands is like a garden, with primroses, violets, and bluebells lining the roadsides and climbing with tall stalks up to the hedgerows. The village children pick tight little bunches of them, and yet so many are there that they do not seem to have robbed the countryside. The roads which go up the Hambletons are called 'banks,' and in spring these are shady bowers with wood anemones spangling the sides and pale forget-me-nots making misty carpets in the woods which overhang them.

Above the woodland the purple flowers of the bell heather are a vivid summer covering, and are scarcely brown before the ling itself comes into bloom. Patches of bilberries hung with their deep red flowers line the hollows and glow amongst the heather, and here and there the flatness is broken by clumps of wild raspberry bushes, or in spring plantations of larch-trees add their fresh bright green.

At intervals on the flat summit there will be a square of cultivated land with a farmhouse in the middle, and only a wire

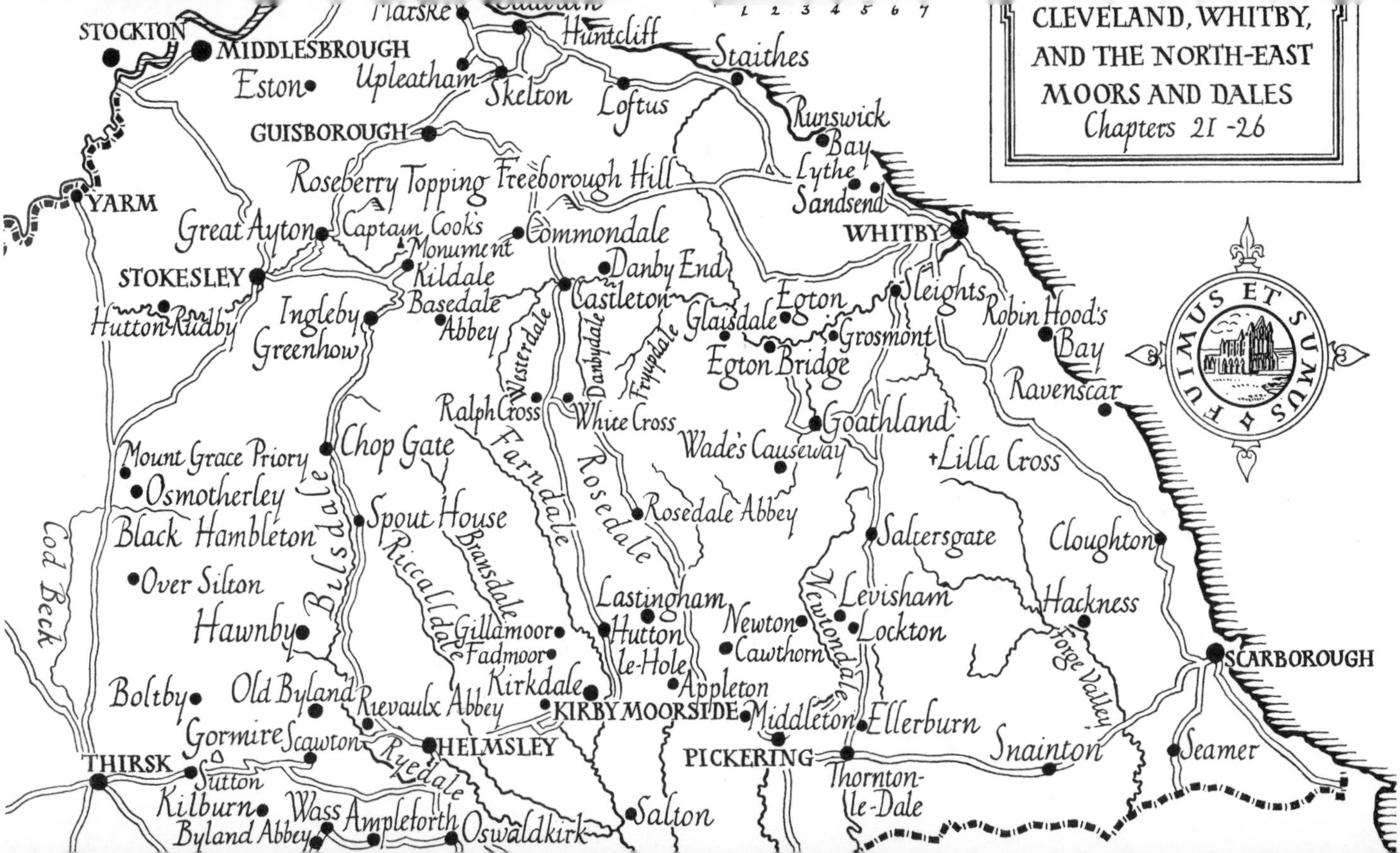

CLEVELAND, WHITBY, AND THE NORTH-EAST MOORS AND DALES
Chapters 21–26

ET SUMUS FUIMUS

1 2 3 4 5 6 7

STOCKTON
MIDDLESBROUGH
YARM
Eston
Marske
Upleatham
Skelton
Loftus
Staithes
Runswick Bay
Hunt Cliff
GUISBOROUGH
Roseberry Topping
Freeborough Hill
Captain Cooks Monument
Great Ayton
Kildale
Ingleby Greenhow
Commondale
Danby Ends
Castleton
Kildale
Basedale Abbey
STOKESLEY
Hutton Rudby
Mount Grace Priory
Osmotherley
Black Hambleton
Over Silton
Hawnby
Boltby
Gormire
Sutton
Kilburn
Wass
Byland Abbey
Oldstead
Ampleforth
Oswaldkirk
THIRSK
Cod Beck
Bilsdale
Chop Gate
Spout House
Bransdale
Riccaldale
Ryedale
HELMSLEY
Rievaulx Abbey
Old Byland
Cawton
Gillamoor
Fadmoor
Kirkdale
KIRBY MOORSIDE
Appleton le-Moors
Lastingham
Hutton le-Hole
Newton
Cawthorne
Middleton
Salton
PICKERING
Thornton-le-Dale
Ellerburn
Levisham
Lockton
Newtondale
Saltersgate
Snainton
Forge Valley
Hackness
Cloughton
SCARBOROUGH
Seamer
Lilla Cross
Goathland
Wade's Causeway
Rosedale Abbey
Rosedale
Farndale
Westerdale
Danby
White Cross
Ralph Cross
Tripdale
Egton
Grosmont
Egton Bridge
Glaisdale
Leaths
Robin Hoods Bay
Ravenscar
WHITBY
Sandsend
Lythe

fence enclosing it from the moor.   Deep bracken-lined ravines run up into the heather, or a village creeps up from the end of a valley.   It is a country of surprises, of breath-taking glimpses, such as Byland seen from Wass Bank or Rievaulx in its wooded setting from across the bridge as you approach it from Scawton Bank.

Sudden dips in the moor open out extensive views, now of the humpy hills of Ryedale running down to Helmsley and up to more brown moors, now across to where the Howardian country rises to the Wolds, now from Sutton Bank over the familiar expanse of the Plain of York.   In two or three miles on this moorland plateau an enormous circle of Yorkshire can be seen.

Immediately below Sutton Bank, cradled in the smaller hills, which seem like pieces fallen away from the main ridge, lies the lake of Gormire, looking like a mirage in the otherwise dry country.   Probably because there is no apparent outlet for the water, legends have grown about this lake.   It is said to have no bottom, to cover a buried city like Semerwater, and

> When Gormire riggs shall be covered with hay
> The White Mare of Whitestone Cliff will bear it away

refers to a legend of a white mare jumping with its rider over the cliff to its death.

Sutton Bank, the main road to Helmsley from Thirsk, climbs the steep cliff with a sharp hairpin bend half-way up. Before its surface was improved people used to gather at the top on Sunday afternoons to watch cars attempting the hill. Modern cars take it easily enough, but the habit remains, and now the motorists themselves stop and watch the gliders soaring over the hill or sailing above the plain.   The Yorkshire Gliding Club has its headquarters on Roulston Scar at the southern end of the cliff, and on a summer evening, with a good breeze blowing, there will be as many as eight or nine gliders out at the same time, looking like great birds as the sun catches their shining wings.   In these troubled days when we have come to associate flying so much with warlike purposes it is soothing to sit here on the heather, and watch the 'air yachts' sailing above, knowing that they are being flown purely for the love of sport.

As the Hambleton Hills run northwards they become fiercer and rise into separate peaks of over twelve hundred feet. Three hundred years ago the name of one of these, Black Hambleton, was applied to the whole range, and it is still used for much of the northern area. An old drovers' road to Yarm goes along the top of the ridge, and horse-races were once held here.

Time seems to have been arrested where Helmsley, the focus of this moorland region, stands with its ruined castle above the river Rye. The town lying round a cobbled market square with a cross in the centre, and ancient cottages, one half-timbered, rubbing shoulders with more ambitious buildings, is like a picture painted a century ago. It was an important centre of the hand-loom weaving industry. Two hundred years ago most of the people were employed weaving linen and linsey-woolsey, which was a mixture of linen and wool. An old poem says:

> My stockings did my mother's taste display,
> Black and white wool she mix'd to make them grey.
> My shirt, of hemp, so coarse, but now I fear,
> Many though poor would be ashamed to wear,
> Although the richest woman in our town
> Would go to church in a linsey-woolsey gown.

The raw hemp and flax came by pack-horse from Hull, the industry growing up here because of the natural bleaching fields. Old people remember their grandparents working in the bleaching fields, now called Beckdale. The weavers wore leather breeches, white aprons, and paper caps, and are said to have been merry men, singing at their work and fond of amusement. The market-place at Helmsley seems to wait expectantly for the sound of their looms or for the voice of one of the villagers reading the weekly newspaper aloud as the rest gather round him in the square.

Ryedale, the only long valley cutting up into the Hambleton Hills, starts as a dale at Helmsley, and almost immediately makes a setting for Rievaulx Abbey under wooded hillsides which end in purple moors. The valley is narrow; three times as the great monastery grew the monks moved the channel of the river further west to make room for it; and because of the lie of the land they built their church due north and south.

Rievaulx Abbey

Let us catch our first glimpse of Rievaulx from the terrace which runs as a long lawn on the hill above. This, another ambitious eighteenth-century idea, was made by Thomas Duncombe as part of the grounds of Duncombe Park, which his grandfather had built in 1718 after designs by Vanbrugh. There are temples at either end, one with a ceiling painted by an Italian artist. At intervals along it openings are cut to give views of the abbey through the trees which cover the hillside. It seems to echo to the voices of men in light tailcoats and women in crinolines, carrying little parasols and peeping through the openings to admire the views. We see the same majestic ruins, but they are better cared for now, and trim lawns surround them instead of the hillocks covered with wild roses and shrubs which Dorothy Wordsworth admired.

Rievaulx Abbey was founded in 1131 by Walter Espec, and became the mother of many Cistercian abbeys, of which Melrose is the most famous. The church was begun at the end of the twelfth century, when the monastic buildings were complete, and its nave is the oldest large Cistercian nave of which anything is left standing in England or France. The Norman builders used yellow stone from a quarry to the north, but the Early English builders used a much whiter stone from a quarry on the south, and the two colours mark their periods in the ruins.

There is nothing now to suggest the 'place of terrible loneliness and horror' which the monks are said to have found, but it remains a hidden corner. The abbey resembles Tintern, but where Tintern seems displayed for attention, Rievaulx in its hollow has to be sought. The village itself is deeply rural; a few thatched cottages cluster along the lanes near the abbey, and a miller grinds the local farmers' corn in a mill built from the abbey stones. With only this tiny village to plunder its walls for stone, enough is left to show the wealth and magnificence of this monastery, which by the middle of the twelfth century had one hundred and forty monks and six hundred lay brothers, 'so that the church swarmed with them, like a hive of bees.'

Children's voices sounding in the playground of the school below and the clink of the mason's hammer as he works on repairs give for a moment the illusion that time has swung back and the abbey church is rising here amid the life of the monastery. But the sight of its pulsing life is not for us who only come as pilgrims to its ruins. Thousands of people visit Rievaulx every year, coming on foot, in cars, or in buses from the coast. The processions pass into the grounds, each person reacting differently to the first glimpse. About an hour later they drift back, some discussing the architecture, some the general beauty, some the wealth of the monks, but the majority talking of outside things, letting the picture slide gently from their minds to be for ever vague.   Then the buses and cars grind up the hill to give place to others.

From now onwards Ryedale is a tempestuous valley tossed into rounded hills covered with corn and patches of woodland, and owing their origin to the river Rye and its tributaries wearing away the soft clay from the limestone and sandstone. The village of Hawnby straggles up the side of one of the hillocks, and roads start from it over the Hambleton Hills. These are all fine moorland ways following old tracks.   The most northerly runs beside the Rye almost to its source, turning under the shadow of Black Hambleton, where it joins the old drovers' road.

Presently along the road we come to Chequers Inn.   The little house stands in the midst of heather, a rough stone building with a red-tiled roof and the famous inn sign: 'Be not in haste, Step in and taste, Ale to-morrow for nothing.' Geraniums nod cheerfully through the window, and a turf fire burns in the clean, cosy kitchen.   The inn has been in the same family for over two hundred years, and as far as is known the fire has never gone out during that time.   It is one of several turf fires in this district with similar records, the custom having started in the first place for convenience before the days of matches, so that the fire had not to be lit each morning.   The last thing at night a piece of turf is placed on the ashes, and in the morning this is poked up into a flame.

Turf requires a particular kind of fireplace.   Being only the top layer of the moor pared off and dried, it is not so solid as peat and would burn away quickly in a modern range, and the hearth is merely a wide open space with a grate slightly raised from the ground.   The oven is heated by pushing the hot turf into a space under it, and kettles and pans hang from hooks over it.   The proper way to cook turf cakes, which are a kind of scone very popular in this district, is in a large covered pan standing on the fire and with red-hot turf piled over it, but this method has almost died out.

Sitting round the fire at Chequers with the two old ladies who live there, we reflected how two succeeding lives as long as theirs had begun and ended in the life of this fire, and we wondered whether the end of a fourth life would see the fire still burning and the inn unchanged and unspoilt.

This is the last northern spur of the Hambletons. The village of Osmotherley nestles on their western slopes, cradled in bracken- and heather-clad hills. It is a rural place, but there is a faint atmosphere of industrialism in its wide street, a lingering memory of the time when there were alum works and ironstone mines among these hills as there are still in some parts of Cleveland.

As we arrived, a man calling out in a jargon strange to the district that he had herrings for sale came up the street with a horse and cart. He told us that he lived at Stockton, and that trade was not what it used to be, though even as he talked people came running out with dishes and plates and soon the last herring had gone. He gave us a sudden realization of the nearness of the river Tees and the towns beyond, and of the sea. Then the farming life of the community effaced the thought of them, as he explained that his horse had shed a shoe in the road and the blacksmith was away helping with haymaking. 'But I 'll manage somehow,' the fishman said. 'I 'll finnd a nail and fix it up mesel' somehow,' and he went whistling away over the green, passing a curious stone table on which butter used to be placed at the markets.

As Byland Abbey might be called the beginning of the Hambletons, so Mount Grace Priory might be called the end. The Carthusian Order with its rule of continual silence has a peculiar attraction, and this is the only place in England where the plan of its monasteries can be studied in existing remains. The cells grouped round the cloister were individual houses, each with its own strip of garden and hatch for food, and arranged for a hermit's existence in a large community.

Bilsdale, which branches from Ryedale, near Hawnby, to follow the river Seph, is a large, wide dale, shut in by high hills, yet carrying the main road from Helmsley to Stokesley and Guisborough. A few cottages and houses cluster together to form the little villages of Fangdale Beck and Chop Gate—at Fangdale the two parts divided by the beck are known as the Town and the Street—but for the most part the hillsides are dotted with scattered farmhouses. Many of these nestle above the becks which run down from the moors, and in the evening light seem to rest in a fold of slate-coloured hills. They are stone houses with red-tiled roofs and square chimneys, and they make, with the small round stacks and groups of leaning pine-trees, a picture on the hillside. A flight of outside steps leads to a loft, against which a heap of manure will be piled, and hens, geese, and pigs wander round the stone flags in front. The fields which surround them are half grass, half ploughland, and a grassy hillock will be topped with a level field of corn. They have a look of a self-contained existence.

The dale keeps its own vigorous life, supporting its feasts and sports, and maintaining its hunt of which there are records from as early as 1668. It was a belief in Bilsdale that Peg Humphrey, a witch always known as 'Owd Peg,' used to turn herself into a hare and give the Bilsdale hounds many a good run. There are pictures in the new inn at Spout House of Bobby Dawson, a famous huntsman, drinking after a meet with his followers in the thatched building which used to be the inn.

This old building at Spout House is one of those perfect relics of the past that almost seem unreal. Its walls and its plan show more clearly than any description could do the life which was lived in these dales up to half a century ago. It is a long, low building with Tudor windows along the front and on the gable, and windows which are little more than peepholes under the thatch. These tiny windows start at the floor of the upper rooms, which are open to the roof, so that in them you see the beams and cross-pieces on to which the first layer of straw is tied. No candles or lamps were allowed to be taken upstairs for fear of fire. One of the rooms has a bed fixed into the wall, a common feature of the dale cottages. Though large families were brought up in the inn, this room and another were always given up to the shooters in the autumn.

The building is used as an outhouse now, but it is easy to imagine the cosy atmosphere of its large main room and the groups sitting round the fireplace, for here again the turf fire is kept continually burning, and much of the cooking for the new inn is done on it. Times have changed, but the topics of the farmers who gather at Spout House now are still corn and cows and markets, and life and death in the dale.

Hutton-le-Hole

CHAPTER 22

THE NORTH-EAST DALES

DARK moors predominate in this district of which the old name was Blackamore, immense heather-clad stretches which seem to roll on everlastingly. Green hollows sink into them, now and again a farmhouse shows on a high slope, and for a moment where the moor dips a little there will be a quick glimpse of a cultivated valley. A summer haze turns the valleys into blue mysterious country, and always there is something remote and detached about them, like the sudden snatches of scenery which you catch from a railway train or an aeroplane, and scarcely realize as places where people live and work and sleep. The road sweeps you on over the moor, and they are out of sight. When at last you start out specially to explore them it is with the feeling of venturing into unknown and almost sacred country.

One reason for the seeming isolation of the north-east dales is that these glimpses from the moor are the only distant views of them. They do not open gradually to the lowlands as

RICCALLDALE

do the larger Pennine dales, but instead a long wooded hill ridge separates them from the Vale of Pickering. The rivers cut their ways through this in narrow gorges, but the roads which lead to them must climb over it. These roads are many of them tarred now, but when they were yellow tracks they must have added to the romance of journeys to the hidden dales. It is usual to find the larger villages on the high roads rather than in the valleys: Carlton, Fadmoor, Gillamoor, Appleton-le-Moors, breezy open places with clean streets and an attractive bareness.

Each dale has its own distinction, but is an essential part in the pattern of the whole, like a section in a piece of embroidery, and has much in common with the rest. Unlike the Pennine dales, which were there before the Ice Age, these were cut by the action of glaciers and are of a less rugged character. Bounded as they are by heather- and bracken-covered moors, there is more colour in the valleys themselves, for they have arable land, and corn and turnip fields make a patchwork with the meadows and pastures. The pastures are round the becks and rivers in the bottoms, and the cultivated land stretches up the hillsides, presenting what is always a startling sight, a field of corn close to the heather moor. The fields are lined with hedges instead of walls, and though the houses themselves are built of stone the roofs are of red pantiles or occasionally thatch.

The high entrances over the nabs give sudden vivid pictures, as where tall pine-trees silhouetted against the sky make a gateway through which you see the whole of the lonely, intense valley of Riccalldale, where the houses lie almost on the line of the heather and seem to be beckoning the cultivated land further.

Near the head of the dale the road goes over the moor, and a row of boundary stones parallel with it marks an old track now lost in the heather. The present road crosses over to the head of Bransdale, the next valley, where a shooting-lodge, a little church, and a handful of houses form the hamlet of East

Moors.   Then along a ridge above the valley and through the upland village of Fadmoor, the tour of these two valleys ends at the exquisite church of Kirkdale by the beck.

Kirkdale church is famous for its Saxon sundial with an inscription declaring that Orm, the son of Gamal, bought and rebuilt the church in the days of King Edward and Earl Tosti. Prehistoric bones of men and animals have been discovered in a cave near the church.   The continuity of life is strongly felt in this sunken valley from the time of the first men in the cave to the families from the moorland and lowland farms whose graves are in the shady churchyard.   So strong has been the influence of the church, that the name of the valley changes here from Bransdale to Kirkdale, and the beck, not to be outdone, changes its name from Hodge Beck to the river Dove.

In these dales you meet again with the tradition of Hob, that elf or hobgoblin originating from dwarfish races who was believed to help or hinder farmers.   Every valley had its particular one; there were Hodge Hob of Bransdale, taking his name from the beck, Hob of Chop Gate, and Cross Hob of Lastingham.   The most famous was Hob o' the Hurst of Farndale, of whom the tale is told of his attaching himself to a certain farm and proving so mischievous in spoiling the butter and upsetting all the work that the farmer decided to move.   As he was driving with his belongings down the road a man passing by called out: 'Ah see thoo 's flittin'?' and a voice from the churn answered: 'Ay, we 'se flittin',' and the disheartened farmer turned his cart round, saying: 'Eh, way— if thoo 's theer we may as 'well gan yam ageean.'

Hob of Lower Farndale was a kind, helpful elf who was said to use white magic.   He was always known as Elphi.

> Elphi, little chap,
> Thoff he wer so small,
> Wer big wi' deeds o' kindness;
> Drink tiv him yan an all.'

is the end of a poem written about him in 1699, and the charm of the little verse fits the valley of Farndale with its fairy-like beauty.

The tradition of Hob survives in the name Obtrusch Roque, given to a Bronze Age barrow on the moor between Bransdale and Farndale. Roque comes from the Old Norse *hraukr*, meaning rook, a pile or heap. There are hundreds of such barrows on the moors, and many are given the name of howes. This particular one with its distinctive name is supposed to be haunted by goblins.

Farndale is the largest and most populous of these dales. The same patterned valley creeps up to the moors, but it has a wider cultivation, and a road runs along both sides of it. All the qualities of the other dales seem concentrated here, so that knowing it you know something of the rest. From near Gillamoor one of those first surprising views beckons you to a dale with a self-contained life.

Farndale is familiar to many people because of its wild daffodils. Annual pilgrimages are made to see these growing for eight miles along the sides of the river Dove, their fresh delicate flowers swaying in the breeze, bringing the gaiety of spring and the promise of summer to the valley. Later the hedges are thick with wild roses; cranesbills and harebells line the banks; the meadows are white with marguerites; and fox-gloves raise their tall spikes along the beck sides and the edges of the pastures. It is sad to reflect that much of this will go if the scheme for using the valley as a reservoir for Hull materializes.

The pendulum swings back as you enter this flowery dale, and find a simple life close to the land. Some of its old-worldness is intentional, as in the case of the thatched houses which would not have survived but for the lord of the manor, Lord Feversham. There are more straw-thatched houses in Farndale than in any other part of Yorkshire, and as well as adding their picturesqueness to the scene they have helped to retain the original architecture of the houses with their long, steep roofs and small single-pane or dormer windows in the thatch.

A thatcher is kept busy on the estate for most of the year, and is only occasionally able to spare time to do a roof in another part of the county. We found him working on a thatch which had not been touched for fifteen years, though the average life of one is ten. He was using straw from wheat grown at Gillamoor. The pile which lay ready for the day's work had been soaked overnight in water, for a thatch made with dry straw would not turn the rain. He worked from the bottom upwards, 'stobbing' the bundles of straw closely into the old thatch, moving his ladder as he went. When he reached the top he took the blade of a scythe and, working downwards now, cut the straw into a smooth hard surface. As this was merely a new layer going on to the top of the old one, there was no tying to be done—only the first layer of a good straw thatch need be fastened to the roof beams. The line of the fresh yellow straw shows clearly for a year before it darkens to the colour of stone.

In an upper room of an eighteenth-century cottage higher up the dale we saw the ropes with which the first layer of thatch was tied to the beams. In a smaller cottage lower down, plaited straw had been used for this instead of ropes. This last cottage nearly approaches a 'cruck' building, for the gable beams rest on a very low house wall. The beams are crossed at the top and fastened with two wooden pegs, and the top balk rests on the cross. The old man who lives there is very proud of the thatch. 'Isn't it wonderful, isn't it?' he repeated as he gazed at it. 'And feel at them beams, hundreds of years old, and still good and sound.'

The rest of the cottage is in keeping with the thatch. The stone floor in the kitchen is scoured in a pattern round the edge, and a cupboard-bed occupies a recess along the greater part of one wall. Its occupant can pull the doors to and be completely hidden, but has no light and little air. These cupboard-beds were a common feature of dale cottages, and were generally used for the 'bairns,' several of whom could be dumped into them and shut away out of sight.

The garden was a delightful jumble of cottage flowers, lilies, sweet williams, stocks, dahlias, growing amongst patches of potatoes, rows of peas and scarlet runners, and clumps of gooseberry and currant bushes. There was no room for weeds, but the old man lets the golden feather grow because he regards it as a medicine. He was spending most of his time that summer sawing and breaking up an oak-tree which had fallen. He took the logs to burn in his cottage, but collected the small bits into 'pokes' (bags), and sold them for kindling. He had found a wood pigeon's nest among the branches, and a bat's nest in the hollow trunk.

Now where a track goes to Ingleby Greenhow the tossed hillsides show where they have been worked for jet. In spite of their thick covering of bracken the tippings give an un-natural surface to the hill. Within recent years bracken has taken a strong hold on these eastern moors, in many places crowding out the heather before it recovers from its periodical burning. Their auburn leaves give a rich effect through the autumn and winter, but there is no feed in bracken, and experiments are being made to weaken it by continual cutting and crushing.

The farmhouses spread almost to the head of the valley, but all have arable land. In a single farmyard here you may see hay, corn, bracken, and turf stacks, and their variety gives a look of plenty to the highest houses. Above the last farm we met a man bringing down a load of dried turf from the moors on a sledge. Turf is still the chief fuel here where it is so easily reached, and many of the farmhouses burn no coal at all. The turf, which consists of peat, soil, roots, ling and moss— the top layer of the moor—dries quicker than the solid peat cut on the Pennines, but the method is much the same. The pieces are tilted up against each other, then built into small stacks, called rooks, on the moors, and finally brought down to be stacked in the farmyard. Some farms will have two or three stacks. 'They cost us nowt but wark,' a farmer said, 'but theer's plenty of 't to turf getting.'

The corn and roots are grown for the farmer's own use, and are not often sold.   A corn mill is still working in the valley, but many of the farms have their own small grinding machines. A threshing machine now visits most farms, but one on the east side still uses a horse threshing machine.   Close to the roadside you may see the two horses harnessed to wooden beams, walking round in a circle to drive the mill inside the barn.   It is a last sign of this hidden dale running itself without much help from outside, as country districts used to do.

A road out of Farndale leads to the village of Hutton-le-Hole which occupies almost the whole of a small dale.   You drop suddenly from the dark open moorland into the green sheltered hollow, and if you are not expecting anything out of the ordinary the sight is amazing.   A beck runs down the middle of it, and the roads which go on either side cross and recross it by water splashes.   There are few trees, but it seems cosy in contrast with its dark background.   The houses perch above the beck beyond stretches of grass, and between them is the new village hall, made of stone from the disused iron smelt mills in the next valley of Rosedale, and roofed with local pantiles.   It is a modern building which enhances instead of spoils the charm of the village.

As you watch, a man on horseback stops to let his horse drink; an old man comes along a path from the woods on the ridge carrying a bundle of faggots on his back; a car splashes through the water; a farmer wades across in rubber boots; and a group of school-children clatter over the foot-bridge.   Sheep graze on the green, and presently a girl riding a pony drives them out of the village, and you see her following a long grey line of them up the moor.

A road leads over rolling country to Rosedale, passing near the tall chimney which took the fumes from the smelt mill. It seems ironical that Rosedale with its rural name should have been the most exploited for iron of all these dales.   The industry went on here for about sixty-five years and ended in 1925.   There are still signs of it in the dull rows of houses built for its workers, the tippings on the hills, and the track which carried the railway round the basin-like valley to collect the ore, though the country is gradually healing itself, going back in spirit to the time when its priory for nuns stood on the banks of the river Seven.

The iron was taken up the hillside, under the roadway from Hutton-le-Hole to Cleveland, and thence by overhead trolleys to Ingleby Greenhow.   This part of the moor is called Blakey Ridge, and a humble little inn, the Lion, seems to dream of the days of drovers and iron workers, and turn unseeing eyes on the traffic of to-day.

There is a tang of the sea on this moorland which stretches almost to the coast — salt and heather and peat mingling in the bracing air which seems to shorten the miles.   It is here that you find the many crosses which are scattered over the moors, and whose chief use seems to have been to mark roads many of which have vanished.   White Cross, or Fat Betty, as it is called locally, lies on the road from Rosedale. It is the stump and head of a cross which shows evidence of having been more elaborate in design than most.   Ralph Cross, which stands in sight of it on the Castleton road, is a tall plain pillar marking the junction of a road from Westerdale. It has a hollow in the top into which passers-by used to put money to help poor travellers.   The crosses tell, as do the stones in Riccalldale, of old forgotten journeys.

It is of old events that you think as you come to the village of Lastingham, cradled in the country between Hutton-le-Hole and Rosedale.   A Saxon monastery was founded here at the request of King Æthelwald by Bishop Cedd, and was probably destroyed by the Danes in the ninth century.   It lay in ruins until 1078 when Stephen and some monks from Whitby began to rebuild it, but eight years later they moved to York, and their church became a parish church.   Part of the chancel and crossing and the whole of the crypt belong to that second building.   The crypt is a miniature church in itself with nave, aisles, and apse, and it echoes the stirring ecclesiastical history of this hidden corner which might easily have come to shelter a great monastery.

Now over the ridge through Appleton-le-Moors, where the plain houses have a windswept air, and geese walk sedately across the clean streets, we come down to Kirby Moorside.

Kirby Moorside, between Helmsley and Pickering, is one of the three market towns which are centres for the dales. It had once two castles, but only a fragment of wall remains from that which belonged to the Nevilles. The plan of the town is different from that of Helmsley. It lies up a steep main road lined with Georgian houses, a few of which are fine examples of the period. The tolbooth, said to have been built with the stones of one of the castles, stands on one side, hiding the market cross. Its two large inns and its memories of historic families tell of an ample life which has not altogether vanished.

It is a change to turn from the old streets to the factory where most of the gliders used in England are made. Long trailers wait outside to carry the gliders to their destination, and inside there is the air of importance of a new industry with its quickly changing designs and fresh ideas and improvements. Large wings hang from the roof, the shining bodies are raised on tables, and there is the odour of newly cut wood and varnish. There is much of the craftsman's art about the making of gliders. No nails are used; the thickness of the sides is made by sticking many layers of plywood together, the smaller joints are glued, and the larger ones sewn with a machine.

You step from its essentially modern atmosphere into another building where a blacksmith forges hand-made hinges, gates, and ornamental iron work, and is proud of his job as the old craftsmen were. Kirby Moorside gives these quick changes. Walking up the main street we saw clouds of smoke pouring out of the open doorway of a barn. It came from a large turf fire built up in the middle of the earth floor, and having no outlet for the smoke but the door. Beside it a wheelwright was making preparations to turn a wheel. Only a few blazes escaped through the black mass of turf, but he told us that it would burn up very quickly and that nothing made so intense a heat for welding as turf does. We could not stay to watch the wheelwright finish his job, but when we passed an hour or two later a glowing heap of fire and a newly shaped wheel told that the work had gone well.

Pickering

CHAPTER 23

ROUND PICKERING

PICKERING town caught in a gleam of winter sunshine, its mellowed red roofs rising up to the light stone spire of the church, with a glimpse of the castle behind, leaves an unforgettable memory. In summer it is more hidden among trees, but in winter the leafless branches, lovely in themselves, make clear-cut patterns against a brilliant background.

The town itself is as interesting as that distant prospect suggests. It runs along four roads, lined with trees, and with a market square in the centre. The houses are built of yellow limestone which the inhabitants could take free from the nearby quarries, and the pantiled roofs are toned with age. The very beautiful old roofs here and in the surrounding district are due to the fact that the making of pantiles was one of the trades of

Pickering. The industry declined when slate was introduced, and the formula for making the tiles died with the owners. One of the unfortunate features about nineteenth - century building was the popularity of blue slate with its cold, hard tones. Present-day builders have realized the mistake and are using tiles again in this district where clay is obtainable, but the industry has not actually returned to Pickering.

Tourists are attracted to the town largely because of the magnificent fifteenth-century frescoes in the church. These are some of the finest in England and show what is always startling to the twentieth-century mind, the warmth and colour which once filled our churches. There are the familiar subjects, the most striking being an enormous figure of St Christopher, placed, as is usual, opposite the door.

The castle stands on the hill behind, reached by a wide, quiet road whose houses seem to belong to the past as much as does the ruin. The curtain wall with three towers and the shell keep, which were added in the early fourteenth century to the castle founded by William the Conqueror, remain, but Pickering Castle's charm is in its position, looking on one side on to the roofs of the town and on the other across rolling country to a horizon of moorland.

In the midst of this country, almost due north from Pickering, is the Roman camp of Cawthorn, which was an important station on the Roman road from Malton over Wheeldale Moor to Goldsborough near the coast. Deep ditches surrounded the four camps, one of which has a raised platform thought to have been the tribunal from which the commanding officers inspected and addressed the troops, but now bracken and heather cover their faint shapes on the hill, and the silence is broken only by the calls of sheep and birds.

Old records mention a chapel of St Nicholas in Pickering, but all Camden could say of it in the sixteenth century was, 'It is gone.' It was believed that this chapel was in the castle, but in 1938 the foundations of it were discovered near the pond at Keld Head at the west end of the town. Keld Head is an ordinary-looking pond which appears to do nothing more spectacular than to give birth to the sluggish river Costa, but actually the water comes from numbers of springs, one of which pumps up five hundred gallons a minute, and the water for the town is supplied from it.

The marshy land through which the Costa flows on the south is now used for growing watercress. Large channels are cut in it and the cress planted along the sides at different stages through the season. Its cultivation gives work to a number of men, and girls are employed to tie up the bunches. Farther along the water is drained into tanks for a fish hatchery. The river Costa itself is one of the best streams in Yorkshire for trout fishing.

This low-lying land, which we now know as the Vale of Pickering, was once a lake draining Blackamore on the north and the Howardian Hills and the Wolds on the south, and having an outlet to the sea near Filey. Lake dwellers lived on it and succeeding races of people settled on the northern margin, the most powerful being the swordsmen of the Iron Age, who drove the early tribes to the moors. Traces of their dwellings, the tracks which led to them, and many flint and bronze implements have been found. The lake gradually settled into a morass, and was eventually drained to become good agricultural land, watered by the Derwent, the Rye, the Dove, and the Costa.

To understand Pickering and its life you must realize the extent of this vale to which the town gives its name and of which it remains a centre. It is sparsely inhabited in the flat area in the bottom, being chiefly divided into large farms and a few sleepy villages. The names of Marishes, Yedingham, whose priory used to be called Little Maries, and Kirby Misperton, whose old name was Kirkby Overker, tell of land reclaimed by drainage. Here and there a village such as Great Edstone stands on an isolated hill which overlooks the whole vale. The church here possesses a Saxon sundial with a word missing, as though someone had called the carver away and he had never returned. But for the most part the older and larger villages lie on the lower slopes of the hills which enclose the vale.

These places stand in a dignified line on either side of Pickering, one of the loveliest of them being Thornton-le-Dale. Some years ago this village won a prize for being the most beautiful in Yorkshire, and it has been a little self-conscious ever since, but it remains very beautiful with becks running beside the streets and bridges crossing them to the houses. An old thatched cottage, which has recently been restored, makes one think of the straw hat maker who in 1837 had a thatched shop where the villagers bought their best bonnets. From here eastwards the connection with the sea is felt. It does not sound fantastic to hear of the three thousand red and white herrings which the abbot of Whitby was required to give annually to St Leonard's Hospital, York, being handed over at the four cross-roads where the market cross now stands.

Wool, hemp, and linen were all woven in the district, and as late as 1830 there would be forty webs stretched in the fields round the bleaching mill at Ellerburn. Now as you stand in the quiet corner by the hidden little Norman church at Ellerburn, the only sounds come from the ducks startled at the sight of a stranger. Numerous tiny dales open out here like the teeth of a comb as the moors lower slightly towards the coast.

The village has had its characters. Old Willie Ecclesfield who died in 1872 used to play the piccolo in the church band, and when it was proposed to buy an organ, Willie's one thought was, 'Will she gang to ma fluett?' For one or two Sundays after it was installed he piped in with his flute, until the rector remonstrated with him, and Willie never came to church again.

A character in our own time was Jimmy Green, the gamekeeper, who died in 1937. Many visitors in the district would not have thought a holiday complete without a visit to Jimmy Green; naturalists and archaeologists sought him out because of his finds in fields and woods and his enthusiasm over them. When he heard that we were interested in collecting skulls on the moors, he raided his gamekeeper's larder for us, and a week or two later a gruesome parcel of skulls arrived by post.

Remembering all these places let us take another road out of Pickering, and revive our memory of the dales, which have had as strong an influence as these on the town's life, and whose children to-day mix with the children of the plain in its progressive grammar school. The road goes through the wind-swept upland village of Newton to Stape, where there are two farmhouses, one of which used to be an inn. They have a band at Stape collected from the farmers round, and the players practise in a small empty room which is not heated in the winter. A visitor, asking one of their wives if they did not feel the cold, was answered, 'Nay, they warm thersels wi' blowin'.'

The hamlet seems an end, but the road climbs on past Manley Cross over the moors to Egton Bridge. A track turns from it to where a line of farms appears suddenly on the summit of the moor, their cultivated land so well won from the peaty ground that there are cornfields among it. Fenced off from the heather and with the flat open space all round them, these farms have the feeling of ranches.

The dales as well as the villages on the vale help to make up Pickering's life, and to keep its market busy. Market day is one of the best times to see the town, not so much for the market scene itself as for the traffic coming into it from all these parts; ancient traps threading a way through; a man selling baskets of mushrooms which he and his family have gathered in the fields; and perhaps among it all the bellman calling a proclamation through the streets.

Pickering of the nineteenth century was much more an obvious farming town itself. Shops and garages in the main street were then farmhouses with crofts stretching behind them to the crofts of farmhouses on a higher road. There were six corn mills where local corn was ground into brown flour, and a village bakehouse to which people took long brown loaves to be baked during the night in a round brick oven After bread, bacon and ham were the chief foods. Every cottager kept a pig, and cured the ham and bacon with salt in the old Yorkshire way. There are old people in Pickering who remember these times, but the life of which they tell seems far from the fast-moving life of to-day.

An old man and his son still make besoms from ling gathered on the moors, and there is a good local sale for these, the best kind of brooms for sweeping cobbles. At one time large numbers were sent all over the country, and they were always exchanged at the local shops for provisions. Their handles are made of ash or birch and the ling broom is bound on to them with strips of ash obtained by soaking the wood for days in water. When the besom-maker was young he went to Liverpool to show workpeople there how to make besoms. He stayed for a few months, and the employer was anxious to keep him. 'But I didn't like t' town,' he said, 'it were all houses and people.' To-day his son makes modern-shaped brushes with ling bristles.

The old man was one of a family of twelve for all of whom his mother knitted stockings, and made suits till they were fourteen. His father was a joiner whose gates and wheel-barrows were in great demand for their good work; gates which he made in 1860 are still in use. He chose his wood well, not, as the son said, picking up 't' fust piece he could lay hand on. Nowadays they wean't last five-and-twenty minutes.' He had often to wait twelve months for his money after de-livering his barrows, but he did not feel this hard, for grocers, shoemakers, and tailors were all paid annually. 'Nowadays,' said the old man, 'when yer send annybody to t' shop, before yer back 's turned, bill 's at hoose.'

But joinering, even by a master at his craft, did not bring in a fortune, and the children had to make their own way early. 'We couldn't all stop at home hodding out wer hands.' said the old man, 'so I saved a bit o' money, and went intu t' market. There were some geese left ovver, and I said: "I'll gi' thee so mich for t' lot." T' owner wouldn't listen to 't at fust, but he cam round a bit later, an' said: "Yer can 'ave 'em." I kept 'em

K

till t' next market-day and sold all t' lot for a profit. Next week I took t' money and went to York market, an' spent it all on geese. I didn't know 'ow to git 'em 'ome. I couldn't put 'em intiv a truck, they 'd 'a been all atop on each other and deed, so I walked 'em all through t' neet, an' kept sittin' down a bit when I were tired. When I got to Spitalbeck a man put his head out o' t' window and said: "Is thou t' man wi' t' geese?" "Aye," I says, "they 're mine." '"Od on a minute, an' I 'll come down," he said, an' I sold 'im a few tired yans fra t' tail end.' The old life of Pickering seemed to come back as the besom-maker talked, and we saw him arriving home with his geese, and the squire letting him put the birds in his croft until he sold them. No words were good enough for the squire.

An industry which flourished at this time and until the advent of motors was the selling of coach horses. These were mostly Cleveland bays, bred usually on the farms in the dales where dealers would go and buy the foals. Many of them were sold to the London General Omnibus Company, but the best went for state coaches. They were supplied regularly to the King of Italy and our own royal family. One of King Edward VII's coachmen was a native of Pickering.

The town also did a large trade in exporting bacon. One man used to salt over two hundred pigs a year, and send the cured hams to London and Edinburgh hotels. They were packed in hogsheads which had come to Pickering with refined moist sugar from Scotland. Salted pork was also sent to Whitby to supply whaling boats. As at Thornton-le-Dale, there is here a strong connection with the sea, either with Scarborough along the plain or with Whitby over the moors. Many of the large houses were occupied by retired sea captains or families connected with shipping.

We leave the town for the moorland road to Whitby, starting above the valley of Newtondale. A particular breed of hawks used to nest here, and by an ancient law the farmers were obliged to attend to them. The last nest was destroyed about the middle of the nineteenth century. On the left the villages of Lockton and Levisham face each other across a deep ravine. Levisham's old church stands at the bottom between them, but these Anglian and Danish settlements cherished for centuries a fierce antagonism, and even to-day have little combined life.

Above Saltersgate there is a sudden view of the valley of the Levisham Beck as it opens out into a round basin known as the Hole of Horcum, where the one or two farms seem shut away from the world. The road then drops to Saltersgate, whose name came from the salt which was taken inland along this way from the sea. The annual hound trials held here combine with the Goathland Hunt to keep alive some feeling of the forest of Pickering where boars were hunted up to the seventeenth century.

There is a suggestion of a hamlet at Saltersgate, where a turf fire burns continually at the Wagon and Horses Inn, and beehives stand in rows round the gardens and meadows. Then the road sweeps up to the moor again, giving a glimpse of the railway which was so marvelled at when it was made from Pickering to Whitby, and which we shall find again at Goathland. Small mounds on the horizon are burial howes, dating from 1500 to 800 B.C. The most famous is Lilla Howe, which is nine hundred and twenty feet above sea-level, and has a moorland cross, probably dating from the seventh century, on its summit. This is sometimes thought to have been erected in memory of Lilla, who died saving King Edwin's life; gold rings and ornaments have been found in the howe. It is situated on the old track from Whitby Abbey to Hackness.

The moor is unenclosed here, and sheep wander freely over it. These black-faced mountain sheep are remarkably clever at finding and remembering the moorland springs, to which they walk long distances in time of drought. In spring plovers haunt the strips of grass which the sheep nibble close at the edges of the road, standing at intervals along it as if they had been placed there as sentinels, and rarely moving for passing cars.

Suddenly there appears a distant view of Whitby town stretching along the cliffs, with the ruined abbey rising above it, and the sea beyond. A first view of the coast with its sudden sign of an end is always arresting, but to catch it across moors is perfection. Whitby, slung between the heather and the sea, is one of the most vivid pictures which Yorkshire gives.

Whitby

CHAPTER 24

WHITBY

WHITBY WEST CLIFF is like many another pleasant seaside resort with its open cliff-top, spa, and hotels showing the various styles of building from the time when it became a holiday resort in the early nineteenth century. The promenade ends where the monument to Captain Cook faces out to sea above the estuary of the river Esk.

From here you look down on to the Whitby which he knew, the old fishing and shipbuilding town. In all variations of weather or season or time of day this view of Whitby harbour is fascinating. It has an artistry of placing which has come naturally, and there is colour and contrast in the red roofs rising in jumbled rows up the cliff side towards the dark walls of the church of St Mary and the ruined abbey, and ending where the valley of the Esk runs. As time has mellowed the dipping roofs and worn the stones of church and abbey, so it has inscribed the history of Whitby in this

261

scene round the harbour. Here the broad outlines are displayed, but as you explore the narrow streets and alleys you pick up details which fill pages in that history.

To understand Whitby's story you must go back to the moors, turn the modern highways into rough tracks, wipe out the railways from Pickering and along the coast, and find, at the mouth of the Esk, a small village whose chief communication with the rest of the county was by sea.

It was by sea that St Hilda came from Hartlepool in 657 to be abbess of the Saxon monastery. She ruled here over men and women, making the abbey into a training school for saints and bishops and encouraging the vision of the cowherd Cædmon by bringing him into the monastery to put the sacred history into poetry. Kings sought her counsel, and it was said that 'all that knew her called her "mother" for her singular piety and grace.' It was while she was abbess that the Synod of Streonshalh, which decided on the Roman rather than the Celtic church ritual and date for Easter, was held. Legends grew up round St Hilda, of birds alighting to bow before her, and of the ammonites on the cliffs being snakes turned by her into stone.

Towards the end of the ninth century the Danes destroyed Hilda's abbey and, settling in the district, named the fosses, wykes, and scaurs, and villages such as Ugglebarnby, Aislaby, and Upsal. They changed the name Streonshalh to Witebi. It was two hundred years before Reinfrid founded another monastic building on the cliff, and twice the monks fled from this because of robbers and pirates. But the abbey grew to become a power in the district again, owning the port and market and the surrounding deer parks. Whitby as we know it was formed under its rule.

Probably no other ruin has so identified itself with the place in which it stands. You cannot imagine the cliff without its west front silhouetted boldly against the sky, the walls weathered and worn by salt and wind. It was all its life connected with the sea, and when it was dissolved the ship in which the bells

PLANTING THE PENNY HEDGE AT WHITBY

THE PLOUGH STOTS AT GOATHLAND [PAGE 276]

and the lead from the roof were being taken to London was wrecked and sunk outside the bar.

A memory of early days survives in the custom of planting the Horngarth or Penny Hedge. In the sixteenth century a romantic legend was attached to this ceremony. It said that in the twelfth century the lords of Sneaton and Fylingdales were hunting a boar in the woods, when a hermit opened the door of his cell to shelter the terrified animal. The two lords, in their anger, mortally wounded the hermit, and the Abbot of Whitby declared that they must be punished by death. But the dying hermit pleaded for them, and they were spared on condition that every year they made a fence down to the river, using a penny knife, and that the words: 'Out on you! Out on you!' should be called at them as they worked.

The real origin of the hedge-planting is much earlier, and probably dates from the time of the kings of Northumbria, under whom a condition of the tenure of certain land was to help to make the Horngarth or enclosure of the deer park. The service continued under the monks, and still remains in respect of one farm at Fylingdales, above Robin Hood's Bay, though now only a few feet of hurdle are built on the riverside.

The modern ceremony follows the legend, but in its simplicity catches the antiquity of the original custom. It takes place on the morning of Ascension Eve, before the holiday season begins. At nine o'clock on that day in 1938 we watched a few townspeople and those taking part come down the steps to the beach on the east side of the estuary. A man carried the stakes and branches with which Mr Isaac Hutton, who has performed the ceremony for fifty-one years, was to build the hedge. The stakes were hammered in, the cross pieces and branches interlaced, and a perfect hurdle six feet long rose before our eyes on the sandy beach. When it was finished, the bailiff of the manor blew a horn, and called the old invective 'Out upon you! Out upon you!' Then the procession turned away, the children ran down to the beach to take a closer look before they went back to school, and the staithe was deserted again.   A few hours later when the tide was high we saw the hedge just showing above the water, and again still standing firm when the tide had gone down.

From the beginning the monks at Whitby made use of the natural harbour formed by the river estuary, and by the time of the Dissolution they had developed a good shipbuilding trade.   From 1600 the industry increased rapidly and many shipyards were set up.   The harbour was improved in 1730, four years later the first dry dock was built, and by the middle of the nineteenth century Whitby was the busiest port between the Tees and the Humber.   Sailing ships were built on the west side of the river and fishing boats on the east.

In those days the ships' masts in the estuary were said to be like trees in a forest, the town echoed with the clang of caulking hammers, and there was incessant activity.   A launch was a great event.   The people would stand on the banks and cheer and sing as the ship took the water, small ones being floated across the river and large ones down it.   Many of the boats in which Captain Cook sailed were made at Whitby; and the French and American wars brought much trade.

There were also industries connected with shipbuilding, and of these the principal ones were rope and sail making. These at first included flax dressing and bleaching, and spinning and weaving were done in the cottages.   In the period between 1796 and 1805, three hundred and eighty-five thousand yards of sailcloth were made each year.   In 1807 the first factory was opened, and more of these sail lofts, as they were called, followed.   The sails were lowered from them by chains hung on wooden beams which still remain.

In 1753 Whitby mariners started whale fishing, and boats, called brigs, built in Whitby would go out to the far seas and bring their catch back to the port where a big trade was done in extracting the oil.   A few mariners who sailed whalers into Greenland waters from here are still living, and they tell of the terrible cold and the horror of encountering icebergs.

At that time the port did a large coastal trade between

London, Newcastle, and Scotland; its boats carried alum from Sandsend and Whitby to different parts and brought back wood and coal; later they dispatched emigrants to Quebec. Boats were also brought in for repairs.

The climax came in the month of February when the ships prepared to set out. The white-sailed boats left the harbour carrying cargoes to distant countries, on voyages of exploration, or on whaling expeditions; and the watching women knew that it would be years before they saw their menfolk again, and that it might be never. The sailors would return with strange tales of other lands which seemed as near to Whitby people as the interior of Yorkshire from which the moors divided them.

Ships and shipping bounded the lives of the people. Most men of any standing owned a few ships, and as soon as the poorer folk had saved enough money they would buy a share, generally a quarter, in a fishing vessel or collier. Farmers would come to market with butter and eggs in baskets the bottoms of which were covered with sovereigns for their purchase.

A retired captain who ended his working days in command of a steamship, but began them in sailing ships, lives within a few miles of Whitby, and his experiences sound like old romances. He describes his ship heeling over as he and his men rescued a crew from a sinking ship during a storm in the Pacific, and tells of tornadoes in the West Indies when the riggings of ships whose captains were not used to hurricanes were blown away like rags. Once his ship had to wait three weeks off the coast near Dublin for wind to sail it, and when they finally moved they had only a few biscuits left for food.

After the days of sailing ships Whitby made iron ships which were towed to Stockton for their engines, but this trade soon declined because the shallow water and the bridge across the river made it difficult to launch the larger boats. There are still shipping companies, but no ships are made here now. The yards up the river Esk are decaying, the dry docks are full of water, and the chains hang limp from the sail lofts as mute

* K

reminders of past usefulness. Those who regret its decline and vanished romance see it as it was then, not as the noisy, smoky concern it would have become. A sailor's son, a boy of about twelve, said to us of a sail up the river: 'It's a nice pull up when the sun's shining, and it's all green country round.' It would not have been 'all green country round' if the ship-building had not slipped away when it did.

The fishing industry developed along with the sailing ships, one trade helping the other. As iron ships began to be made, it became more centred in the villages round Robin Hood's Bay, Runswick, and Staithes, but when the shipping declined it returned to Whitby. Since trawlers and motor boats have taken the place of cobles, fishing is not what it was, and the Scottish herring girls no longer come for the season, but a number of Scottish keel boats are still owned, and there is a bustle on the quay when they come in with their catch, and the fish is spread on the ground and sold by auction.

Further along the quay fishermen prepare bait for the next voyage, mussels for haddock and gurnet for crabs and lobsters. Crabs and lobsters are the most important catches, their season lasting from March to December. Making and mending the pots is continual work through the year, for many are damaged or lost from their pitch during heavy storms. 'They've to stand all 'at comes,' said an old sailor in a blue, hand-knitted guernsey, as he skilfully wove a net across an end.

And there are still the salmon. Fresh life comes to the town with the news of the appearance of the first salmon. The regular fishermen, who because they fish all the year round call themselves winter fishermen, are now joined by a number of young men who take out a licence for the salmon season, and go on the dole for the rest of the year. The fishing-ground is beyond the harbour where the fresh water meets the salt. An hour before the tide turns, the men lean over the old stone pier watching for the fish darting; then one by one they go down to their boats. The nets, called jazz-nets, are weighted at the bottom, and every few minutes the two boats to which they are attached draw together to haul them in.

As we watched, more men and boats arrived, and some began to move down the harbour, which is out of bounds. This was early in the season when one salmon was worth as much as several later on. There was a rolling sea, but the men stood up in the boats shouting and waving their arms. As two drew together to haul in the nets, another pair would dart past them further up the river. A loud cry went up whenever a salmon was netted.

It was a wild, unforgettable scene with the swaying figures hauling up the nets as if their life depended on it. Watching it we could understand how years ago angry fishermen chased a Salvation Army man through the streets because he had said that a man who had died was burning in hell. We might have been back at the time of the rough tracks over the moor when a new resident was looked on with suspicion, and people asked each other: 'What has he done?' Or perhaps a little later, when the promoters of the holiday resort were putting railings round the cliff, and the inhabitants of the old town whose children played there—escaping often from rooms with no windows—repeatedly tore them up.

The first houses at Whitby stood in little patches of ground called tofts. As his sons married, a man would build each of them a cottage, attached to his own house or in some part of the toft, until there evolved a conglomeration of cottages with narrow alleys running between them. The main streets were eventually straightened, but the alleys remain, turning at queer angles, breaking now and again into flights of steps, and giving unexpected views of the sea or corners of the harbour.

The church of St Mary looking down on them is essentially a seaman's church. It was ships' carpenters who, in 1612, lowered the tower and the roof of the nave, and later inserted dormer and sash windows in it. You feel their hand in the medley of galleries which run in all directions in the interior —they were built to hold the growing population, and seats in them were sold to raise money. A memorial under the tower is to fishermen whose lives were lost at sea; a rope ladder was kept in the church to help in saving crews of vessels wrecked under the cliff; the parish chest was recovered after being robbed and thrown into the sea; a chair in the sanctuary is made from the timbers of a wreck; and part of the crowded churchyard has fallen down the cliff to be washed away by the sea.

As the town grew to the west, people found the walk to the old church, and particularly the climb up the one hundred and ninety-nine steps, the church stairs as they were called, too strenuous, and a new church was built in the town. Now it is chiefly holiday makers and sightseers who wear the steps hollow. Parallel with, and just below the steps is the Church Lane or Donkey Road, which was a shorter way than the carriage road. When Lord Mulgrave of Lythe was courting Ann Elizabeth Cholmley of the Abbey House, he used to drive a coach and four up the Church Lane, two of the horses hitched behind serving as brakes when he went back. He married the lady in 1787.

The Cholmleys are a famous Whitby family. Sir Richard Cholmley bought the abbey lands from the Yorke family in 1555 and pulled down the cloisters and most of the south side of the church to build the Abbey House. Sir Hugh Cholmley, the most famous member, restored the family's fortune partly by running alum works. He fought in the Civil War, first against the king and then against Parliament, and had finally to flee to France; and we hear of his coming to the Abbey House to collect his belongings before he left. The Cholmley pew is the most ornate in St Mary's Church. It stands on twisted wooden columns and crosses and partly hides the Norman chancel arch.

Towards the end of the eighteenth century the first diligences and coaches began to run across the moors to Pickering on the way to York, but the making of the railway from Pickering in 1830 was the first strong influence in opening out this part of the coast to the interior. It brought more visitors, and it had much to do with the development of the jet trade.

Jet found in Bronze Age barrows shows that it was worked here four thousand years ago. The Romans used it, and it is often mentioned in the abbey rolls. It owed a great deal of its later popularity to the fact that Queen Victoria bought it for mourning. By 1870, twelve hundred men and boys were employed in the industry, and the yearly output was valued at £20,000. We talked to a man who was apprenticed to the trade for seven years, and though at the end of that time it had already declined, as that was the only trade he had in his hands, he stuck to it and is one of the few left. These now amount to not more than half a dozen men, but they are genuine craftsmen. In a shop in Henrietta Street, where jet ornaments are still made and sent all over the world, they have beautiful exhibition pieces with intricately carved figures and heads.

The popularity of jet rested on the insecure foundation of fashion, a whim started by a queen. Whitby suffers in its decline for it is an asset for a holiday resort to have a speciality of its own, to provide an easy solution for a present-buying public. Its popularity had already died when one of us as a child bought a jet penholder for our first schoolmistress. She would probably like it, because she was an old lady and cherished a deep reverence for the memory of Queen Victoria.

The old box pews in St Mary's Church have the names on them of the townships, such as Hawsker and Sneaton, for which they were reserved. They show Whitby as the centre of a country district whose people come in to its market. But more than the inland villages, Whitby reflects the small fishing villages which lie on either side of it, and are miniatures of it and its fishing life. Robin Hood's Bay is most closely attached to it, and has much of the character of the larger town. Journeying to it you see from the Hawsker road the sweep of the coast towards the headland of Ravenscar, and the village of Thorpe immediately below resting in a grassy hollow between the moors and the sea. A little to the north the red-roofed cottages of Robin Hood's Bay climb down the steep cliff side.

Here again the plan of the village has come from that habit of the father building a house in his own garden for his son, and there are the same tiers of houses and narrow alleys. The steep road to Bay Town from the new residential part at the top of the cliff ends abruptly at the beach, which is covered at high tide. This and the absence of a harbour are among the reasons why the fishing has left Robin Hood's Bay. The boats, normally anchored in the bay, have to be hauled up into the streets during high tides, a comparatively easy matter with the old cobles when there were plenty of men to help, but difficult with heavy motor boats and few men. In the nineteenth century numbers of ships were owned by the people, and a big trade was done in exporting coal. To-day there are not enough fishermen in the Bay to man a lifeboat.

But neither the lack of fishermen nor a superabundance of visitors can take away the thrill of this place. It leaves vivid remembrances of cottage flowers in gardens and windows—asters, phlox, dahlias, marigolds, gladioli, and people carrying country bunches of them through the streets; of farm carts, laden with bracken and pea-sticks, taking short cuts across the beach from the pastures which run down to it; of butchers' boys riding horseback across the sand to the farmhouses on this land; of captains' and sailors' wives at Thorpe watching through field glasses their husbands' boats sail along the horizon; of women gathering periwinkles on the shore, working until the last minute and then racing the tide along the beach and carrying the heavy sacks up the steep hill to the station, from where they are sent to the Norfolk town of King's Lynn, where there is a particular demand for winkles.

Before the railway came, girls used to walk ten miles from Staithes to Robin Hood's Bay to gather limpets for bait. At Whitby they would probably join one of the stone causeways which are a feature of this part. That running beside the

present road from Robin Hood's Bay to Hawsker was part of a
road along which fish was carried inland.

Between Whitby and Staithes the quaint hidden village of
Runswick nestles into the sloping cliffs, the flowers in its
gardens overhanging the roofs of the lower houses. Though

Staithes

visitors claim Runswick, and bungalows dot the cliff at one
end, it still keeps some crab and lobster fishing and mans its
lifeboat, which the women have been known to launch when
some of the men were away.

Staithes runs beside two becks to the shore, where the little
bay is shut closely in by rocky headlands, so that it has no view
but the rocks and open sea. Of all the small fishing places
Staithes retains its own life most. The fishing has suffered
because the stone piers built nine years ago for the harbour were
planned actually on the fishermen's road in, but a sufficient

amount is caught for it to be sold by auction each day on the quay. The chief buyers are women who take it to Redcar and Middlesbrough to sell. You can tell that fish is landed here by the number of sea-gulls. After their morning's feed they settle down to the quieter hours of the day, folding their wings and perching like weathercocks on the chimneys. Their white feathers present a vivid contrast to the black walls of the Cod and Lobster Inn, tarred to keep the wet out when the sea dashes over it in winter.

The time has gone by when the people of Staithes used to throw stones and fish-heads at strangers as they appeared down the hill, although quite young people can remember visiting it in winter when every one rushed out to see them. There is still a hint of native costume in the sun-bonnets which almost all the women and children wear. They are made of print gathered fully at the back, and are of various colours with a few black ones worn for mourning by the older women. It is a communal place where the women hang their rugs and the weekly washing on the rails of the bridges and the harbour. You can imagine how the inhabitants would unite to help the smugglers who were very active here. A door covering what looks like a cave above the river opens to a smugglers' passage wide and high enough for a horse and cart to pass through. It led out to the moors and smuggled goods were left in it until it was safe to take them away.

In 1669 the village of Runswick slipped into the sea, but no one was hurt because the inhabitants were all in one cottage attending a funeral wake. In 1829 the village of Low Kettleness, which was half-way down the cliffs, also glided into the sea, taking with it an alum shop. Alum was then being worked on the cliffs between Whitby and Staithes, and the inhabitants sought refuge in a ship which was waiting to load a cargo of it.

Sir Thomas Chaloner discovered alum in this district at the end of the sixteenth century, having noticed a peculiarity in the rock formation and in the colour of the vegetation. He and his family had much to do with the development of the industry. It was worked first at Guisborough, then at Sandsend where the old village of East Row which follows the beck into the woods was built chiefly to house the workers. It was also found further north at Boulby where, after the alum works were closed, the cliffs, the highest in Yorkshire, caught fire and burned for seventy years. An 'alum house' where the mineral was smelted stood under the cliff at Sandsend and coal brought from Newcastle for smelting was landed at the jetty here and tipped out on the beach. The industry declined when it was found that alum could be made from chemicals, and the last load was sent from Sandsend in 1867.

The dark, shaly cliff of Kettleness Nab, quite bare of grass, remains to tell the story of an industry whose workings once made a line of smoke along this stretch of the coast. Kettleness Nab is a strange, ominous cliff, and there are more wrecks on it than at any other part of the Yorkshire coast.

Goathland, Wade's Causeway

CHAPTER 25

ESKDALE

OUR most vivid recollection of the river Esk is of seeing it
after heavy floods in the autumn of 1931. We had travelled
up to the coast in a storm which ended a week of almost un-
ceasing rain, and had seen bridges washed away and roads
turned into rivers. Next day the fury and ecstasy of the
storm were exhausted, the river went down, and the sun came
out, but the desolation it had wrought lay over the land. At
Ruswarp, tea gardens and huts had been swept into the water,
sodden carpets were drying on the walls, and mud and sand
were being dug out of the flooded inn. The bridges at Sleights
and Egton Bridge had been washed away, leaving yawning
gaps in the road.

The flood told of the many becks which flow into the river
Esk from its source in Westerdale down to Ruswarp. Many
of these becks rise in the moorlands of the Cleveland Hills
and come down lonely dales with farms scattered on the strips

274

of cultivated land. The villages chiefly lie outside them in the wider valley of the Esk. The stream of the Mirk Esk is an exception. It comes midway in its course to the large village of Goathland in a hollow of the moors.

Goathland is more a series of small hamlets than a clustered village, and modern building has retained the scattered plan. The houses are placed in a seemingly haphazard manner round the edge of an open common which fades into the moor with no hedge or wall enclosing it. The space and openness and the moorland breezes blowing over it make much of the charm of the village. Sheep grazing on the green are so tame that they nuzzle into your hand for titbits, and chaffinches, sweeping in little flocks over it, follow you from one end to the other hoping for crumbs. Paved causeways which cross it and are gradually being recovered from the grass are over three hundred years old. There are wooded waterfalls on the river, and the sunken hamlet of Beck Hole lies in a ravine by it, but the heart of Goathland is its green swung on the moors.

Nearly seventy years ago an aunt of one of us went with her grandfather, who was a Unitarian minister in Whitby, to visit a family in Goathland. She remembers arriving at a small farm on the edge of the village, and that the woman, who was working in the fields, saw them and came down to let them in. There was one main room with a floor of earth and a fire in the middle. A pot hung over the fire, and near it a baby lay asleep in a wooden cradle, and a dog guarded it while the mother worked on the land. She remembers, too, that the woman went out and fetched her a mug of warm goat's milk.

Country houses and modern villas make up a large part of Goathland to-day, and the cottage has gone, but it is still easy to imagine the simple building and the lives of its tenants here. As recently as 1811 a farmhouse on the green was built from start to finish in a fortnight, using local stone and tiles and mud from a nearby pond for mortar. John and Martha Pierson were the builders, but one feels that the whole village must have joined in helping to finish it so quickly.

At the back of this house a barn with the date 1663 on a coping-stone has a pair of crossed rowan twigs over the cow-shed door as a charm against witches putting a spell on the cattle. A more elaborate precaution, of which there is an example in a cottage in Danby, is that of building a witch-post into a house to keep witches away.

These are relics of a belief in the power of witches which lingered in this valley until recent times. An old man who died not long ago used to keep dried calves' hearts stuck with pins in his chimney to draw witches from their hiding-place. An old lady of eighty tells how one day she was playing cards with Nanny Pierson, the Goathland witch, when Nanny suddenly disappeared into a cupboard full of china, and presently emerged without having smashed a thing. Nanny, who had followed her mother and aunt in the profession of witchcraft, was believed to turn herself into a hare at will. Two other Goathland witches were said to turn themselves into cats, and the story goes that one night these were shot at, and the next morning one woman had a broken leg and the other's clothes were torn.

Pierson is a common name in the district. Old William Pierson was a local character. We hear of him going to buy his Christmas cheese, and asking for some which had 'a grip i' t' gob.' Another time when asked why he did not keep bees, he replied: 'Nay, I 'll nut 'ave my money fleein' aboot i' t' air.'

These people and customs lived long after the railway came to Goathland in 1830. Yet the railway connecting the moorland village with the coast and the interior did much to alter it. The opening of any new line was a triumph for its promoters and the people benefiting by it, attended with celebrations and much cheering and feasting, but with the completion of the line from Pickering to Whitby it not only seemed to the people that distance had been eliminated, but that the moors had been conquered. It was hardly a normal railway. It ran downhill on its own momentum, and relays of horses pulled it up the steep inclines. Old pictures show the passengers walking up the slopes to relieve the horses. The horses gave way to trucks holding tanks of water which pulled the train by gravitation. At Goathland a steam winding engine superseded the trucks to draw the train up the steep slope from Beck Hole, and the walled enclosure which held it is still there. The present line takes a curve to avoid the slope, and the station has been moved, but the early line ran through the village. Near where it crossed the road a cottage was occupied rent-free by the man who opened and shut the gate.

Some of the first outside people to come and live here were shipowners and sea-captains from Whitby who seemed to have a liking for moorland scenery. Then more newcomers built houses, hotels sprang up, and finally came the modern villas, some in keeping with the local architecture and some not.

The Plough Stots revived at Goathland by Mr F. W. Dowson bring back an echo of the old life. The ceremony is performed on Plough Monday, the first Monday after 6th January, old Christmas Day. It is a relic of a pagan ritual to bless the sowing of the corn and Christianized into the belief that this was the day on which the plough was put into the ground after the Deluge. The play and the kind of jumping dance which accompanied it are now lost, and sword dances which were introduced into the district by the Norsemen have been added to the day's celebrations.

The steps of the dances were collected from remembrances of old men who, however, refused to perform them themselves, so that the first revival had to come through the school children, and from them to the young men. The most famous was originally a dance of triumph round a victim, a tree, or a sacrificial altar. The morning of Plough Monday used to begin with the lighting of candles for a blessing on the work of the year, and part of the collections, which are now for Whitby Hospital, used to go to buy candles.

We first caught sight of the dancers in Darnholme, the costumes of the performers showing up against the grey background. Half wore pink coats and half blue, a nineteenth-century innovation to satisfy Whigs and Tories. The fiddler's coat was of both colours. A King and Queen led the procession, and were followed by 'Toms,' dressed in patchwork coats, and the 'Owd Man' and 'Owd Woman.' Now and again the 'Owd Man' entered the ring of dancers and was supposed to be beheaded as he was caught between the locked swords. It was probably a quieter ceremony than those of which it is a revival, but it brought back the atmosphere of the days when people, though by then they had lost the meaning of the ceremony, felt it to have some significance in the life of the valley.

About a mile south of the village the Roman road from Malton crosses Wheeldale Moor. You see it as a grey track from a long distance, for the road is now registered as an ancient monument, and one and a half miles of the rough surface, with occasional kerb-stone edges, have been exposed. It seems almost a living thing as it sweeps over the moor which hid it for centuries. Above the rippling note of the curlew and the hoarse call of grouse, you imagine you hear the tramp of Roman legions, and a faint song to Mithras as they march. The road is known as 'Wade's Causeway' from the legend that it was made by the giant Wade, so that his wife, Bell, could go dryshod over the moor to milk her cows. Wade was said to have built Pickering Castle while Bell built Mulgrave Castle, near Lythe, the two using one hammer, throwing it across the valley to each other as they required it.

It is loveliest here just before darkness comes, when shapes are softened in the evening light, and the moor seems to draw the road back to itself in sleep; but local people advise you not to stay too long on the moor at this time, for there are ghosts of more than Romans on it. Hob comes out to haunt the becks and bogs in a wraith of mist, and utters a peculiar cry which it is not lucky for men to hear.

From Goathland a gated road goes over the moors to Egton Bridge on the river Esk. An iron bridge has taken the place of the stone one which we saw washed down in the flood of 1931, and an island which until then was a lawn with a tea-garden on it is now strewn with mud and stones; but Egton Bridge is still a lovely place. The sunken wooded valley comes as a quiet haven from the moor.

It was the day of the 'Berry Show' when we came down, and the villagers were carrying baskets of gooseberries to the hut near the inn where the show was held. The prizes were arranged on a table at one end, looking very tempting among vases of sweet peas. They are presented for the largest single berry, a pair of berries, or a plate with a given number. Each berry is weighed separately and in secret on glass scales in a little room near the door. When they finally arrive on the show table the sight is astounding; it seems unbelievable that this bloated-looking fruit is the humble gooseberry. The largest that year weighed 27 dwt. 4 gr., but the record for the show is one weighing 30 dwt. We sat with the villagers on forms opposite them and gazed at the green and red balls with the skin stretched so tight over their fleshy bodies that the hairs on them bristled. 'They doctors 'em,' an old man said, but it was obvious that no gooseberry would grow like this unless it were doctored. 'They sits wi' umbrellas ower 'em when it gets near the day,' another man remarked.

The Berry Show was started over a hundred years ago to encourage the local growing of gooseberries. At one time it was made into a fair day, and stalls on the roadside stretched from the inn to the bridge. At night twopence was charged for dancing on the island, and the money was given to Whitby Hospital. The fair has gone, but the show remains, and the gooseberries must have grown beyond all expectation of its founders. Almost every little garden has a square netted over to protect the fruit from the birds, and tending the bushes is work for much of the year.

Above Egton the valleys are like the fingers of a hand. Glaisdale, which has been spoilt by ironworks, we remember chiefly for the beauty of the Beggar's Bridge across the river Esk at its foot. It was built by Thomas Ferres who as a poor boy was nearly drowned by falling off the stepping-stones as he was crossing the Esk in a flood. He eventually made a fortune in Hull, and in 1621 built this bridge. Legend has provided a more romantic story of a lover who often found it difficult to reach his sweetheart across the river, and, having made a fortune in foreign lands, built the bridge so that future lovers should be spared his trials. Mr Pannett, who gave the Art Gallery to Whitby, was once driving in a hurry to Glaisdale to make a man's will when his cab was wedged on this bridge. The driver climbed over the top and pushed at the back whilst Mr Pannett remained fastened in the cab, expecting every minute that the horses would take fright and jump the low parapet. The carriage road was then over a ford. Now the bridge is sandwiched between a railway and a modern road bridge.

Four miles higher up the valley the Esk is crossed by Duck Bridge, which was built about 1380 by the Nevilles to carry the road to Danby castle on the hillside above Little Fryup Dale. When Robert de Brus received the Danby estate soon after the Conquest he built his castle at Castleton. It came eventually to the Latimers by marriage with Lucy, the heiress of the Thwengs of Kilton, and the castle at Danby was built in the early fourteenth century. This was an occasional home of Catherine Parr, and Henry VIII is said to have stayed here.

Danby was the earliest castle in Yorkshire to be planned round a quadrangular court, its four towers being placed diagonally at the corners. A farmhouse and barns built into it blend harmoniously with the few remains. Stone steps lead from what is now a farmyard into the great hall where the court leets were held for centuries after the castle was deserted.

The dales here come in quick succession: Great and Little Fryup, separated by a moorland crag, Danby Dale, Westerdale, Baysdale, Commondale; rich little valleys with cornfields among the meadows and trees surrounding the red-roofed farmsteads, but all of them running up with a kind of mellowed grandeur to the moors.

Danby Dale is the best known because of Canon Atkinson's book, *Forty Years in a Moorland Parish*. It was a remote, backward place when in 1847 he came as a young man to be vicar at Danby. He tells how on the journey from Whitby he saw ten oxen and ten horses pulling a load of freestone up Stonegate Gill.

The village which many people call Danby is really Danby End, and is on the other side of the river Esk out of the dale. The red-tiled houses climb up a steep green where sheep graze between them and the road, and it has an air of being a gateway to the moors. The real Danby was a hamlet half way up the dale, vanished now except for the church and one farmhouse. The church is curiously planned with the tower over the south porch, but it has character and dignity, and the spirit of the green valley broods over it. Canon Atkinson found it in a ruinous neglected state, and his first work was to put it in order. You picture him, an old man with a white beard, gathering dalesmen to rest in the churchyard where he himself now lies.

The flagged paths whose hollow stones tell of the many dalespeople who have trodden them on the way to services at the church; two women coming out to talk to us from Stormy Hall; the amphitheatre of bracken enclosing the head of the dale; the farmhouses nestling under the hill; a farmer driving a cart along the narrow road; two owls sitting on trees in a wood by the parsonage: these are among the pictures which Danby Dale has left on our minds.

The habitation of the valley is now in small scattered farms running along either side of it, and a hall at the end. When the estate was sold in 1647 most of the farmers bought their own farms, thus becoming yeomen, known in this part as freeholders. The farms have expressive names like Honeybee Nest, Crag House, Stormy Hall, Lumley House. Many of the freeholders were converted to the faith of the Quakers; George Fox visited Danby several times, and a strong Quaker community grew up here. Until the meeting house was built at Castleton meetings were held in the various farmhouses; and three Quaker burial grounds remain in the dale.

Any early story of the Quakers is one of journeys, of Friends coming long distances to hear George Fox or one of the leaders speak, of a group of Friends in one dale walking or riding miles to attend a meeting in another; and the road from Danby to Rosedale was so much used by them that it was known as 'The Quakers' Road.' Near the farmhouse of St Helena on the west side of the dale it is still called the Quakers' Way.

The Friends took a leading part in the life of the dale. Some of them, under the leadership of George Baker of Honeybee Nest, journeyed to York in 1807 to vote for Wilberforce and the abolition of negro slavery. In 1820 George and Sarah Baker removed from Honeybee Nest to Askham Fields, near York, and we are told how on the journey their six-year-old son James wore a white hat, and was teased so much about looking like a Luddite that he hid among the furniture while they went through the streets of York.

Castleton, the largest town in the upper dale, has an industrial air due to old ironstone mines and the ganister quarries and clay pits which are still being worked. It straggles up a hill, pauses at the modern church built very attractively in brown stone, climbs again, and then suddenly ends at the moor. Only an unnoticeable mound at the roadside shows where the first castle for the Danby estate stood. It was dismantled in 1216, and it is said that its stone was used to build Danby church.

Above Castleton the road starts over the moor to Hutton-le-Hole and Rosedale by Ralph Cross and Fat Betty, but the river Esk turning south runs parallel with it into Westerdale. Here where the wider dale is ending there is a village with a church and vicarage and an inn amongst the cottages and farmhouses. Just beyond it, looking out over heather and bracken, is a cottage, now derelict, to which two centuries ago an old sailor named William Bulmer came to retire where there is a tang of the sea when the wind is in the east. In the overgrown garden there still stands a monument which he built. It is a thick stone shaft with crude figures of boats sculptured on it, and lettering cut round it, regardless of corners, tells of the foreign lands to which the sailor had travelled, and how he was saved from a wreck in 1729.

Branching from the Esk is the lonely dale of Baysdale. This is crossed at its foot by a white road over the moor, but it has no road up its higher reaches, although almost at its head there is the site of the nunnery of Baysdale Abbey. At the Dissolution the church at Baysdale Abbey was described as having fourteen little glass windows and a roof of lead. Besides the monastery buildings, there was a 'water mylne . . . a cowhouse, oxe-house, swyne-cote, hey-house, barn and turf house,' all covered with thatch.

The white road goes on over Commondale Moor, and now on all sides, as on the Danby moors, there are prehistoric remains. The numbers of tumuli, circles, ditches, enclosures, and pits where iron has been dug show that there must have been a heavy population on this high land. The idea that moors are places which have never been lived on or changed by man is particularly wrong in the Cleveland district. You feel the memory of man as you walk over them here, of an eager life, now vanished, which lasted for hundreds of years.

The high bleak moorland was avoided by early people, and the first dwellers on these hills were the Urn people of the mid-Bronze Age, driven here by more progressive tribes from the Wolds and the Vale of Pickering. These tribes stayed on during the Roman occupation, and were left unmolested by the Angles who also avoided the high land. When the Scandinavians came to people the remote valleys they absorbed many of the Britons, though some groups remained in separate communities. The long and comparatively late occupation of the moors led to the mingling of Celtic and Norse legend of which there is so much evidence in this part, and the looks of the people are inherited as much from their Celtic as from their Scandinavian ancestors.

We turn eastward to Crown End on Commondale Moor to find one of the enclosures. It is difficult to distinguish in the deep heather which makes a distant view of it impossible, but gradually the extent of the settlement reveals itself—the surrounding ditch with slabs along it, the standing stones, irregular fields, one or two huts, and a large circle with a terrace below it. It has a commanding position looking down Eskdale and to the north across Commondale, where modern brick and pipe works are using the local clay which the early Britons used for their pots.

Great Ayton and Roseberry Topping

CHAPTER 26

CLEVELAND

THE north-eastern slice of Yorkshire which the Norsemen named 'the hilly land' is a district to itself, a low semicircle with the Cleveland Hills on the south and the coast and river Tees curving round on the north. It is rolling country with villages and old-world towns tucked into the hollows. Trees clothe the lower slopes of the hills, and bracken covers the jagged peaks, which are so formed that when a mist hides the summits you can imagine them the bases of tall mountains.

Many of the hills show signs of ironstone workings. These are mostly silent and finished now, but the hilltops look over miles of green country to a conglomeration of tall chimneys which mark where the industry has gone to the towns of Middlesbrough and Stockton.

Eastwards the country stretches through wooded land in which feudal lords built their castles to where the high cliffs of the coast drop gently down to the estuary of the Tees. It is a strange mixed country where superstition and legend die hard. Many of the small humpy fields are ploughed, and the newly turned furrows gleam like mahogany, for this is Cleveland in the clay, where you 'bring in two soles and carry one away.' It is a great hunting country, for foxes abound among the bracken-covered hills. ' I want foxes' has been the slogan of the Master of the Hunt, and game on the moors has had to take a secondary place. Cleveland Bays are crossed with thoroughbreds for hunting this district.

We will enter it at the west by Stokesley, which lies on flatter land by the river Leven with these hills as a tempting background. A southern lady touring the north of England two summers ago pronounced Stokesley the loveliest country town she had seen. She was amazed at its unspoilt character, and said that had it been near London it would have been developed as a show-place. Like the other market towns of north Yorkshire, it makes no attempt at display, but stands as the centuries naturally made it. The winding entrance leads past a green to where cottages, shops, and tall, dignified houses line the long main street. This broadens on the north into a large market-place, and then dwindles away at the bridge which crosses the river Leven. The green grass, the red roofs, and the fine weathering of the stone make a more colourful picture than most Yorkshire towns present.

' Aye, Stokesley, Yarm, and Guisborough are t' audest spots i' t' North Ridin',' said an old man, looking down at the town with its red-roofed houses and cobble-edged road. Then unconsciously he left out the others. ' Aye,' he said, 'it's an aud spot is Stokesley.' He seemed to sense the age behind the present town, which is itself old. Its plan was influenced to some extent by the nearness of the Scots border, its narrow ends could be efficiently barricaded against raiders, and the large green on the south would provide food for the stock until the danger had passed. No market is held in the square now; that went to Stockton with the railway; but at the time of Stokesley Fair a large travelling feast fits into it with room to spare.

The river runs behind the houses, and a series of bridges crossing it make it a distinct part of the town. The old corn mill on its bank is still working, though only cattle food is ground here now. Our friend remembered it running day and night grinding local-grown corn into brown flour. When he was a boy no white flour was used, and the chief food of the people was brown bread and treacle. There were three bake-houses in Stokesley then, and people used to take what they called 'night loaves,' which weighed a stone, to be baked in the ovens all night.

At that time a labourer got twelve shillings a week, and out of that he had to find a shilling for rent and something for 'Sunday meat,' but most of them brought up large families. They managed all right as long as the harvest was good. In the year 1880 they had to eat black bread all winter, and sometimes this was so soft that it ran under the oven doors when it was being cooked. They relied a great deal on the corn which they were able to glean. A hundred Irishmen would reap one field, and after the corn was tied into sheaves the townspeople were allowed to glean what had been 'slathered.' They threshed it themselves with rolling-pins, and carried it in a sheet on to the village green to winnow before they took it to the mill. One family would glean enough to make flour to last them into the new year, or to feed a pig which they would kill at Christmas. 'We 'ad to do it to live,' the old man explained. 'Ther was no gaein' to t' pictures or football matches i' those days,' he went on, 'but we was content. We 'ad to mak wer own amusements, an' we did it. We used to play cricket and "knur and spell" on t' green. Nowadays they 're allus rushin' off on t' buses, an' gaein' to t' pictures. They 're laitin' pleasure an' nivver finndin' it.'

Great Ayton lies further into the hills, running at one end beside the river Leven and at the other round a large green. One side of the green is almost taken up with the buildings of the Friends' School, which was founded in 1841, originally for an agricultural as well as an educational school. The only tulip tree in the north is in the school gardens, casting its ample shade over the playground. When we saw it in July it was flowering with green tulip-like blooms.

Great Ayton has become famous throughout the British Empire because Captain Cook spent his boyhood here, though he was actually born at Marton, a village near by. In 1927 the cottage in which the Cooks lived was removed to Australia, and all that remains now is a monument to say where it stood, and a rather melancholy little museum in the village. Cook's father was farm man at Airey Holme on the lower slopes of Roseberry Topping.

The curious conical-shaped hills of this part are given the name Topping. Roseberry, which dominates the village of Great Ayton, is the most remarkable of them all. It is not the highest, but it is so placed that it can be seen for long distances, and when you are near it it seems to have a definite personality. The local people use it as a weather prophet, for:

> When Roseberrye Toppinge wears a cappe
> Let Cleveland then beware a clappe.

Its oldest name of Othenesberg probably indicates that it was a centre of the worship of Odin. The 'r' at the beginning of its name has come with the running on of that letter from the word 'under' in places such as Newton-under-Roseberry.

Legends have become attached to this and most of the individual peaks. Freeborough Hill further east was thought in pagan days to be the abode of the Great Earth Mother. The names of Nanny and Old Wife given to standing stones and mounds on these moors show the survival of pagan religions. Nanna, the wife of Balder the Beautiful, was the Viking goddess of nature, and Old Wife seems to be the Earth Mother. A Scandinavian name for her was Carlin, and the custom, still kept up in Cleveland, of eating carlins, that is brown peas, on Carlin Sunday, the week before Palm Sunday, is a relic from these early times.

Echoes of these religions survived after the coming of

A FOREST PRIORY

Christianity in the practice of witchcraft, and in Cleveland this persisted until recent times. Almost every place in it had a witch. *T' Hunt o' Yatton Brig*, Richard Blakeborough's dialect poem, tells of the terrible things which befell a Great Ayton man who did not carry out the instructions of a witch whom he had consulted. Mary Marshall, the witch of Stokesley, was supposed to be condemned to crow three times when a hen crossed her path. Stokesley had also that antidote for witches, a Wise Man who claimed to break their spell. Wrightson of Stokesley, who died at the beginning of the nineteenth century, was the most famous Wise Man in the north, and his help was sought when people or cattle were ill. He was the seventh son of a seventh daughter, and it was claimed for him that he knew before they told him why people had come to consult him.

From the top of Roseberry you can see the sea on the east coast, the Pennine Hills to the west, and to the north the distant smoky haze which obscures the iron works of Middlesbrough and is only broken at night when the furnaces send their red glare into the sky. The industry, which has left these hills now, has cast its shadow over Guisborough, where the depression has brought poverty to an extent which a purely rural town would not have known. After the decline of this and its alum works Guisborough is slowly slipping back into a country town, of whose existence the market cross with a sundial and ball is a proof.

It centres to-day, as it did before industry came to it, round its church and the peaceful ruins of the priory. The east front of the priory is the only substantial relic of a church which had a greater length than Beverley or Byland, but this is so beautiful that because of it Guisborough takes its place among the finest of Yorkshire abbey ruins. The arches and window tracery make a frame for the sky and the green country, which has the essence of Cleveland in it. They are of the Decorated period, for the Early English church was burnt down in 1289 through the carelessness of a plumber repairing the leads.

L

There is an atmosphere of retirement about the grounds, in which a dovecote and fragments of a cloister are hidden amongst trees and bushes. One part is taken up by a lofty chestnut tree whose lower branches have drooped to the ground and taken root, so that the mother tree stands surrounded by a circle of trees now almost as large as herself; and the process continues. It is said that the original tree is four hundred years old, so that it would have been a little sapling when the priory was dissolved.

The history of the church and priory is wrapped up with that of the Brus family of Skelton from which King Robert the Bruce of Scotland sprang. Their castle stands as one of a series which lie at the foot of the hills but look over the flat land between Guisborough and the sea. Rebuilt in 1788, it faces towards Upleatham where the nave of the old church now makes the smallest church in England. Wilton Castle to the north of it was forfeited by the Bulmers after the Pilgrimage of Grace. Kilton Castle, on a ravine by Kilton Beck, was founded in 1135, and was the birthplace in 1279 of the notorious Lucy de Thweng who married William Latimer of Danby.

Where Kilton Beck runs down to the sea we come to the ironstone district of Skinningrove, Loftus, and Brotton. Here are smoke and dirt and rows of dingy houses, but all is on a comparatively small scale with something still of a country industry about it. The drifts, or 'winnings,' are driven into the earth, and the iron works with their great blast furnaces rise on the top of the cliff. Skinningrove lies along the steep sides of a ravine whose upper slopes are covered with allotments, to one of which each cottage has a right. Vestiges remain of the old village, which must have been very lovely; and the manor house is now an inn. The houses run down to the shore, and the last row, facing the sea across a narrow street which might be in a town, has a peculiar effect on a coast otherwise given over to holiday resorts. But the houses are clean and neat, and paths lead from them on to the open cliff where a man can walk and detach himself from his working surroundings. Seen from this distance the works have a grim kind of beauty. Below them a ship waits for the tide to bring it in to the jetty, from which the smelted iron and steel is shipped by sea.

The industrial area stops abruptly on Huntcliffe Nab, where there was another Roman coast fort and which has given its name to a particular kind of Roman pottery common in the fourth century. Across the ravine of Skelton Beck, the modern resort of Saltburn-by-the-Sea stands on the cliff. Old Saltburn, a cluster of whitewashed cottages, lies close to the shore below it under the isolated hill of Cat Nab.

Wooden huts and buildings have somewhat spoilt this old corner round which there hangs the romance of a smugglers' haunt. The goods were landed under Huntcliffe, and taken inland up the Skelton valleys. Almost every cottage had an underground cellar where these could be hidden till it was safe to move them. When a row of houses and an inn under Cat Nab were pulled down they were all found to have deep cavities under the floors. The Andrews, a famous smuggling family who lived at White House Farm on the hill behind, had their hiding-place in the stable under a stall always occupied by a vicious mare.

The landlord of the Ship Inn was in sympathy with the trade, and stirring tales would be told in his inn parlour. The secrecy of those days seems to hang in the dim corners of the rooms with their dark cupboards and old fireplaces and a ship's figure-head gazing stonily across the bar. A message that 'William's cow had calved' meant that a load had been landed, and would quickly empty the bar. Perhaps tales were told of the smugglers of Marske, the next village, where the horses were so well trained that, with a keg of brandy fastened to either side, they would make their way alone at a good pace inland to Stokesley, and after being unloaded return home by themselves.

As soon as smuggling was put down, the fishing village of Old Saltburn began to decline, but when the new resort grew on the cliff, this part of the beach through which the road from Brotton passes was at first the most frequented. The bathing machines, wooden ones with high wheels and steps leading up to them, were here. They stand yet in a long row near the Ship Inn with their wheels deeply embedded in the soft sand. About 1810 visitors from as far as Redcar came at least once during a holiday to drink tea and eat 'fat rascals' at Old Saltburn.

The new resort on the cliff was the idea of one man, Henry Pease of Darlington. He was struck with the beauty of the site, and in 1865 persuaded the railway to run a branch line there and to build the Zetland Hotel. The town was planned with two shopping streets, an open front, and streets, named after jewels, running at right angles to it.

One side of the ravine of Skelton Beck was made into pleasure grounds whose walks lead eventually to the Italian gardens, where rarities such as egg plants flourish. The central oval-shaped bed laid out with greenhouse and tropical plants, has scarcely changed in pattern this century. Pre-War lovers of Saltburn remember these gardens illuminated with night lights in little coloured glass bowls. Until the War the resort fulfilled itself as its originators hoped, but to-day it seems to require another genius to rise up and finish its planning.

The firm golden sands on which motor races are still held stretch to Redcar through Marske, where Mr Pease's grandfather built Cliff House overlooking the sea. When his two aunts came from Darlington to stay there, they rode in their open carriage on a truck attached to a passenger train, and thus made the journey from door to door. A modern road now runs from Marske to Redcar close to the sandhills where the donkeys which carried fish to Stokesley used to graze.

Redcar itself has become a holiday reflection of the iron and steel towns towards which we are drawing. Workers from them can reach it easily and cheaply for a day or longer, and they swarm on to the sands and the pier. The town is un-ashamedly given up to providing for them and offers in its pleasure palaces, stalls, and shows a gaudy attraction. It has a robust spontaneity which compensates for its lack of natural beauty.

Redcar started its existence as a resort very differently. Its popularity came with the fashion for sea bathing in the beginning of the nineteenth century, largely because it was safe, and the absence of cliff, which to-day emphasizes the crowds, made it suitable for invalids and children. In 1810 Mr William Hutton of Birmingham stayed at the principal hotel, where he paid eighteen shillings a day for himself, his daughter, his coachman, and two horses. He told how it was difficult to walk on the streets because of the 'mountains' of drifted sand. The visitor, he said, may 'sport white stockings every day in the year, for they are without dirt; nor will the pavement offend his corns.'

A woman named Diana Carter had the first bathing machine, and when the season was over she would harness her horse to the van and travel inland to the Northallerton district, calling on her various summer patrons, and occasionally staying a few days in their houses. She made a little money on the journeys by selling packets of tea which she made up herself.

Six hundred years ago salt was being made at Coatham, which now joins Redcar, using sea coal to evaporate the water. The canons of Guisborough Priory and the nuns of Basedale Abbey owned salt works. These industries must have made little difference to the shore, for a Cottonian MS. of the sixteenth century tells how a sandbank here 'entertaines an infynite Number of Sea fowls, which laye theyr Egges heere and theere scatteringlie in such Sorte, that in Tyme of Breedinge one can hardly sett his foote so warylye, that he spoyle not many of theyr Nests.'

The ironworks which now surround it tell a different story. They have seized and claimed this country. Their chimneys and works line the mouth of the Tees to Middlesbrough, and turn out smoke to blacken the land, kill the vegetation, and cast a grim dreariness over everything. Only when the smelt furnaces pour out their molten refuse does any brightness pierce the gloom.

The town of Middlesbrough has grown purely because of the ironworks. In 1801 it was composed of a few houses scattered over a marshy plain, but in 1829 it was made a railway terminus, and was planned as a town by a group of Quakers negotiating with the railway company. Benefiting by that plan, its streets are wide, its buildings lofty, and it is not so depressing as it might have been, but its atmosphere remains that of a busy ironworking town. Echoes of its quiet past are felt in the two convents which lie in wooded gardens behind high walls; and in a modern museum which shows the antiquities of the district, many of them prehistoric finds on the Cleveland hill of Eston Nab. Our old friend at Stokesley would, no doubt, have classed Middlesbrough as 't' newest place i' t' North Riding,' but very little away from it, beyond his ancient town of Yarm, industrialism on the Tees ceases, and it becomes a country river running down from the Pennines.

Egglestone Abbey

CHAPTER 27

TEESDALE

TEESDALE'S story is one of roads and journeys. Yorkshire is ending here; the river Tees, forming the northern boundary of the county, only half belongs to it, though its larger tributary dales run down from Yorkshire hills.

At Scotch Corner near Richmond, the Great North Road forks, one part keeping directly north to cross the county boundary at Piercebridge, where there was a Roman station on this main route to the Wall, and the other, the Roman Watling Street, going north-west through Bowes to Carlisle.

This, which we take, runs along a lonely ridge of hill, and it is said that on the fifteen miles between Scotch Corner and Bowes its wide verges provide a hundred acres of roadside grass on which cattle can graze. Milestones dated 1774 point with a hand to 'Greata Bridge.' The villages, like those near the Great North Road, lie a mile or so on either side: Gilling, where the Saxon lords of Richmondshire had their castle:

Ravensworth, round its green with the ruins of its Norman castle on the fringe; Kirkby Hill, with the ancient grammar school backing into its churchyard, reminding you of its curious custom of electing wardens for its almshouses by wrapping the names of the applicants in wax and picking them out of a bowl of water; and beyond the wind-swept street at Barningham, the ruins of a tower-house at Scargill.

A far-off glimpse of the whitewashed houses of Teesdale, and then the road comes to Greta Bridge, which has long been a resting-place for travellers. A proof of this is found across the bridge where the large, modern hotel, the Morritt Arms, has its private golf-course on the earthworks of a Roman fort.

When in 1838 Charles Dickens put up for the night at Greta Bridge on his way to Barnard Castle, the Morritt Arms was only a small hostelry, and he stayed on the other side of the bridge at the George Inn, now the farmhouse of Thorp Grange. This coaching and posting house was then at the height of its prosperity. To-day it is a large homestead looking out to where the coaches drew up in the cobbled courtyard. Occasionally its patrons would include a runaway couple on the way to Gretna Green.

Some travellers, attracted by the loveliness of this corner, remained for a time at Greta Bridge. Sir Walter Scott stayed with the Morritt family at Rokeby Park, and immortalized it in his poems. But probably more than any part of Yorkshire this has been a place loved by artists. Turner found inspiration in it, and some of Cotman's earliest and most beautiful work is of its wooded streams and bridges. His picture of Greta Bridge, now in the British Museum, has caught the magic of the country.

It is dreamy wooded land where trees hang low over the river banks, but its gentleness is not that of the lowlands. The brown water, turning to a deep olive colour as it flows over the mossy rocks and golden over the smooth white ones, tells of the peat moors over which it has come. Ruined buildings add their interest and romance to the scene. The old church of Brignall stands where an amphitheatre opens out of the hills near to Brignall Banks which Scott found so entrancing. It is roofless now, but thorn- and holly-trees bend over it, and forget-me-nots creep up to its crumbling walls. Among its neglected gravestones is that of two postmasters of Greta Bridge, Christopher and Henry Thwaites, who died in 1693 and 1748.

Near where the Greta meets the Tees down a wooded lime-stone scar, is Mortham Tower, a sixteenth-century tower-house built round a courtyard, and giving even in decay a feeling of a stately life passed in this wooded country. A mile to the north, raised high above the Tees, the ruins of Egglestone Abbey stand near the Thorsgill Beck. The footbridge which the monks built over the beck remains, and you can picture them crossing it after fishing in the river. John Wycliffe, whose birthplace is at Wycliffe, a few miles lower down the river, was taught in this abbey by the monks of Egglestone.

Forgetting for a time the traffic sweeping by on the Roman Watling Street, we take the quiet tree-lined road beyond the abbey to Barnard Castle and Teesdale. Barney, as the people call the old town, lies across the river in Durham, but it is the chief market town for Teesdale, and its ruined castle still seems to guard the gateway to the valley.

A journey up Teesdale is remarkable not so much for the continued loveliness of the dale as for special points of beauty which surpass in grandeur those of the other dales. It has in Mickle Fell the highest hill, and in High Force the finest waterfall, in Yorkshire, and the expanse of fells at its head is greater than that of the other dales. Of the rare flowers found on these hills the most interesting are the blue gentians on Cronkley Fell.

We come first to Cotherstone, which used to be famous for a special kind of white, rather rich cheese. The mistress of a farmhouse in Baldersdale has started to make this again, and her shelves are crowded with cheeses ordered for three or four months ahead. She is carrying on the tradition of the farm by drying her cheese-cloths on a solitary hawthorn-tree planted long ago in the yard and kept trimmed for that purpose.

The Quakers were strong in the Cotherstone district, and their meeting house in a field outside the village is still used. The first person to be buried in its graveyard was a black boy who died at Woden Croft, one of the 'Yorkshire schools.' He could not be buried in the churchyard because it was not known whether he had been baptized, and so the Friends received him into their burial ground.

At Romaldkirk there are stocks on the village green, flowery gardens behind high walls, and the church has a beautiful Decorated chancel. Roads lead from it to the branch dales of Lunedale and lonely Baldersdale, which is now almost filled with reservoirs.

Above Middleton-in-Teesdale the valleys follow the bold curves of the fells. Scattered along them are the white houses of which we caught a glimpse near Scotch Corner. Standing out sharply as if painted on their dark setting, they are a particular mark of Teesdale, for it is a condition of renting them that they shall be kept white.

The main road up the valley, the magnificent moorland road from Middleton to Alston, goes on the Durham side of the river, but looks over Yorkshire; and the waterfall of High Force comes down in two falls, one of which belongs to Yorkshire and one to Durham. This moorland road was made in the eighteenth century as a way for transporting lead and coal by the London Lead Company in conjunction with Greenwich Hospital. From 1699 to 1905 this Quaker company owned and ran numbers of lead mines in the district, but their activities were most vigorous just over the border at Nenthead, where they built a village for the workers, a school and church, and eventually a corn mill, so that the people had not to pay so heavily for the carriage of corn. They were a remarkably early example of a company run for the benefit of the workpeople as well as the owners. Most of their lead mines are closed now, but their monument

remains in the roads which they made over the fells.   Running
across the fells to Stainmore, over the hills to Durham, and
from one dale to another, they still connect the life of the
valleys.

Until the early nineteenth century pack-horses were the chief
means of transport, and these were known as 'carrier galloways,'
contracted to 'galls.'   In Teesdale there are to-day branches
of a family who came from Durham in the seventeenth century
bringing pack-horse trains to carry lead.   When the pack-horse
days ceased they became farmers in Wolsingham and Lunedale.

The road up Lunedale to Brough in Westmorland is one of
the finest of the London Lead Company's roads.   It runs up
the side of the valley, and then on to vast open tracts and the
unchanging solemnity of the moors.   Westmorland seen from
their summit seems another land from these fierce exhilarating
heights.

At the head of Lunedale the farmhouse of Grains o' Beck
settles into a hollow of the fells where the two becks of the Lune
and Long Grain meet.   Until recently this house was an
inn which for three hundred years had caught the first and last
traffic over the bleak moorland road.   If you come this way
one day in late October you will find a sheep show, promoted
by the Swaledale Sheep Breeders' Association, taking place in
a field near the inn.   A group of spectators lean over the wall
and watch the judging in the field below, but it is all very
solemn and serious, and there is little noise to disturb the
silence of the fells.   Bread, cheese, and butter are shown in a
barn behind the house.   Inside it great fires burn in every
room, and farmers coming in for a meal rub their numbed
hands before its glow, for often there is a covering of snow on
the fells or blinding rain blows from them for Grains o' Beck
Show.

We started the climb up Mickle Fell from Grains o' Beck,
going past Arncliffe House, the last farm in the valley, and near
the mountain tarn named the Fish Pond.   Mickle Fell, though
it is the highest hill in Yorkshire, is not so well known as

Ingleborough or Whernside, probably because of its more remote position and its less striking shape. Early topographers
seemed unaware of its existence. There was a long climb over
rough heather and two ridges before we arrived at the heel of
what is known as the Boot of Mickle Fell. From here we looked
across the dip of the instep and along the sole to where far
away at the toe was the distant summit. We sat by the cairn,
and looked over the narrow wedge of land on which Yorkshire

Bowes

juts into Westmorland and Durham. The line of the Westmorland fells lay on the west; northwards the waterfall of
Cauldron Snout poured down the Tees near a rocky scar.
Lifted into this quietness, it seemed strange to remember the
little sheep and cattle sale which we once saw outside the
Langdon Beck Hotel, and the farmers buying their winter
clothing from a motor van, fitting on coats and mackintoshes
between buying and selling sheep.

We join the Roman road again at the village of Bowes. Here
the softness of Greta Bridge has gone and we are in a moorland
community. The grey houses of Bowes climbing either side
of a steep hill have the gravity of the moors about them and a
tradition of long habitation in these high places. This was the

Roman station of Lavatrae on Watling Street, and Bowes Castle tells of other powerful occupants in Norman times. The old Unicorn Inn half way up claims to have been an inn for six hundred years. It became a famous coaching and posting house in the eighteenth and nineteenth centuries, and the front of the house, facing the cobbled courtyard, is much as it was in those days.

Travellers still stop here for hospitality for a night, and then pass on as they did in the coaching days. The inn will be almost empty during the day but full by evening. Staying there one year at the beginning of August, we came down to breakfast to find a mixed crowd of people, all ready to make a fresh start, and all eager to say where they had come from and where they were going. There was the excitement which travelling to Scotland gives, as if the English still looked on it as a foreign land. Some were on their way to climb the Cairngorm Mountains, some to visit Edinburgh, Inverness, Oban, or Skye, and some to shoot on the moors. Only two of them had deviated from the road on the journey up, one to see York and one to see Richmond. They all expressed amazement that we too were not going on, but when we spoke of Stainmore, Mickle Fell, and Cronkley Fell, they seemed to pull themselves up, to realize with almost grudging surprise that this moorland country in which they had rested for a night was itself very beautiful.

At the upper end of Bowes is the house where Mr Shaw held his Yorkshire Academy. This is often claimed to be the original of Dotheboys Hall in *Nicholas Nickleby*, but, though Dickens visited it when he was staying at Barnard Castle, he declared that he drew his 'Yorkshire schools' from many sources. It was here, however, that Dickens heard of boys going half-blind from lack of attention, and George Ashton Taylor, who died in 1820 aged nineteen and whose grave is in Bowes churchyard, was the original of Dickens's Smike.

These schools were not always kept by Yorkshiremen but often by outsiders who saw them as a means of making money.

There were several in Bowes, taking altogether eight hundred pupils, and when these were closed as a result of Dickens's exposure their loss was felt in the village, for however poorly the boys were fed and clothed they necessarily brought a large amount of trade. The tuck - shops kept by Mistress Ann Sayer, Mistress Nanny Denham, and three others, and where the children spent what pocket-money they managed to keep, did not survive their going. You can pick out the substantial houses which were the schools as you go up the village street. They are boarding-houses or ordinary residences now, and some of the rooms where the boys slept, four or five in a bed, are empty. At Dotheboys Hall the flagged and cobbled yard and the pump and trough where the boys used to wash and quarrel over the soap and the two towels remain behind the house.

Bowes has a pathetic memorial in the grave of Roger Wright-son and Martha Railton, who died in 1714. The parish register record them as 'Buried in one grave: He died in a fever, and upon tolling his passing Bell she cry'd out My heart is broke, and in a Few hours Expired, purely thro' Love.' Mallet made them the subject of his ballad, *Edwin and Emma*.

Time swings back centuries as we stand by the meagre ruins of Bowes Castle, which is actually on the site of the Roman fort. There are Roman altars and inscriptions in the church, a Roman bath has been excavated, and aqueducts discovered on land behind Bowes show that water was brought to this from Levy Pool two miles to the north.

We set out from Bowes one showery summer morning to discover Levy Pool, the Roman Laver Pool, expecting to find it on Deepdale Beck. We took the road over Bowes Moor, and a little way down a rough lane saw the house which is called Levy Pool, and forgot the Romans. This was something much nearer to ourselves, and yet as much of the past as they. The thatched, stone farmhouse facing the hill has the mystery and tragedy of the moors about it, and all their fascination. It would make a perfect setting for some wild romance of the moor.

We found the house derelict and the stable roof falling in, but presently an old man came along to feed the hens which are now its only occupants, and he told us that only a few years ago his son had lived in the thatched house, and how warm and comfortable it was. 'It's old-fashioned, like me,' he said, 'an' now there's scarce a man i' the district could thatch wi' ling.' Its farm has been attached to the next one, and the farmer lives in the house there. We came back to Bowes without finding Levy Pool, which only seems to remain now in the name.

The river Greta, still lovely, flows below Bowes and the road to Stainmore, and is crossed in one place by a natural limestone bridge, wide enough for a cart-road, and known as 'God's Bridge.' Stainmore, stretching for miles with no shelter from the wind, is one of the wildest Yorkshire moorlands. It is said that when coachmen reached the Bowes inn after crossing it they were often frozen so stiff that they had to be lifted down from their seats. This is the moor we looked over from Tan Hill Inn in Swaledale, and now across the immense space we see that whitewashed building on a rise of the land.

Almost to the summit of the pass there are farmhouses, but these have a wild, grim air, in keeping with their surroundings. It was at one of them, the Spital, that the gruesome Hand of Glory, the hand of a dead murderer, was used by robbers to prevent sleepers from waking. The house gets its name from having been a guest-house belonging to Marrick Abbey in Swaledale. It is now an ordinary farmhouse, but Saxton's map of 1577 marks it as 'The Spitle on Stainmore,' and in the seventeenth century Thoresby calls it 'the notorious Spittle on Stanmore.'

On the summit of the moor, fourteen hundred and sixty-eight feet above sea-level, stands the Rey Cross, an old boundary stone cut and worn through long years of weather. Standing by it we think of the men and women who have used this road through the centuries. Few have travelled idly on it, for this

is a highway from north to south and east to west. Turning
from it we gaze across the county through which it has come
and whose end the cross marks. We have journeyed over
much of it, seen the beauty and the ugliness, the sheltered
valleys and the wind-swept heights, the bright and dark corners
of our heritage. We trace its progress by what each generation
has contributed, and wonder what impression our troublous
times will make on those who come after.

BIBLIOGRAPHY

A Tour through England and Wales, Daniel Defoe.
Yorkshire Archaeological Society's Journals.
Transactions of the Yorkshire Dialect Society.
Victoria County History.
The Oxford Dictionary of English Place-names.
The Archaeology of Yorkshire, F. and H. Wragg Elgee, 1932.

WEST RIDING

Diary of Ralph Thoresby, 1677–1724.
History of Nidderdale, William Grainge, 1863.
Diary of Abraham de la Pryme (Surtees Society, vol. liv).
The History of Thorne, 1874.
A Glossary of the Dialect of Almondbury and Huddersfield, A. Easther, 1883.
Yorkshire Diaries (Surtees Society, vol. lxv).
Old Eland, Lucy Hamerton, 1901.
Sheffield in the Eighteenth Century, R. E. Leader, 1901.
The Yorkshire Woollen and Worsted Industries, Herbert Heaton, 1920.
The Story of Old Halifax, T. W. Hanson, 1920.
The Hurts of Haldworth, Sir George Reresby Sitwell, 1930.
History of Wakefield, J. W. Walker, 1931.
The Leeds Woollen Industry, W. B. Crump, 1931.
The Ancient Parish of Giggleswick, T. Brayshaw and R. M. Robinson, 1932.
The Parish of Kirkby Malhamdale, J. W. Morkill, 1933.
History of the Huddersfield Woollen Industry, W. B. Crump and Gertrude Ghorbal, 1935.
Notes on the Cutlers' Company of Hallamshire, J. H. Whitham.

NORTH RIDING

The History of Whitby, G. Young, 1817.
A Visitor's Guide to Redcar, J. R. Walbran, 1848.
Forty Years in a Moorland Parish, J. C. Atkinson, 1891.

NORTH RIDING—*continued*

Wit, Character, and Folk-lore of the North Riding, R. Blakeborough, 1898.
Unhistoric Acts, George Baker, 1906.
Early Man in North-east Yorkshire, F. Elgee, 1930.
The History of Scarborough, A. Rowntree, 1931.
Thornton-le-Dale, R. Jeffery, 1931.

EAST RIDING

Primitive Methodism in the Yorkshire Wolds, H. Woodcock, 1889.
The Capital of the Yorkshire Wolds, John Nicholson, 1903.
The Lost Towns of the Yorkshire Coast, Thomas Shepherd, 1912.
Yorkshire Reminiscences, M. C. F. Morris, 1922.
Sykes of Sledmere, J. Fairfax-Blakeborough, 1929.
Place-names of the East Riding, A. H. Smith, 1937.

INDEX

INDEX